Psychology
and
the Stock Market

Psychology
and
the Stock Market

Investment Strategy
Beyond Random Walk

David N. Dreman

WARNER BOOKS

A Warner Communications Company

To my mother and father

Preface _____

    Probably at no time since the Great Depression has there been so much skepticism about investing in stocks. The stock market debacle of 1973–1974, a much larger and more destructive replay of the 1969–1970 drop, resulted in huge losses for both professional and amateur investors alike. It is scarcely 24 months now since major corporations were unable to raise badly needed equity capital, since the brokerage industry tottered one step away from collapse, since the small investor had been driven disillusioned from the market, and the trained money manager stood dazed and bewildered. Stocks traded at ridiculously low prices, seemingly anticipating the total disintegration of the economic system—or that our industry was about to be carried away on the backs of new Mongol hordes.

    Although the market has recovered sharply, the chorus of contradictory opinion bewilders many investors, both professional and amateur alike. A new breed of academic researchers has demonstrated conclusively that professional investors do not outperform the market. Although these researchers present the most far-reaching challenge ever made to professional investment, neither their explanation of this phenomenon nor their approach to investing is really acceptable.

    In this book I hope to show evidence of how extensive samples of professionals made dramatic errors at major market turning points and fared far worse than blind chance with their best investment recommendations. As in David Halberstam's *The Best and the Brightest*, something went drastically wrong with their decision-making procedures, and we shall try to determine what it was.

The book is not written as an exposé or a censure of institutional investment. I have been a professional investor for almost 20 years and, along with many others, am deeply disturbed by such results, for they indicate some striking defect in current investment practice. Even the more successful professionals are guilty of major mistakes which shouldn't have been made. In my own case I followed, and at times eagerly embraced, the conventional wisdom only to be led, like so many others, into serious investment blunders. Such errors and the repeated observation of many leading analysts and money managers faring poorly in stock selections—far worse than the law of averages—made me begin to probe for better answers than seemed currently available. The book presents the answers I have been able to find. It will demonstrate, I believe, why the investment theory we are all schooled in, while essential, is simply not sufficient by itself for market success. There is a crucial dimension missing which, if ignored by professionals and other investors, leads to a constant repetition of the same major errors and inevitably to poorer market results.

The missing dimension is psychology. A major portion of this work is devoted to showing just how important this influence actually is on the market decisions of amateur and professional investors alike. Without a better understanding of the tremendous psychological pressures influencing decisions, the investor is simply not adequately equipped to cope with the securities market.

The work is not abstract: both major historical and topical market events are used as illustrative material. Our journey will be far-ranging and will lead us through the fascinating world of crowd psychology from markets in the distant past to those of the mid-1970s. As we travel, striking similarities in investment behavior leading to major errors will become apparent. The work will at times appear somber or even gloomy, but it will have its lighter moments as well.

Our analysis of the evidence will lead us to devise an investment strategy which should help us avoid some of the most dangerous psychological pitfalls and even allow us to benefit from the repeated mistakes of market crowds.

The integration of psychological and financial theory is a new and basically uncharted area. I hope this work will persuade the reader of the importance of behavioral considerations both to increase understanding of the market and to improve investment results.

Acknowledgments

I would like to thank the numerous publishers and investment organizations who allowed me to use the valuable tables and other material incorporated into the text. I very much appreciate the help and suggestions I received from a number of my friends, both within and outside the investment field, and from the several who reviewed the manuscript. I owe a tremendous debt to Dr. Susan Dickey, a clinical psychologist who started my writing of this book and then carefully read the entire work. Dr. Solly Dreman of the Hebrew University (Jerusalem) and Dr. Edward Conolley of the University of California (Los Angeles), both psychologists, also reviewed the manuscript and made many helpful suggestions as did Professor Fred Renwick, of the New York University Graduate School of Business. Steven Distler, a graduate student at New York University, provided me with invaluable assistance in research and made many constructive suggestions. Vivian Avery and Carol Davis patiently and expertly typed the many drafts of this manuscript.

David N. Dreman

Contents

Part I   The Professional Record and Its Interpretation

1 The Riddle of Professional Investing   3
A Glance at the Professional Record / The
Performance Treadmill / Bank Trust
Departments and Pension Funds / Mutual
Funds

2 The Academic Onslaught   18
In the Beginning / A Brief Survey of
Technical Analysis / The Fall from Grace of
the Technician / The Blitzkrieg Rolls On /
Testing, Testing

**Part II   Psychological Aberrations of the Market
Crowd**

3 Bubbles, Bubbles, Bubbles   47
Tulipmania / The First Hot New Issues
Market / You too Can Own a Swamp /
1929—Stocks Discount the Hereafter

4 The Tulips of the Sixties   76
Electronic Bubbles / The Rise and Fall of
the Gunslinger / The Common
Characteristics of the Manias

Part III   Groupthink on Wall Street

5 A Poisonous Competitive Environment   99
What Is Groupthink? / A Gun at the Money
Manager's Temple / Institutional
Research—The Great White Hope / What
Went Wrong? / A Limit to Critical Thinking

6 A Flourishing Environment for Groupthink   125
     The Global Village / Evidence of Group
     Conformity / Pressures to Conform Within
     the Organization

7 The Ascendancy of Groupthink   146
     Investment Forecasts Made by a Large
     Sample of Experts / The Herd Mania into
     Concept Stocks / The Top 50 / Market
     Performance of Popular and Unpopular
     Stocks

8 The Amazing Two-Tier Market   168
     The Market's Aristocracy / The Stampede
     into the Upper Tier / Was the Two-Tier
     Market a Manifestation of Groupthink?

9 Panic   189
     The Liquidity Trap / Previous Warnings
     Ignored / The Market Collapse Viewed
     Within Groupthink / The Nature of
     Panic / The Institutional Role in the
     Break / Possible Economic Implications of
     Institutional Investing / The Effect of
     Increasing Institutionalization of the
     Market / Have Things Changed?

Part IV   Can an Investor Beat the Market?

10 Market Information: The Forest and the Trees   217
      The Necessary Assumptions of EMH /
      Interpretive Capabilities—The Story
      of Supersleuth / Accounting—Order Out of
      Chaos? / Imaginative Accounting in
      Action / The Interpretive Problem in
      Perspective

11 The Foundations of EMH—Bedrock or Quicksand? 238
      The Problem of Investor Behavior / A Pact
      with Mephistopheles / Is There Another
      Defense of EMH? / Where Do We Go from
      Here?

12 A Contemporary Investment Strategy   252
        Psychological Variables in the Investment
        Formula / Visibility Revisited / A
        Proposed Investment Strategy / The
        Concept of Earnings Power / Using Expert
        Advice / Other Components of a Successful
        Strategy / Diversification—An Essential
        Ingredient / The Cold-Turkey Road to
        Success / Another Alternative / A Final
        Word

References   275
Appendix   1967-1976; Unpopular Stocks Outperform
        the Market Favorites   291
Index   293

Part I

The Professional Record and Its Interpretation

1

The Riddle
of Professional
Investing

A Glance at the Professional Record

They had come from every state to be there and
from most major cities. Some traveled from Canada and
not a few from Europe. Over 2,000 strong, they managed
large pools of money for bank trust departments, pension
funds, mutual funds, investment advisory firms, insurance
companies, college endowment funds, and other financial
institutions. They were professional investors, and they were
gathered at the Third Annual Institutional Investor Conference at the New York Hilton in early February 1970. As
a group they were intelligent, articulate, extremely well
trained and had the finest, most detailed information from
which to make investment decisions.

The growth of the assets under their control was phenomenal, reaching over $900 billion by the end of 1972, and
expanding at a much faster rate than the national economy. [1]
Only a little more than two years after this conference they
would control 70% of all the trading and almost 50% of
the stock holdings on the New York Stock Exchange. They
were indeed the princes of their profession. Their buying
power was staggering; between 1960 and 1969 they purchased
and sold some $400 billion worth of common stock while
generating $3 billion in brokerage commissions in the process.
By 1975, corporate pension funds—the largest category of

institutional investors—owned one-third of all publicly held stock and invested $0.30 of every dollar of corporate pre-tax profits.[2]

Unlike stockbrokers, who seem to have been under ever mounting criticism since the founding of the first Stock Exchange in Amsterdam in 1602, institutional investors have generally been well regarded over the years. They were said to bring a new depth of knowledge to securities markets. No longer would the stock market be controlled by the whims of millions of uninformed individual investors who, reacting first to greed, would send prices soaring and then reacting to fear, would send them plummeting piecemeal. Now the market would be increasingly in the hands of steely-eyed, informed professionals, and price movements would become far more objective and systematic. The change was welcomed by knowledgeable observers of the financial scene. They urged the uninformed and emotional small investor to realize he was ill equipped to deal personally with the complex modern market and to turn his money over to one of these seasoned experts. Some writers on the subject had gone so far as to state that the amateur investor is "obsolete" in current stock markets.

And so in 1970, with the knowledge of the growing importance they were to play in the future allocation of the nation's financial resources, the professionals gathered at the conference to consider an extensive and sophisticated investment agenda.

Among the blue ribbon speakers to address the conference that year was Bernard Cornfeld, whose spectacularly growing Investors Overseas Services (IOS) mutual fund empire in Europe had recently been sold to the public by a consortium of the most aristocratic European investment banking houses including the Rothschilds. On Cornfeld's board of directors were the son of an American president and a Harvard economist. Cornfeld, short, paunchy, and balding, but with the eyes of a visionary, detailed the irresistible growth path of IOS expansion that would shortly make it one of the multinational financial giants. The audience seemed impressed. It was definitely impressed with National Student Marketing, a company with a phenomenal sales and profit record. In fact, the company's prospects appeared so exciting that in a secret ballot conducted at the conference, the assembled money men voted it as the stock they thought would do best in the marketplace that year. Only five months afterwards, National Student Marketing was down almost 95% in price, while IOS was in its death throes. Bernie Cornfeld would shortly change his address from an elaborate castle near Geneva to a Swiss jail. The investment heroes of 1970 had not fared well.

At the Fifth Annual Institutional Investor Conference in 1972 the airline stocks were picked by secret ballot to be the best performing industry for the balance of the year. Within 1% of their highs at the time the poll was taken, they dropped 50% as a group for the remainder of the year and 75% by the spring of 1973.[3] The following year, the chastened investors as a group voted to avoid airline stocks.

In late 1971, *Institutional Investor,* one of the magazines most widely read by professionals, interviewed more than 150 money managers in 27 states, each of whom picked five stocks he thought would do the best in 1972. Although over 400 different stocks were mentioned, the article stated that the top ten choices received remarkably wide backing from professionals as diverse as a Midwest banker, a West Coast fund manager, the portfolio manager of a southern insurance company, and an aggressive New York performance manager. The magazine warned investors that consensus had never proved itself to be the best forecasting tool for picking stocks.[4] The advice proved accurate. The top ten increased an average of 1.3% in 1972,* a year in which the Standard & Poor's (S&P) 500, a broadly based market index,† increased 15.6%. The next year these stocks declined an

*All the following comparisons are January 1 to December 31.
†This widely followed index includes 425 industrials, 25 railroads, and 50 utilities and comprises more than three-quarters of the value of all securities listed on the New York Stock Exchange.

average 40% versus a 17.4% decline for the S&P 500.* The magazine published 50 other frequently selected favorites. The 50 also did worse than the average in both 1972 and 1973, performing almost nine times worse than the market for the two years.

Of course anybody can be wrong once, so the survey of professional investors was repeated in 1973, using even a wider sample of portfolio managers—160, each from a different institution. Their top ten selections were down an average of 40.4% that year, again more than twice as much as the S&P drop of 17.4%. For the two-year 1973–1974 period, this group of stocks declined an average of 67.0% against the S&P's drop of 41.9%. After the top ten of 1973, 26 other favorites were chosen which were again decisively outperformed by the S&P 500 in the 1973–1974 period. To no one's surprise, the *Institutional Investor* contest was discontinued after 1973.

What conclusions are to be drawn from the tepid performance of professional investors described above? According to financial lore it is the rational and unemotional professional investor who is able to gauge value and coolly move in and buy securities at bargain levels in periods of panic when the public is selling them without regard for their worth. The portfolio manager, so Wall Street legend goes, will also sell stocks in periods when the public is intrigued with securities, and prices in the ensuing speculative mania go too high. In fact, evidence compiled by the Securities and Exchange Commission suggests strongly that the much abused and supposedly emotional individual investor sold securities near the 1968 market top† and was a buyer in the market bottoms of both 1970 and 1974. The institutional investor, on the other hand, was a buyer near market tops and a seller at the market bottoms.

---

*Neither the S&P nor the group is adjusted for dividends. The decline would appear worse if they were, as these stocks had a significantly lower yield than the S&P.

†In 1968, the year the broadly based Value Line Composite Index reached its all-time high, the public sold a record $12 billion in securities, about double the amount they liquidated on balance in the next few years.

In the August–November 1974 period when the lows of the ravaging 1973–1974 bear market were established, a large survey that covered 261 banks, insurance companies, investment advisory groups, and mutual fund organizations indicated that cash reserves climbed to 19% of assets versus 13.5% a year earlier. For the most part, the cash reserves were increased by the selling of stocks. In October 1974 the 100 funds most actively seeking capital gains had 23.9% in cash.[5] The institutions surveyed were thus aggressively selling stocks at the very bottom. Near the market high in 1968, 1971, and 1972, the funds' cash position was near 7%. The institutional pattern of buying heavily near highs and selling near market bottoms has not gone unnoticed. One financial columnist proposed that a new market indicator could be developed from such facts. The more optimistic mutual funds were, as measured by the investment of their cash reserves in the market, the more likely the market was to decline; conversely, the greater the cash reserves of mutual funds in anticipation of a falling market, the more likely that a market upswing was imminent.

Further evidence corroborating the uninspiring record of many professional investors was recently provided by Frank Russell and Company, a firm specializing in the measurement of institutional results.[6] In an extensive survey of 342 institutional investors,* it found only 17% outperformed the 37% gain of the S&P 500 in 1975. Only 7 of 91 bank equity funds (7.7%) and 11 of 90 advisory firms (12%) beat this index. Table 1 lists the average annual returns of each class of institutional investor for the one-, four-, and eight-year periods.

What does one make of such results? Benjamin Graham, the dean of security analysts and widely acknowledged to

---

*The sample included 91 bank equity funds (wherein the funds of many clients are pooled together or commingled); 31 bank special equity funds (similar but more aggressive); 22 equity funds operated by insurance companies; 90 accounts of investment advisors; and 50 growth mutual funds. Balanced and income funds that contain a higher percentage of bonds and preferred shares have been omitted from the table as the comparison to the S&P is less meaningful.

TABLE 1. Annual rates of return.*

	1975 % Return	1971–1975 % Return	1967–1975 % Return
S&P 500	+37.1%	+0.6%	+2.7%
Bank Equity	+26.0	−2.9	+0.6
Bank Special Equity	+31.8	−9.7	n.a.
Insurance Equity	+30.1	−3.2	+0.3
Investment Advisors	+25.1	unchanged	n.a.
Growth Funds	+32.8	−5.4	−2.2

*All periods end December 31.
n.a. not available.
All figures include dividends and interest.
Source: Frank Russell and Company.

be the most important single influence shaping modern investment theory,* recently mused,

> In the past ten years Wall Street has given a poorer account of itself than at any time in its history. . . . You can almost despair of expecting any rationality if you look back over what has happened . . . after new highs were made for the indexes at the end of 1972 and the beginning of 1973 . . . we saw another kind of collapse very similar in terms of the figures to what we saw in 1970. How people could have had the lack of prudence to reestablish those late 1972 and early 1973 values is something I don't think I'll ever understand.[7]

By people Graham meant professional investors.

Graham's comments are particularly worth considering, for after the debacle of 1969–1970, portfolio managers conducted an industry-wide post-mortem. Hundreds of professionals solemnly reviewed their major errors in the "go-go" years of 1967 and 1968, such mistakes as buying "concept stocks" without proper investigation, concentrating heavily in thinly traded issues that would be difficult to sell, and paying too high a price for companies with good prospects. They were convinced that the mistakes that led to the calamity

---

*Benjamin Graham died while this book was in press. His book *Security Analysis*, coauthored with David L. Dodd is considered the classic work in the field. First published in 1934 it has been updated three times since. The latest edition was published in 1962.

would not be allowed to happen again. Yet they did. Within only a matter of months of these reappraisals the same mistakes were being made by many professionals on an even larger scale. The repetition was the market equivalent of the U.S. Navy allowing its fleet to be caught napping twice at Pearl Harbor within six months.

The Performance Treadmill

Strangely enough the more professionals tried to improve their results the worse their records seemed to become. Many of the worst investment decisions of the late 1960s were made in the name of "performance," which, in brief, means beating both the market averages and other professional investors. As we shall see the pressure on professional investors to "perform" came from virtually all sides.

Along with the sharp rise in mutual fund sales beginning in the early 1960s, the public concomitantly began to scrutinize more closely the performance records of institutional investors. This interest sparked a frenzied competition among financial professionals to outperform the market averages and each other. The competition grew in intensity as the decade progressed. In the latter part of the 1960s the top performing investment professionals were treated by their colleagues, the financial press, and the investment public with the adulation that teenage crowds reserve for rock heroes. Not only was their professional stature enhanced by outdoing the averages, but outstanding money managers (like Gerald Tsai and Fred Carr of the Manhattan and Enterprise funds, respectively) attracted a veritable flood of highly profitable new business. In early 1967, McGeorge Bundy jarred even the most conservative professionals into paying more attention to investment results. As head of the Ford Foundation, he stated:

> There may be room for great improvement here. It is far from clear that trustees have reason to be proud of their performance in making money for their colleges. We recognize the risks of unconventional investing, but the true test of

performance in the handling of money is the record of achievement, not the opinion of the respectable. We have the preliminary impression that over the long run caution has cost our
colleges much more than imprudence or excessive risk-taking.[8]

Trading on the major exchanges was stepped up considerably by the mid-1960s in an attempt to improve performance. Mutual funds that turned over 13% of their stock
portfolios annually in 1953 increased this to 22% by 1965
and 51% by 1969. Between 1965 and 1969, pension fund
turnovers rose from 11 to 21% of their portfolios annually.
Even staid life insurance companies got into the act. Their
trading rose from 14 to 29% of common stock holdings in
this time span.[9] The combination of rising flow of funds
to institutions and the higher turnover they generated resulted
in institutions becoming the most important single source
of trading on the big board. Excluding stock exchange
member trading, the institutional share rose from 31 to 68%
of the total between 1971 and 1974, while the public's dropped
from 69 to 32%.*[10]

The outcome of the performance derby was scarcely
breathtaking. After Bundy's speech, *Fortune* magazine irrev-
erently tested the results of the Ford Foundation for the
decade between its 1956 and 1966 fiscal years and concluded,

> The foundation's investment performance over the decade was
> not exactly scintillating. It did not even approach the gain made
> by the Dow Jones Industrial Average, a rather modest measure
> of investment performance. . . . For the 10 year period, the
> Foundation holdings showed an adjusted gain of only 35%,
> while the Dow had a 63% gain.[11]

Fortune noted that the Foundation would have improved
its results if it had retained its original holdings of Ford
stock instead of selling a portion during the decade to diversify
into other equities. By 1975, the foundation's portfolio losses
had become so extensive that it was planning to lay off a

*The importance of institutional trading on market direction will be discussed
in Chapter 11.

large part of its professional staff and reduce its philanthropic programs by 50%.*[12]

The Ford Foundation is only one case; far more important is how professional investors have done overall. To answer this question let us briefly examine the records of the major institutional investors, bank trust departments, pension funds, insurance companies, and mutual funds.

Bank Trust Departments and Pension Funds

Trust and pension funds account for well over half of institutionally managed money in the country. Bank trust departments by themselves administered $378 billion in assets at the end of 1974.[13] There was a significant amount of concentration among the major banks, with the trust operations of the 50 largest banks controlling over 50% of the total.[14] A large percentage of pension fund money is also run by the trust departments of the banks.

A good trust officer has an intimate relationship with his (or her) client, providing advice not only in stock market and financial affairs but very often on an extensive range of personal matters. Trust officers have been known to pay off blackmailers, arrange abortions, and even identify corpses. One trust officer with an acute fear of dogs was forced on occasion to walk the poodles of a wealthy dowager client.[15]

Though the call of duty has perhaps at times carried him far afield, the main responsibility of the trust officer is, naturally, to manage his client's money. A measure of how satisfactorily this job is done may be gauged from the commingled funds of bank trust departments. Small- and medium-sized accounts with the same investment objectives are merged into a pool, or "commingled." Each account receives far more intensive attention than it could be given individually, while providing the bank with greater operating efficiency. Most large banks run both equity and fixed income funds, tailoring the exact proportions according to the client's

*The 1970–1975 losses were about equal to those of the market generally.

individual requirements. The performance of the pooled funds is often used to spotlight the bank's ability to manage money for potential new accounts. Thus, although these pools are only a small portion of the bank's administered assets, such fund indexes are a valuable window through which to observe their investment performance, since no other information is consistently available to judge such operations.

A comparison by *The New York Times* indicated how the commingled funds of ten of the largest New York City banks have fared each year from 1971 through 1974 and for the entire four-year period. The banks have combined trust assets of over $90 billion, a little under 25% of the industry total, with Morgan Guaranty, Citicorp, Bankers Trust, Chase Manhattan, U.S. Trust, and Manufacturers Hanover (in that order) being the largest trust operations in the nation. (See Table 2.)

TABLE 2. Annual returns of commingled equity funds for employee benefit accounts (year ended 12/31).*

	1974	1973	1972	1971	Compound Annual Returns for 4 Years
Bank of New York	−23.3	−11.2	+19.7	+19.5	−0.5
Bankers Trust	−30.5	−28.4	+20.5	+25.1	−6.9
Chemical Bank	−20.6	−16.3	+11.4	+25.9	−1.7
Chase Manhattan	−27.3	−17.9	+ 6.5	+15.1	−7.5
First Nat'l City	−27.6	−18.3	+22.4	+22.8	−2.9
Irving Trust	−29.6	−18.4	+22.5	+18.8	−4.4
Manuf. Hanover	−32.8	−20.2	+25.1	+22.8	−4.7
Marine Mid. N.Y.	−11.9	−21.0	+11.8	+10.5	−3.7
Morgan Guaranty†	−36.1	−20.8	+25.9	+18.1	−6.9
U.S. Trust	−34.1	−22.9	+21.9	+28.4	−5.6
S&P 500	−26.5	−14.8	+18.9	+14.3	−3.9

*Total rates of return, with income reinvested.
†Morgan's 1974 figure is not from its commingled equity fund, which the bank would not supply. It is the result of a $200 million General Electric Savings and Security Program. It is not necessarily typical of all Morgan pension trust and profit-sharing funds.
Source: *The New York Times*, February 20, 1975. © 1975/1976 by The New York Times Company. Reprinted by permission.

For the four-year period, four banks—Bank of New York (−.5%), Chemical (−1.7%), First National City (−2.9%), and Marine Midland (−3.7%)—managed to surpass the performance of the S&P 500 (−3.9%). None of the returns was positive.*

With total assets currently exceeding $200 billion, pension funds are the largest institutional holders of common stock. Because of the increase in contributions to pension funds dictated by the passage by Congress of the Employee Retirement Investment Security Act (1974), these funds should become an increasingly larger part of institutional holdings in the future. The banks' trust departments manage over 80% of pension fund assets. Since banks use their commingled accounts as a showcase of their performance, pension fund results not surprisingly fall pretty much into line.

The Chicago-based Becker Securities Corporation is the leading firm monitoring institutional results. In recent years Becker's data base has measured the performance of over 3,000 funds. The comprehensive results are striking. In the decade ending December 31, 1975, the S&P 500 increased 3.3% annually while the median rate of return of pension fund stock portfolios was 1.6%. The S&P outperformed 88% of these portfolios for the ten-year period and 90% for the most recent five years.

Becker's data bank also contained information on how pension fund managers have performed relative to the S&P over the past seven market cycles. In only one of these cycles did more than half of the funds outperform the index. During the other six cycles, the S&P beat the funds 75% of the time on average. In the 1962–1975 time span, a period which included four full market cycles, the S&P outdistanced fully 87% of all funds.[16]

---

*Unless specified, all rates of return including S&P 500 figures include dividends reinvested. The S&P 500, measured in this manner, is probably the most widely used yardstick with which professional money managers compare their results.

Mutual Funds

Because their performance is almost always measured on a daily basis, mutual funds are the goldfish bowl of professional investing. Buying the right stock or selling the wrong one or being in or out of the market at the appropriate time is immediately known. As in George Orwell's *Nineteen Eighty-Four*, the harsh eye of "big brother" constantly watches every move. Making the correct decisions can mean the difference between substantial inflows or outflows of funds by approving or disenchanted investors. As a result, mutual fund managers are among the most active in the pursuit of "performance."

One of the first studies of results was undertaken by the SEC, which measured the record of investment companies from the late twenties to the mid-thirties. The report stated, "It can then be concluded with considerable assurance that the entire group of management investment companies proper failed to perform better than an index of leading common stocks, and probably performed somewhat worse than the index over the 1927–1935 period. . . ."*[17]

A number of exhaustive studies of mutual fund performance have been completed by academic researchers in recent years. The most comprehensive study was that of Friend, Blume, and Crockett of the Wharton School in 1970.[18] The report was widely read and discussed in both professional and academic circles. One hundred and thirty-six funds produced an average return of 10.7% annually between January 1960 and June 30, 1968. During the same period the average share on the New York Stock Exchange appreciated 12.4% annually. (If value weighted, the average New York Stock Exchange share increase was 9.9%.†) The study was extended for the year ending July 1969. The average

*The investment companies studied were closed-end. This type has a fixed number of shares outstanding. Unlike mutual funds, closed-end funds do not continually offer and redeem their shares. Purchase and sale of existing shares are normally transacted on a stock exchange.
†Weighted for the number of shares of each company outstanding, thus giving more emphasis to the changes of larger companies.

return on the funds in this period was −3.8% compared to −3.3% for the value-weighted investment in all stocks on the big board. The report concluded that there was no evidence that mutual funds could outperform the market.

What then do we make of these statistics? Some cynics and financial writers (I'm never sure the two are not at times synonymous) believe the figures indicate professional money management is inept. The most important service investment management could perform for their clients, they might say, would be to walk dogs or identify corpses. Other pundits have cheerfully suggested that blindfolded chimpanzees heavily fortified with martinis could outperform the experts by throwing darts at the stock pages.

When they are not poking fun at the professionals, many serious observers of the financial scene are admittedly perplexed by the problem. They know through their contacts with market professionals that these people are by and large anything but inept.

It is generally acknowledged that the men and women running money today are the best trained in market history and for the most part are bright, hard-working, and highly motivated. Yet their overall lack of success remains both obvious and disturbing.

The failure is not found in the comprehensive statistical record alone. Contained within this evidence are both constant repetitions of similar errors and significant deviations from the rational decision making which is supposedly the hallmark of fiduciary investment. How for example could large numbers of thorough and prudent experts have heavily purchased Levitz Furniture, one of the top ten institutional favorites in both 1972 and 1973, near its high of 60, only to see it plummet to under 2 within months? Or how in mid-1973 could the concentrated buying of professionals have pushed the market value of Avon Products higher than that of the entire U.S. steel industry and the value of McDonald's above that of U.S. Steel? Both Avon and McDonald's were dwarfed in comparative size and profitability and dropped sharply shortly thereafter. Something apparently went drastically wrong with the decision-making processes of experts in these and hundreds of similar cases.

One of the most conspicuous and alarming features of institutional thinking has been the tremendous convergence on a course of action which has turned out to be markedly wrong. Such conformity is at times startling. For a period in 1972 and 1973 a large part of the mainstream of American institutional opinion believed there were only 50 to 60 stocks worth buying out of a population of 11,000 public companies. The experts strongly defended this position publicly and in hearings before Congress, only to diametrically shift their opinions within a matter of months. Most peculiar of all, the most common reason put forth for buying these stocks (high inflation) was now given as the explanation of why they were being sold. The same reasoning had led the leaders of many of the nation's largest financial institutions in a full circle!

We must question the effectiveness of the investment theory that professionals are schooled in since it has not proved to be of any help in preventing either their poor performance or the major errors that have been made. To develop a more realistic explanation of stock market behavior, we must first examine the following important questions:

1. Why do professionals not outperform the market averages and often fare more poorly?

2. How could institutions repeat many of the worst mistakes of the disastrous 1967–1970 market on an even larger scale only months after the decline had ended?

3. Why are the majority of intelligent, sophisticated, and well-trained professionals repeatedly wrong at important turning points in market cycles?

4. Why is there such widespread consensus of favored industries and stocks which is very often incorrect?

5. Why is each new institutional favorite chosen by utilizing the same guidelines and selection procedures responsible for the previous failure?

If we can find good answers to these questions we should have not only a better understanding of how the stock market operates but also, perhaps, a reasonable chance of doing better than the market averages.

Academic researchers on securities markets have developed new and basically revolutionary answers to some of these questions. We shall look at their explanations next.

2

The Academic Onslaught

The evidence on the poor performance of professionals has not gone unnoticed by academia. With diligence, indeed at times with undisguised glee, the professors have put the figures through their computers and have provided us with chapter and verse on the professional record. Their analysis of the problem and theoretical explanation form the subject of this chapter. It is worth examining in some detail, for if the professors are correct, their theory undermines the foundations of investment practice as it is currently carried out.

In the Beginning

It all started peacefully enough when Louis Bachelier, an outstanding French mathematics student at the turn of the century, examined the fluctuations of commodity prices in his doctoral dissertation.[1] He found that commodity price movements appeared random. Recent price data were of no help in predicting future price movements. His was the first formulation and test of what became known as the random walk model, although he did not call it by that name.

Bachelier's work lay dormant for 60 years until it was rediscovered in 1960. At about the same time, other researchers had started to study stock price movements. One early work showed that randomly chosen series of numbers when plotted together resembled actual charts of a stock's price movements over a period of time.[2] Another study demonstrated that stock price fluctuations were remarkably similar to the random movements of minute solid particles suspended in fluids and known as "brownian motion," after the Scottish botanical explorer Robert Brown, who had first observed this activity in 1827.[3]

In the first half of the 1960s, evidence of the random movement of stock prices mounted. Almost all the statistical evidence, now considerable, buttressed the hypothesis that successive price changes were independent of past price movements.* The statistical methods involved in these studies are complex; a knowledge of higher mathematics and some background in the method are often required to follow the course of the experiments. For the most part, the random walk findings were published in scholarly journals, so it is not surprising that very few on Wall Street knew of the results for years.

The principle of a random walk is relatively simple. Suppose you are with a friend, well into his cups, and you take him outdoors for some air. If you let him walk alone, his movements, providing he can walk at all, will appear random. He may stagger two steps to the left, one forward, three to the right, and again one to the left, following no discernible pattern. You could not predict where or how far he will go in any direction from his past movements, since they are entirely aimless. His next step could just as likely be to the left, the right, or straight ahead, or he might possibly turn around completely and lurch purposelessly in the opposite direction.

The random walk theory of stock price behavior states that "the past history of stock price movements, and the history of stock trading volume, do not contain any information that will allow the investor to do consistently better than a buy-and-hold strategy in managing a portfolio."[4] A buy-

*Nobel prize-winning economist Paul Samuelson contributed one of the most important papers on this subject: "Proof that Properly Anticipated Prices Fluctuate Randomly," *Industrial Management Review*, Spring 1964.

and-hold strategy means exactly what it implies. Investors should simply buy securities and hold them; they cannot outperform the market by analyzing price and volume information to trade stocks. The market has no "memory"; what has happened, like the drunken friend's last steps, will provide no clue to the next movement. No matter how definite a trend looks, the tossing of a coin will give the investor as much of a chance to be right. Statisticians tell us that if a true coin is tossed, and heads come up 10 times or even 12 times in a row, on the next toss there is still a 50–50 chance to toss heads again.

Needless to say, the investment professional's reception of this theory has been something short of enthusiastic. The theory is certainly contrary to our intuition and has important implications for the formulation of a stock market investment strategy. If it is correct, it means that technical analysis, one of the two methods of investment widely used by professionals and other knowing investors to outperform the market, should be abandoned.

A Brief Survey of Technical Analysis

Let us then look at the technical approach to buying and selling stocks. Technical analysis is used to cover a fairly wide range of techniques, all based on the concept that past information on prices and trading volume of stocks gives the enlightened student "a picture" of what lies ahead. It attempts to explain and forecast changes in security prices by studying only the market data rather than information about a company or its prospects (as fundamental analysis does). John Magee, whose book *Technical Analysis of Stock Trends** is considered a classic for technical analysts, says:

> The technician has elected to study, not the mass of fundamentals, but certain abstractions, namely the market data alone. He is fully aware that this is not all . . . also he is aware that what he is looking at is indeed a fairly high order of abstraction

*Coauthored with Robert Edward, the book has recently been revised in both English and Japanese.

and that back of it lies the whole complicated world of things and events.

But this technical view does provide a simplified and more comprehensible picture of what is happening to the price of a stock. It is like a shadow or reflection in which can be seen the broad outline of the whole situation.

Furthermore it works.[5]

The technical analyst believes the price of a stock depends on supply and demand in the marketplace and has little relationship to value, if any such concept even exists. Price is governed by basic economic and psychological inputs so numerous and complex that no individual can hope to understand and measure them all correctly. Many technicians refuse to even look at economic and company-related data, finding them distracting. John Magee, for example, works from an office with boarded up windows so as not to be affected by the weather and does not allow himself to read *The Wall Street Journal*, except to get prices, until it is two weeks old, in order to remain uninfluenced by fundamental information.[6]

The technician thinks the only important information to work from is the picture given by price and volume statistics. The proper technical system is the key that unlocks this treasure and provides the answer of when to buy and sell stocks for superior gains.

The technician sees the market, disregarding minor changes, moving in discernible trends which continue for significant periods. A trend is believed to continue until there is definite information of a change. The past performance of a stock can then be harnessed to predict the future. The direction of price change is as important as the relative size of the change. With his various tools, the technician attempts to correctly catch changes in trend and take advantage of them.

Technical analysis includes bar charts and point and figure charts, moving averages and other trendlines, advance-decline ratios, statistics on new highs and lows, odd-lot and short-interest ratios, and numerous other measurements.

Most technicians generally have one favored tool but use a variety of others to confirm or reject its predictions.

One of the oldest and most primitive methods of technical analysis is tape reading which was so popular in the board-rooms of the twenties. As a boy I had an opportunity to watch this practice firsthand when visiting my father's small brokerage firm in Canada. The firm had a merry little group of customers who carefully watched the tape spew out its price and volume data, chatting among themselves as they did so. Periodically, conversation ceased and attention was riveted on some important new pattern of prices determined on increasing volume. Then one or two would spring into action and place orders based on the messages received from the tape. A dedicated tape reader is convinced that if he watches the tape intently hour after hour, day after day over the years, a special "feel" develops which leads to fortune. This belief is what the 1920s pool operators exploited so successfully. By manipulating prices, they convinced the public a major move was forthcoming, inducing them to rush in and buy as the pool unloaded. As a youngster I was fascinated by how these priests and priestesses of the tape would magically derive such information. As I grew older, I found that, unfortunately, none of our small sample ever made much money, and were lucky to break even. In any case, the office was warm, the group hospitable, and the temperature often went down to $-20°$ outside.

Of course this method is considered primitive by the bulk of technicians. Most technical analysis today is substantially more sophisticated. We will briefly touch on the principles of some of the more important techniques.

Charting is the most widespread form of technical analysis and the most common type is the vertical line chart. An example is given in Figure 1(a).

Price is plotted on the vertical axis and each time period on the horizontal axis. Such charts are plotted on a daily, weekly, or sometimes monthly basis. For each day in our example we have a thin line, indicating the day's trading range. The small tick across each line is the closing price.

Figure 1. Vertical chart techniques.

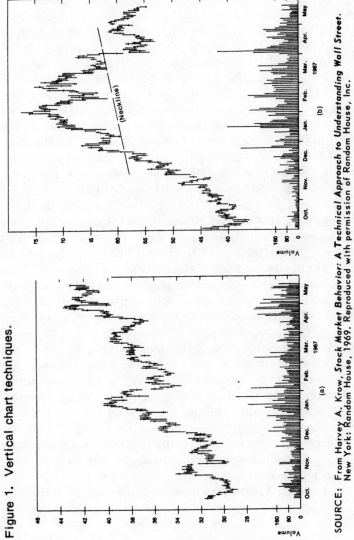

SOURCE: From Harvey A. Krow, *Stock Market Behavior: A Technical Approach to Understanding Wall Street*. New York: Random House, 1969. Reproduced with permission of Random House, Inc.

The vertical lines on the bottom of the chart indicate the daily stock market volume.

A chartist works from dozens of separate patterns of prices. One of the most widely recognized is the head-and-shoulders formation shown in Figure 1(b). Such a pattern appears normally after a major advance in market prices over a period of weeks and sometimes months. In this pattern the first peak, the left shoulder, would be formed with rising volume on the way up and declining volume as the price falls. The volume pattern is the same in the formation of the middle top, the head, but the volume is often somewhat less. In the head formation, price does not decline from the peak below the nadir of the left shoulder. The right shoulder is the key. Volume is less than in the previous rise, indicating declining upward momentum. If on the decline, the right shoulder breaks through the neckline, the sell signal has been given. Had the right shoulder started moving up before reaching the neckline on rising volume, and eventually broken through to higher ground, this would be construed as bullish.

Trendlines are an important charting tool because of the technician's belief that once a trend has started it is not easy to halt or reverse. Chartists believe that the major move is often broken by movements in the opposite direction often canceling from one-third to two-thirds of the primary move without nullifying the original trend. Trendlines are drawn to connect the series of reactions to the primary move.

In Figure 2(a) we have an up-trendline, with the trendline connecting the reaction lows on the bottom of the channel. In Figure 2(b) the opposite is true, and there is a down-trendline at the top of the channel. Trendlines can also be drawn to curve upward to fit the intermediate bottoms, as in Figure 2(c), or downward to fit the intermediate tops, as in Figure 2(d).

The Dow Theory (not to be confused with the Dow Jones Averages), proposed by Charles Dow shortly after the turn of the century and extended in a book by Samuel Nelson[7] after Dow's untimely death, is one of the oldest technical methods still widely followed. There are many versions of this theory, but essentially it consists of three types of market

Figure 2. Some typical trendlines.

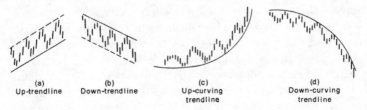

(a)	(b)	(c)	(d)
Up-trendline	Down-trendline	Up-curving trendline	Down-curving trendline

SOURCE: Krow, loc. cit.

movements: the major market trend, which can often last
a year or more; a secondary intermediate trend, which can
move against the primary trend for one to several months;
and minor movements lasting only for hours to a few days.
The determination of the major market trend is the most
important decision to the Dow believer. A rising major trend
is one where each new peak is higher than the last and
each reaction low holds at a price higher than the previous
low. In a primary downtrend the order is reversed. (See
Figure 3.)

The Dow Theory utilizes support and resistance levels,
a concept widely used by chartists. After the market has
fallen back from a previous peak, it will have difficulty going

Figure 3. Primary trends.

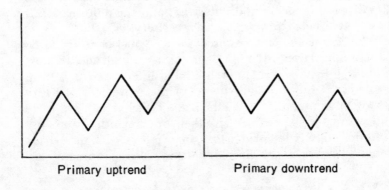

Primary uptrend   Primary downtrend

through this peak on the next upswing. This becomes a resistance level. If it does go through, it is a definite buy signal. If there is a double or triple peak, the resistance level is much tougher to break through. If the market breaks out from this point convincingly on the upside, it is a very strong buy signal. Similarly, in a decline, once a bottom is reached and the market is up from the valley, this point becomes a support level. It is difficult for either the market or an individual stock to penetrate this level. A number of these valleys near the same price make the support level that much stronger. But once a support level is definitely penetrated, abandon ship! It is a clear-cut sell signal, or for the more courageous, a time to sell short.

Price-volume systems are another popular technical method. When the market moves up on rising volume, there is increasing buying interest and prices should continue to move higher. The opposite is true when a stock declines on rising volume. The investor should buy stocks moving up on increasing volume and sell stocks moving down on larger volume.

There are many other technical systems, often more elaborate. Relative strength is one enjoying increasing popularity. Although there are many variations, the basic idea is to select stocks which are performing better than the market and to eliminate from your portfolio those which are performing more poorly. How much better or worse and for what period of time can depend on the user. With the computer, of course, it is quite easy to find the best and worst acting stocks and industries, and this information is widely circulated by various advisory services.

Filter techniques are used when a stock appears to be reversing a trend. If a stock has reached a high and declined 10%, it may be a rule to sell it, or if it has risen 10% from a low, to buy it. The amount of the movement will vary with the user of the method. Such techniques are quite common and appear to have their origins in the "stop loss" order which is designed to limit an investor's loss if the market does not rise as anticipated.* Moving averages are another

---

*The stock is sold if the price declines to a predetermined point.

popular tool. A 200-day moving average is a line drawn parallel to the price action of the stock on a chart. For each individual day's price it shows what the average price for the previous 200 days is. When a stock climbs sharply above this moving average, it is considered bullish and when it falls substantially below, bearish.

The chartist can either custom make his charts from the available information, or he can subscribe to one of numerous services which provide charts, with varying information on them. One service provides charts once a week on each stock on the New York Stock Exchange and major over-the-counter issues, as well as the strongest and weakest 50 stocks on each exchange and the relative strength of various industries. [8]

Technical analysis has, of course, become computerized and the chartist can get more and more complex information almost instantaneously. With a computer, calculating relative strength and moving averages is child's play. Computers multiply many times the technician's informational inputs. A chartist can test a method that appears promising by programming a computer to recognize the pattern it has stored (for example, a particular head-and-shoulder formation to determine where to place the sell order), and then see how the method would have worked on past prices. The system can then be modified as needed.

There is a wealth of charting and other data available to the technician which our discussion has only briefly touched upon. Most chartists use a variety of such techniques, relying on their individual judgment to choose the proper combination of methods. Judgment is extremely important both in extracting the meaning of the information from the price patterns which often appear most obscure to the layman, as well as in the choice of the method to do this.

On the outer fringe of technical analysis there are any number of exotic schemes to outdo the market. Sunspots are still thought by some to influence both economic conditions and security prices. Others read tree stumps to determine market movements. One unfortunate investment advisor, Frederick N. Goldsmith, several decades ago was brought to trial when it was discovered he got his market "signals" through the interpretation of the dialogue of characters from

a popular comic strip of the time. He had discovered this
method in a seance where he contacted James R. Keane,
the famed turn of the century Wall Street manipulator.
"Bringing Up Father" was Goldsmith's favorite comic strip
source. The signals took skill to ferret out. If Jiggs, the hero,
placed his right hand in his pocket it meant "buy." Once
at the theater Jiggs said "The intermissions are the only
good thing about this show." This of course indicated Mission
Oil would move sharply. The advisor recommended it, and
it went up 15 points the next day. At the trial, many customers
gave evidence of the substantial profits made, and Goldsmith's
sister testified that she had gone to a medium, made contact
with the spirits and asked "Could you give Fred a little advice
on how to make money?" They replied "Fred knows more
about that than we do." The judge obviously not impressed
dismissed this evidence, and the successful but unorthodox
advisor was banished from the business.[9]

The Fall from Grace of the Technician

While most Wall Streeters practice fundamental analysis,
which will be discussed next, technical analysis is followed
exclusively by a not inconsiderable minority and is used to
some degree by almost everybody. The attack on technical
analysis thus undermined an extremely widely followed investment method. What evidence did the academicians provide to support their contention that such methods were
worthless?

Basically two techniques were employed. A number of
detailed studies were made in the early sixties which demonstrated that stock movements were random, that the proof
of trend vital to the technician could not be found. Such
tests were performed by Arnold Moore in 1962, Clive Granger
and Oskar Morgenstern in 1963, and Eugene Fama in 1965.
Fama, for example, in his doctoral dissertation analyzed the
prices of the 30 stocks in the Dow Jones Industrial Average
at varying time intervals between one day and two weeks
for over five years. His results firmly supported the random
walk hypothesis.[10]

If stock prices are random, then no matter what price and volume information you have or how strong a chart may look, it is meaningless as a predictive instrument. The next move is entirely independent of the preceding one. If a stock has moved up seven days in a row, this has no influence on the eighth. It can trade up or down or be unchanged, just as a coin coming up heads many times in a row has a 50-50 chance of coming up heads again on the next toss.

In extensive testing employing rigorous statistical procedures only relatively minor departures from randomness in prices were ever found. Randomness in price movements was found day to day, week to week, and month to month.[11] No evidence to date has been able to refute the random walk hypothesis in the numerous tests conducted. Thus, the central thesis of the technician that markets and stocks display major identifiable trends that may be used to predict future movement seems to have been refuted.

The second argument of the technician was more difficult to handle. "True," they could say, "randomness might be proven day to day or for a number of successive weeks or even months, but aren't these measurements unfair? The tests have measured only total price data and indicated randomness. Could there not be useful direction in price changes within the time periods studied, such as hour to hour? Or trends to be seen by using selective data?" In effect, the technicians were inviting the academic researchers to test the systems used in technical analysis rather than price movements as a whole; which they proceeded to do, with devastating results. Some of the first tests were on different filter systems. The tests showed that after deducting commissions, filters do not work.[12] An investor is as well off with a buy-and-hold strategy. Relative strength methods were also tested, and provided no better results.[13] The popular Dow Theory in its turn was subjected to scientific scrutiny. Peaks, valleys, support and resistance levels, although important to technicians, have no predictive value in fact. Price action was random after both "sell" and "buy" signals were given.

The computer proved fickle. While helping the chartist

when in his hands, it was also turned against him. In one such test, a computer analyzed 548 stocks trading on the New York Exchange over a five-year period, scanning the information to identify any one of 32 of the most commonly followed patterns, including head and shoulders and triple tops and bottoms. It was programmed to act on its findings as a chartist would. It would, for example, buy on an upside breakout after a triple top or sell after the market had plunged through the support level of a triple bottom. The computer measured its results, based on these signals, against the performance of the general market. There seemed to be no correlation between the buy-and-sell signals and subsequent price movements. Once again our old friend the buy-and-hold strategy would have worked just as well. [14]

Price-volume systems met with the same fate. Neither the size of price nor volume changes appears to have a bearing on the magnitude or direction of future price. Stocks going down on heavy trading may just as likely reverse themselves and go up in the next period as may stocks currently going up on large volume. [15]

The tests all indicated that mechanical rules do not result in returns any better than the simple buy-and-hold strategy. [16] The evidence accumulated is voluminous and strongly supports the random walk hypothesis. Some tests have shown dependence (nonrandom price movements), indicating that a number of marginally profitable trading rules and small filters appear to consistently work. The problem is that the numerous transactions involved in such systems generate substantial commissions, which absorb the expected profit. [17]

Technicians will claim their methods work, and if you look at their examples they certainly appear to do so. But as we have seen, their success is only chance in accordance with the law of averages. Also of course their methods work better with hindsight. Technicians, being human, forget their "misses" and remember their "hits." If they are wrong, it wasn't the basic technique but its misapplication, or the fact that another application or supplementary information was required. Technicians have also claimed that some systems work supported by computer evidence of a correlation over certain periods of time. Undoubtedly this is true, but when a portion of these results were tested more thoroughly, using different time periods and more extensive price information, the correlation disappeared, again showing the systems were based simply on chance.

In the end, of course, it is impossible to absolutely prove the random walk hypothesis, for this would mean not only testing all the hundreds of systems but also the hundreds of thousands of possible combinations, with the final decision depending on the technician's own interpretation. An infinite number of tests would be required to do this. Technicians can, quite rightly, say that all systems have not been examined and that in any case their decisions were not based on any one method but were the outcome of judgment and experience. Still, from the substantial evidence accumulated, no system of technical analysis has as yet been found which can put a dent in the random walk hypothesis.

Even though the academic findings have not been refuted, chartists and other technicians continue to flourish. They disregard the findings—if they are aware of them—because "their" system is different, and hope their clients also ignore the research. Occasionally they let off steam at their antagonists, but usually their protests are without factual support.

When they are not warning investors to beware, the academics appear to regard technicians with a detached amusement that others might reserve for witch doctors or primitive soothsayers in bygone cultures (I don't dare include astrologers today). This tough and dedicated cult of financial forecasters has been taking its lumps for many years, not only from academics but also from the proponents of fundamental analysis. Some unkind fundamental analysts I have known would go so far as to propose a new experiment to the academics. A survey would be taken of shiny suits, frayed collars, and sundry holes in the attire of a sample of technicians, to be measured against a control sample of other Wall Streeters. It is believed the findings would show technicians to be far the worse for wear and tear, since most tend to follow their own pronouncements.

On the other hand, most fundamentalists are part-time

dabblers in the technical mystique. Even though fundamental
analysis is dominant on Wall Street, most of this group at
one time or another look "to see what the charts tell us,"
probably more often in periods of crisis but also as a final
affirmation of a decision to buy. We then find that in spite
of the accumulation of evidence for almost two decades on
the complete unproductiveness of the method, it continues
to be widely practiced by investors.

The Blitzkrieg Rolls On

Unfortunately for most money managers and analysts,
the academics did not rest on their laurels after this one
rather clear-cut victory. Beginning in the mid-1960s, a much
more ambitious operation was launched when the academic
researchers challenged whether fundamental analysis is of
any use in obtaining above-average gains in the market.

Fundamental research, as we have already seen, is the
gospel of the large majority of Wall Street professionals.
They have been trained in its many complex nuances and
applications, both in undergraduate and graduate schools,*
and have expanded their knowledge through daily application
in their work.

Fundamental analysis attempts to determine the real worth
of a security. The fundamentalist carefully examines the
company's competitive position, industry and economic
conditions, financial strength, expansion plans, accounting
policies, and the record of sales, earnings, and dividends.
From these and many other similar facts, often supported
by visits with senior officers of the companies, the fundamentalist hopes to accurately estimate the future rate of
earnings and dividends growth. The proper prediction of
the stream of future earnings and dividends, including an
assessment of the risk factor, is considered to be the core
of this method. Valuation formulas are then applied to this
earnings stream to determine whether the security is overval-

*A significant number of academicians still believe in, or at least still stay
employed, teaching these subjects.

ued, undervalued, or properly valued relative to its current price.* If the security is significantly undervalued, the analyst may recommend its purchase; if fully valued or overvalued, its sale.

Fundamental analysis, then, concentrates on the business and economic information affecting a company's position and prospects. The fundamentalist believes the market can very often be wrong in appraising the value of a company. If his analysis indicates a stock to be significantly undervalued, he may recommend that it be bought because he believes that the market will eventually see "the error of its ways." All fundamentalists believe that some approximation of the real worth of a stock, its intrinsic or "true" value, can be determined; that stocks do not always trade at true value; and that companies far removed in price from such value can be selected for purchase or sale, resulting in above-average market performance.

The difference between the fundamental and technical approaches can readily be seen. The technician ignores all company- and economic-related information that is central to the fundamentalist's determination of value. To the technician, all such information is already reflected in the stock's price. Value is not intrinsic but what the market says it is by its current price action. To the true fundamentalist, market information is a very secondary consideration,† for price will eventually return to true value.

Academics and fundamentalist practitioners basically agree that the size and expected trend of a company's earnings eventually determine the price of its stock. Thus, the accurate prediction of the future course of earnings is most important to successful fundamental analysis. The recent earnings record has always been a very important starting point for estimating future results, for both part-time investors and professionals who practice fundamental analysis.

---

*In the final part of this book, we shall spend some time examining the tenets of fundamental analysis.
†However, many fundamentalists, as has been indicated, attempt to "fine tune" their purchase or sale decisions by studying current price and volume data.

Just how important the recent record is for making future forecasts was indicated by a study of earnings estimates made by security analysts. The great majority of these estimates were predicated on the basis of the recent rates of change in the historical earnings pattern. The earnings estimates appeared to be simple extrapolations of trends in the recent past earnings record, even though the analysis was detailed and often included data obtained from company visits. [18]

The importance of past earnings and the emphasis placed on the direction of their change as a base for forecasting must be questioned in view of some remarkable findings in recent years. Oxford professor I. M. D. Little published a paper in 1962 which studied the earnings patterns of a group of British companies. In an article appropriately entitled "Higgledly Piggledy Growth," Little concluded that the recent course of earnings was of no use in predicting future trends. Earnings growth, as did stock prices, appeared to follow a random walk. [19] This work was expanded into a small book. [20]

Researchers in the United States conducted tests to determine the applicability of Little's findings to the American scene. The conclusions were similar; changes in the earnings of American companies appeared to follow a random walk from time period to time period. One study examined the percentage change in earnings for 700 industrial companies between 1945 and 1964. The direction of year-to-year earnings changes did not continue, and actually showed a slight tendency to reverse itself. The exception was found among companies with the steadiest rates of earnings growth, but even here the correlations were only mildly positive. [21]

At this point the reader might ask how this could be, and might even mention a number of companies that have had years of up-earnings. The answer may be found partly in the fact that for every real growth company like IBM, Xerox, or International Flavors and Fragrances, there are dozens upon dozens of others that appear to be growth companies and which have had consistently good results for years (sometimes by loose accounting) before collapsing.

Each market has scores of new concept companies with

excellent past records whose earnings growth is expected to continue forever—but doesn't. Some readers may remember the extraordinarily explosive earnings of University Computing, Leasco Data Processing, or National Student Marketing in the late 1960s, Levitz Furniture, Research Cottrell, or the catalogue retailers in the 1971–1972 market.

Even the great ones like IBM, Xerox, and Polaroid have had periods of down-earnings. Polaroid, one of the all-time favorites among growth stocks, is a particularly appropriate case. The company had an unbroken chain of earnings increases between 1964 and 1970. But even this truly exceptional company ran into difficult times with the development of a major new product, the SX-70 camera, and earnings declined for a number of years. In this light, the researchers' findings do not appear all that surprising.

In the previous chapter we saw the strongly documented case of the professional's failure to outperform the market. Now we see, perhaps as tellingly, that one of the vital tools of fundamental analysis—the ability to correctly predict future earnings—is based to a significant degree on the continuation of past earnings trends, with only random chance that past trends will persist. A question could then be raised as to whether fundamental analysis can be of any more use than technical analysis in outperforming the market.

Even before the evidence on the randomness of earnings had been found, researchers had begun to ask this question. A new hypothesis was developed, a stronger form of the random walk model, which is increasingly being called the "efficient market hypothesis" (EMH).*

Although the name is formidable, the essence of this theory is really quite simple. Researchers Hagin and Mader have defined it as follows:

> The efficient . . . market theory hypothesizes that all available information is continually analyzed and reanalyzed by literally millions of investors. It holds that in this kind of market, news

---

*Following Lorie and Hamilton, who have written a thorough book covering research in the field, the original random walk hypothesis is designated as the weak form of the efficient market hypothesis.[22]

of, say, an earnings increase, is quickly and accurately assessed by the combined actions of investors and immediately reflected in the price of the stock. The purported result of this efficiency is that, whether you buy the stock before, during, or after the earnings news, or whether you buy another stock, you can expect a fair rate of return commensurate with the risk of owning whatever security you buy.[23]

The efficient market hypothesis predicts that it is highly unlikely that an investor will outperform the market, regardless of his methods. It is unwise to believe the investor or his advisor are smart enough to beat it with regularity. And as we have seen, no proof exists that anyone has. The best strategy is simply to buy and hold a portfolio of securities with the degree of risk preferred. Securities with greater risk offer greater rewards over time. Utilizing modern statistical methods, risk can be fairly accurately measured.*

The market adjusts to new information very quickly, if not instantaneously. Since important news events, both for the market as a whole and for individual companies, enter the market unpredictably, prices react in a random manner. This is the real reason why charting and other technical schemes cannot work. Price changes are dependent on meaningful new information. Nobody knows when the next news will come, whether it will be of a political, general economic, industry, or company nature, and whether it will be positive or negative.

The implications of the efficient market hypothesis are much stronger than those of the original random walk theory.

---

*The volatility of a portfolio or any single stock can be measured against the market's over a period of time and from this correlation, predictions of a stock's future movement vis-à-vis the market can be made. Such correlations have been found to have useful predictive value. Beta is a commonly used term to measure volatility. The market is considered to have a beta coefficient of one. Stocks or portfolios with a higher beta coefficient are more volatile than the market, while those with a lower beta coefficient are less so. Thus a portfolio with a beta coefficient of two should on average move twice as far as the market, in either direction, while one with a beta coefficient of 0.5 should move about half the distance of the market. Some such adjustment for the relative riskiness of different stocks or portfolios is necessary in order to realistically compare them either to the market averages or to one another for any period of time.

In the latter case, we were told only that investors could not successfully predict future price changes from past price information, ruling out the profitable employment of technical analysis. The efficient market hypothesis, on the other hand, rules out the successful use of fundamental analysis. For if enough buyers and sellers have received and accurately measured all information on a stock and have acted rationally, prices always will be in line with basic or intrinsic value. Security analysis, by definition, attempts to discover undervalued or overvalued situations. According to the new theory, such situations do not exist because investors' continual vigilance does not let them exist. Thus the fundamentalist, like his more shopworn sibling the technician, has been told his tools are useless for determining future values with greater than average results. He might as well pack his slide rule, brush the tears from his eyes, and accept the harsh reality of life.*

Now most EMH theorists do not go quite this far. They concede that there can be stocks in some smaller companies or obscure convertibles and warrants not followed by enough sophisticated investors whose markets are not fully efficient. There can also be some exceptionally gifted individuals who can divine major developments from public information. But this ability, and these situations, are believed to be extremely rare. The markets for the stocks of the great majority of public companies are most certainly considered to be efficient. Which means you cannot beat the market.

The extensive evidence that mutual funds did not outperform the market provided major support for this theory. The Friend, Blume, and Crockett report on mutual funds referred to in the last chapter also found other evidence supporting the efficient market hypothesis. Randomly selected portfolios of New York Stock Exchange stocks performed slightly better over the 1960–1968 period than did

---

*EMH theorists acknowledge a peculiar paradox here, for if enough fundamentalists did so, markets would no longer be efficient. Thus the efficiency of markets is dependent on enough fundamentalists not believing EMH to be correct.

funds in the same risk class. It also found if the degree
of risk was kept constant there was no relationship between
a fund's performance in one period and another. Funds
in the top 10% in one period of time might as easily be
in the bottom 10% in the next, and so on. No significant
correlation was found between performance and turnover.
Rapid turnover did not improve results. Any relationship
between performance and sales charges appeared to be mildly
negative, as no-load funds and funds with lower sales charges
performed slightly better. Finally, if the risk factor was kept
constant, little difference was found in the results of funds
of various sizes.[24]

Thus, this exhaustive report on mutual funds provided
strong additional support for the demonstrated difficulty of
outperforming the market with consistency once an adjustment was made for risk. It also seemed to refute the popular
notion that turnover could improve performance and that
paying high initial sales charges for the supposedly superior
management of the load funds would lead to better results.

Testing, Testing

Once the theory of efficient markets was formulated,
academic attention became increasingly centered on whether
any tests could be established to support this thesis. A number
of experiments were devised to measure how quickly a market
adjusts to new information, since according to the hypothesis
it must be done very quickly so that alert investors do not
profit from it. In Fama's words, "Security prices at any point
in time 'fully reflect' all available information."[25]

Researchers investigated the market "legend" that stock
splits increased the value of an investor's holdings.[26] In reality,
when a stock is split, the investor still owns the same propor-
tionate share of the company. The only real benefit would
be if management increases the dividend rate at the time
of the split. This is quite common, and is often done in
the following manner: If Amalgamated Consolidated pays
a $1.00 dividend annually per share, and the stock is split
5-for-4, and the dividend is kept at $1.00 a share, the

shareholder who owned 100 shares before the split now owns 125 and receives $125 in dividends annually, a 25% increase from the previous $100.

To determine whether the market properly understood the meaning of a stock split, a thorough investigation was made of all splits of 25% or more in the New York Stock Exchange in the 1926 to 1960 period, some 940 in all. The study found stock splits were understood by the market. The stock prices after the splits maintained about the same long-term relationships to market movements as before.* The work is regarded as strong support for the hypothesis.

The market's awareness of earnings changes was also examined. Earnings changes in 261 large corporations were scrutinized between 1946 and 1966.[27] The companies were divided into two categories, those whose earnings increased and those whose earnings decreased relative to the market in a given year. It was found most often that companies with increasing earnings rose in price relative to the market and those with decreasing earnings fell through the year preceding their announcement. The authors concluded that only 10 to 15% of the information in the earnings report had not been anticipated by the reporting month. This, too, provided evidence of market efficiency.

A third test was a study to determine the effect of sizable secondary offerings (the sale of substantial blocks of stock held by either large individual or institutional investors). Normally the knowledge that a large holder is selling is

---

*Something rather curious occurs in this experiment. By demonstrating that the relationship between the sample of split stocks and the market had not changed after the date the new stock was distributed, the researchers concluded that the meaning of new information (in this case the effect of a stock split) is rapidly understood by the market. But the news of the stock split is normally announced between 60 and 90 days before the actual distribution date. Thus, the researchers should have started their measurements at this earlier time rather than at the distribution date in order to properly gauge the effect of the news. Their studies clearly showed that between the time of the announcement and the date of the stock distribution the stock prices were sharply ascending relative to the market, seemingly completely contradicting their conclusion that the market realistically discounted the news. The experiment then appeared to provide evidence that the markets are fairly inefficient rather than efficient.

considered unfavorable by the market and results in a decline in price of 1 to 2%. It was found that larger declines occurred when the seller was the corporation itself or one of its officers. Further, the full price effects of the offering were felt within six days. Since corporate insiders do not have to report such sales to the SEC for six days, the market apparently anticipates the identity of the seller.*[28] Other tests of market awareness of developments provided similar results.

The researchers do not claim any one test can establish the theory; rather they say each test provides further supportive evidence. Through the accumulation of such evidence, they believe a very strong case has been established.

Some academic researchers have asked whether a strong form of EMH also applies. They hypothesize that all information, not only published reports but also the kind received by security analysts and money managers in confidential meetings with senior company management, is without benefit in improving results. Also of no benefit is private information known only to company insiders and privileged trading information known only to the specialist trading a security.

The first question we must ask is how much "inside information" do professional investors really have? It would seem on the whole to be very little. SEC corporate disclosure rules† are becoming increasingly more stringent following the landmark rulings in the *SEC v. Texas Gulf Sulphur* and *SEC v. Merrill Lynch* cases.

In the first case, insiders benefited from the knowledge of the discovery of a major copper ore body in Ontario in 1964. Insiders, knowing a public announcement was to be made on April 16, 1964 at a 10 A.M. press conference, put in orders at the market opening, also at 10 A.M. The news came out over the Dow Jones ticker at 10:54 A.M. (although Merrill Lynch had already released a condensed

---

*I am not quite sure how the market is supposed to anticipate the identity of the seller. Perhaps the spirit of the famed speculator James R. Keane is consulted by far more people than just Fredrick Goldsmith, the unfortunate advisor discussed earlier.

†Rules on how broadly material information must be disclosed when given to any one person or group.

version on its private wire system at 10:29). Substantial profits were realized on the early orders.[29] The SEC sued to rescind these profits and won the decision. The important principle established was that anyone trading on the basis of inside information is in effect considered an insider whether he or she is one or not.

The second case involved important information concerning Douglas Aircraft. On June 21, 1966, institutional salesmen from Merrill Lynch, the company's investment bankers, disclosed to a dozen or so mutual funds and other professional investors that the company would shortly report poorer than expected earnings. This news had not as yet been announced publicly by the company. These investors sold 154,000 shares totaling over $13 million. In a major decision in favor of the SEC in July 1971, it was ruled that an investor acting on inside information, in this case a tip from a salesman, violates the law if he is aware the information has not yet been made public. It was also stated that the use of such information is illegal even if the recipient received it innocently or by chance.

At the present time, any information released by a company to any investor must be released to all investors. The New York Stock Exchange also requires member firms to immediately report any significant information about a listed company not being used for investment banking purposes.

It is extremely dangerous today for a mutual fund or other institutional investor to attempt to take advantage of inside information. Any such action could ruin the career of the professional involved. The same danger exists for corporate management. Practically speaking, when it is remembered that most large portfolios may have a hundred or more stocks in them, the overall effect of an inside disclosure must be small, hardly worth the risk of a possible jail term.

There have been a few tests to determine whether specialists and other insiders can outperform the market. One study concluded that specialists on major exchanges could profitably utilize the information on their "books" (about unexecuted

orders at varying prices, most of which is confidential).[30]
A second study found that insiders apparently display some
ability to outperform the market in their trading.[31] These
are the only departures from the concept of a highly efficient
market that have been found, and their effect is considered
to be unimportant to the proper functioning of securities
markets.

The original random walk hypothesis, broadened to include various forms of the efficient market hypothesis, is
by far the most important stock market theory of modern
times. If widely accepted, it will drastically change the entire
nature of investing and the shape of the securities industry.
How valid, then, are its conclusions? To answer this question
we must carefully examine the adequacy of the academic
approach with its sole reliance on wide samples of both price
changes and professional performance records. There is
always the danger that reliance solely on extensive statistical
analysis without the detailed insight and corroboration of
numerous individual examples may be similar to the story
of the blindfolded Hindu youth who attempted to describe
the anatomy of an elephant by feeling only its leg or its
trunk. He may have precisely delineated the parts he examined but this is a small fraction of the whole.

There is little question that the academic researchers have
made an immensely valuable contribution to finance. By
systematically collecting and categorizing a vast amount of
market information, researchers have introduced a scientific
approach to the study of securities markets for the first time.
But, we must still ask if their hypothesis is broad and realistic
enough to explain all the evidence we have viewed to date.
To answer this question we should examine the premises
on which EMH is based.

The efficient market hypothesis makes some very precise
assumptions about how investors behave in the marketplace.
It assumes that enough well-trained investors instantly and
flawlessly understand the meaning of new information and
act rationally upon it to keep prices constantly in line with
true value.

Do investors in reality act in the rational error-free manner that EMH assumes? We have already observed how wide samples of professionals in the surveys discussed in Chapter 1 did worse than the market and were most negative at market bottoms. Further disclaiming evidence was provided recently by *Fortune* magazine.[32] It estimated that corporate pension and profit-sharing plans, the largest class of institutional investors, would have been worth $13 billion more in the 1966–1975 period, if they had only done as well as the S&P 500. This was before deducting brokerage commissions and advisory fees! These findings cannot be explained by EMH. In fact, they directly contradict its most crucial premise that it is the very error-free operations of these professionals that keeps prices consistently in line with value.

As interesting and important as the efficient market hypothesis appears to be, the contradictions are simply too telling not to pursue our examination further. A good scientific theory must be in harmony with all the important facts it purports to explain, including those that are inconvenient or contradictory. EMH does not seem to be able to do this. Thus we should look beyond this hypothesis in an attempt to find a more comprehensive and satisfactory explanation of the evidence we have viewed.

The logical starting point would seem to be the assumption of rationality, the cornerstone of the efficient market hypothesis. Are investors really as consistently rational in their investment decisions as this theory assumes? The evidence on professionals introduced to date appears to indicate not. Let us next examine how well the concept of rationality fits in with the behavior of investors in markets in both the distant and the more recent past.

Part II

Psychological
Aberrations
of the Market Crowd

3

Bubbles, Bubbles, Bubbles

In this chapter we are going to take a brief detour through history in order to observe the actions of crowds, that is to say large groups of investors, in the grip of speculative fever. Our trip will not be that of the economic historian for we are not looking for specific dates or facts per se; instead we are trying to gain an understanding of investor behavior and investor psychology.

Speculative fever or speculative mania is a way of characterizing periods at various times and in various countries when the combination of strong economic fundamentals and investor confidence pushes the prices of stocks or commodities or land far beyond traditionally prevailing standards of value. The prices stay up for weeks, for months, sometimes for years, which of course reinforces investor confidence and pushes prices still higher. To those caught up in such a situation, it can be a heady experience. The everyday rules of the game are discarded. Profits, equal to years of hard work, are made in days or weeks; dreams of a lifetime are realized in months. The climb in prices becomes the single, obsessive topic of conversation, and dramatic stories circulate, usually embellished with each telling, of the fortunes made by individuals who got in early. Those who are still on the sidelines seem to be wasting a golden opportunity, and more and more people are drawn into the boiling market as speculators. It is like discovering a gambling casino where

the odds have changed suddenly and dramatically in favor
of the patrons. When investors see that the wildest gambles
are rewarded with success, caution is thrown to the winds,
and the voices of reason and moderation are shouted down.
The great bubble of hope, unreason, confidence, and greed
floats upward. Of course all bubbles, real or figurative, come
to the same end.

A suitable guide on our ramble through history would
be a Frenchman by the name of Gustave Le Bon who in
1895 published *The Crowd*, a remarkable book which still
has many lessons for us. According to Le Bon, a group of
people becomes a crowd when

> . . . the sentiment and ideas of all the persons in the gathering
> take one and the same direction, and their conscious personality
> vanishes. A collective mind is formed doubtless transitory but
> presenting very clearly defined characteristics. The gathering
> has then become . . . a psychological crowd.

And what are the characteristics of such a psychological
crowd? Le Bon continues:

> Whoever be the individuals that compose it, however like or
> unlike their mode of life, their occupations, their character
> or their intelligence, the fact that they have been transformed
> into a crowd puts them in possession of a sort of collective
> mind which makes them feel, think, and act in a manner quite
> different from that of each individual of them would feel,
> think, and act were he in a state of isolation. . . . The individual
> forming part of a crowd acquires solely from numerical consid-
> erations a sentiment of invincible power which allows him to
> yield to instincts which had he been alone he would perforce
> have kept under restraint.[1]

Keep these ideas in mind as we make the first stop on
our tour: Holland in the early seventeenth century. If the
Dutch, who might be characterized as somber, hardworking,
God-fearing citizens, seem unlikely candidates as wild-eyed
speculators, then the object of their frenzy must appear even
more incongruous—tulips. Not gold or silver or shipping
or colonies in the new world, but tulips.

Tulipmania

Just as the money managers of today often buy a "concept stock"—one whose idea appears irresistibly right for the time—so were the Dutch smitten with a concept. Nobles, weavers, merchants, innkeepers, tax collectors, sailors, servants, chimneysweeps, Lutherans, Arminians, and "Papists" all fell in love with the tulip. Jewelry was pawned, houses mortgaged, crops and businesses sold in order to buy the valuable bulbs. Prices soared, and there seemed to be no end to it all.

Tulips were first imported into northern Europe from Turkey in the 1550s and found their way into Holland somewhat before the turn of the century. From the beginning, they were considered to be a mark of distinction, and connoisseurs displayed them like works of art. By the early 1600s the fashion has spread throughout Europe, and the Dutch became the principal suppliers of bulbs. At the peak of interest, tulips were cultivated in a 40-mile stretch between Amsterdam and The Hague.

Before going on to examine the wild excesses of the tulip boom, it is worth noting that there was, in fact, a sound economic basis for the interest in tulips as an investment. They were a botanical novelty to the professional gardeners of Europe; they were genuinely beautiful; and the climate and soil conditions of Holland seemed to be just right for their cultivation. Since the crowned heads and lesser nobility of Europe were eager to have uncommon varieties of these plants (and could certainly pay for them), a prudent Dutchman might well put some of his money into raising tulips. None of this, of course, explains the frenzy or the folly of the tulip craze in full swing, but it does point up a peculiar characteristic of such speculative manias which we will find to be a common denominator of all such booms: namely, that the mania occurs in the context of a relatively sound, prosperous economy, and that it starts out as a reasonable investment opportunity.

By the 1620s, demand for tulips was rising steadily. Horticulturists in Holland created many beautiful and rare new varieties. They were helped in their efforts by a plant disease which caused strange mutations to the tulip's inner petals. Many lovely new shades of pinks, mauves, yellows, and eye-catching color combinations were developed. Each tulip was given a name, and the Dutch began to pay high prices for the rarer, more exotic bulbs. The Semper Augustus by 1624 was worth 1,200 florins ($1,800 in current dollars). Its large calyx was white, the base lightly flecked in blue and trimmed with bright red vertical stripes.

The trade was limited to horticulturists and collectors until 1633, when the public became involved. It was at this stage that the frenzy began. Prices started to rise rapidly. A house in Hoorn was bought for three tulip bulbs. A single Admiral Liefkens sold for $6,600. The price of a Semper Augustus ranged from $6,000 to $8,250. In Amsterdam one resident made $90,000 from his garden in four months. Rare tulips were more valuable in weight than gold, and people stayed awake at night watching their gardens, or else fixed bells to their beds connected to cords surrounding the precious tulips. Prowlers would trip the cord, ring the bell, and the owner would come aflying.

As the year progressed, turnover quickened and substantial profits were made. One bulb which had been bought for $65 was resold a little later for $800. Market participation was considerably broadened by the sale of the less valuable bulbs by the pound. Like modern market players, who buy lower-priced issues because they cannot afford the more expensive blue-chip stocks, tulip traders could now also buy lower-priced issues. In a raging bull market the "cats" and "dogs" (low-priced speculative stocks) move spectacularly, and it was no different with tulips. Gheele Cruohen, bought for about $30 a pound, was sold a month later at $1,575.

With such spectacular profits to be made, money poured into Holland from abroad to be invested in bulbs. In cities and towns where bulbs were traded, rumors of foreign orders and still higher prices constantly fanned through the exchanges and taverns, and bulbs might change hands as often as ten times a day. A commodities future market in tulips developed as the boom progressed, with payment and delivery to be made at a specified future date. Sellers sold bulbs they did not actually own to buyers who pledged money they did not yet have. Both parties believed they could honor the contract at a profit.

Of course, there were some cool heads who remained unswayed by the spectacle of spiraling tulip prices and refused to enter the fray. These few that stood aside called the investors Kappisten, "the hooded ones," after the hoods then worn by madmen.

There were a few incidents that had a comic aspect—that is, when viewed in hindsight. An amateur English botanist in the conservatory of his host, a wealthy Dutchman, began stripping off the coats of what he believed to be a most remarkable onion. He had cut it into two equal parts, making numerous scientific comments on the onion's appearance when the owner pounced on him in fury and asked him if he knew what he was doing. "Peeling a most extraordinary onion," replied the philosopher. "*Hundert tausend duyvel!*" said the Dutchman. "It's an Admiral Van der Eyek." "Thank you," replied the traveler taking out his notebook, "are these admirals common in your country?" The owner at this point became apoplectic; the astonished Englishman was dragged through the streets followed by a mob to the magistrate, where he found out what he had done, and lodged in jail until he could produce the $6,000 to pay the cost of his experiment.

Even the most delightful dreams eventually end, and when this one did, the awakening was sudden and harsh. One day, in early February 1637, a dealer bought a bulb and found he could not resell it. The individual dealer's predicament, coupled with the obvious abuses of credit in bulb transactions, panicked the other dealers. Everyone tried to sell at once, but buyers had vanished. Previous purchasers would no longer honor commitments because prices had dropped to a fraction of former levels.

How the wheel turns. A few months earlier a man in possession of a few rare tulip bulbs could command house, land, ships, jewels, or whatever else he desired. Now they were worth little more than onions.

Shockwaves reverberated through society and, although attempts to save the situation were made by the tulip growers, the municipalities, and the courts, the damage was beyond repair. The panic fed on itself, and prices continued to sink. Eventually a few honest people who had contracted for purchase paid 1 or 2%, or in rare cases 5%, of the original price. Most paid nothing. By the end of April 1637, the price of the most expensive bulb had dropped from $8,250 to $75. Among the financially ruined were the painter Jan van Goyen and his teacher, Jan Steen. In the rush to acquire tulip bulbs, they had disposed of many pictures, works of art which today are priceless.

The story of these little men in funny hats chasing tulips with unpronounceable names has more to do with us and with the subject of this book than might be immediately obvious. First, it demonstrated an important point about how people determine what is realistic and what is ridiculous. Social psychologists are devoting increasing attention to the importance of recent and repeated experience in shaping our perception of reality. Such immediate situational factors often seem to override well-established previous standards in determining our social behavior. The human animal is apparently heavily influenced by the whims of the moment, rather than by the wisdom of the past.

If, for example, my neighbor tried to sell me a tulip bulb for $5,000 I'd simply laugh at him; that's ridiculous—unless, of course, I had just seen one exactly like it in a shop for $4,975. If I had seen the same bulb elsewhere for $5,025, I might even think my neighbor's bulb was a bargain. The tulip craze, like the manias we shall see shortly, created its own reality as it went along. It is ludicrous to pay as much for a flower as one pays for a house, but if tulips sell for that price every day (repeated experience) and have done so for many months (recent experience), then the whopping price becomes, from the contemporary point of view, "realistic."

Our guide, Le Bon, has some further thoughts on crowds which apply rather neatly to the tulip bulb mania and to others as well.

> A crowd thinks in images, and the image itself calls up a
> series of other images, having no logical connection with the
> first . . . a crowd scarcely distinguishes between the subjective
> and the objective. It accepts as real the images invoked in
> its mind, though they most often have only a very distant relation
> with the observed facts. . . . These image-like ideas are not
> connected by any logical bond or analogy or succession and
> may take each other's place like the slides of a magic lantern.
> . . . Crowds being only capable of thinking in images are only
> to be impressed by images.[2]

Le Bon's "images" bear a striking resemblance to the
"concepts" which so moved investors in the 1960s and to
the tulips, which became the new image of wealth. People
sold or exchanged gold, houses, diamonds—the more traditional trappings of wealth—to get their hands on tulip bulbs.
But like Le Bon's magic lantern, the shifts in images, or
concepts, are abrupt and sudden, and when the tulip fell
out of favor it became almost worthless.

The First Hot New Issues Market

Would you be tempted to play the market if you saw
General Motors rise over 800% in less than five months?
Suppose the President of the United States was GM's previous
chairman, and a good number of senior senators and con-
gressmen had been associated with it? What more could an
investor ask for?

In this case, it was the English who dropped their impecca-
ble cool and were catapulted into market insanity. It began
in 1711 with the formation of a company entitled "The
Governour and Company of Merchants of Great Britain
Trading to the South Seas and Other Parts of America and
for the Encouragement of Fishing." That mouthful was
certainly not likely to give investors concept, and concept
is what fueled fantasy then just as it does now. But the
South Sea Company, as it came to be known, was a happier
choice of name. It conjured up visions of stupendous quanti-
ties of gold and silver pouring out of the vast, almost
inexhaustible mines of South America. These precious metals

would be traded for English manufactured goods on terms making every shareholder rich. It was a name that encouraged daydreams and spawned images.

The company's first years were inauspicious. In return for taking over a portion of the English national debt, the company was granted a monopoly on English trade with the Spanish colonies in America and the Pacific Islands. King George I became its first governor.

The monopoly covered a vast amount of territory, but Spain ruled its colonies literally with a mailed fist and allowed almost no trade with other countries. All that was allowed the company by the Spanish government was a limited trade in slaves and the right to send one ship per year, called the "permission ship," to trade with the colonies. The profits of this one ship was to be divided with the King of Spain. All in all, small pickings. However, we must never underestimate the skill of the concept weaver, even if the material is not the best. In this craft the South Sea Company directors were first rate and could probably have taught many present-day promoters a thing or two.

In 1719 the company took over another government loan, again offering the loan holders company shares in exchange. The directors made every effort to indicate their charter would result in enormous profit, and the debt holders eagerly accepted the stock. Both the government and the debt holders did well, the government because the company reduced its interest, the former debt holders because the stock rose.

The stage was now set for a bold stroke of creative management. England was extremely prosperous at this time, and investment opportunities were limited. Like the Dutch in our last episode, the English were ready for a bold concept, and concept was something the South Sea directors had plenty of (we have just seen that they had precious little else). The company's next move was to attempt to take over the entire national debt of England on terms that would ease the high interest burden to the government. In order to make this work, stock in the company had to be issued at continually rising prices to both the public and the bondholders. The nerve of it is breathtaking. Here was the conglomerate game two and a half centuries before its time. Even Leasco Data Processing or Ling-Temco-Vought at their pinnacle in the late 1960s wouldn't have dared to think of funding Uncle Sam.

The concept looms now worked round the clock spinning exciting tales of what government would give the company for substantially reducing its debt. One of the most persistent rumors was that Spain would give the company major bases in Peru with free-trading rights to the immense wealth of its colonies. The stock, buoyed by such whisperings, began its relentless and necessary flight upward.

At the end of January 1720, the price of South Sea stock stood at £129. In less than six months it had gone over £1,000, reaching a high of £1,050. Naturally, it was not an unbroken advance, and there were moments of profit taking and loss of confidence in which some investors were ruined. One such moment occurred after the stock had run from £550 to £890 in just four days. When the stock declined to £640 in a single morning's trading session, the directors, always on the alert, sent their agents to Exchange Alley (where the stock was traded) to buy, and the rout was stopped.

It is hardly surprising that social conversation of the time was dominated by talk of "South Seas"; and it was considered unfashionable not to hold shares. The pressures on people to conform to the currently popular investment mania (and ask few questions) may be judged from the following fact: at the height of the boom, the South Sea Company stock had a total market value of some £500 million, roughly five times the current cash in all of Europe. Is this rational behavior by competent investors? With the wisdom of hindsight the answer must be "no," but again the concept created its own "reality," thereby reshaping the perceptions and expectations of investors. We might ask just what then is reality?

Social psychologists have devoted a significant amount of time to this question. Our beliefs, we are told, might be thought to lie along a continuum. At one end are those based on incontrovertible physical evidence (for example, my car won't run without gas in its tank, or ice cubes left unrefrigerated indoors will melt within a short time). At the other end of the continuum are beliefs based on little or no evidence. Much of the world that is important to us has few objectively definable criteria, and those that are present are difficult to evaluate (for example, what is the best political party, or how much is a stock worth?).

The more vague or complex the information, the more dependent we are on other people both for clarification and as benchmarks against which to measure our own opinions. The examination of the statements and actions of others reduces the uncertainty we have about our own beliefs. These "social comparison processes," as psychologists call them, provide an anchor for our own opinions, when there is no other way in which to assess them.

Social psychologists have shown experimentally that the greater the uncertainty, and the fewer the objective criteria, the more we measure reality against the opinions of others. The term social reality refers to how a group perceives reality. Because a group can combine both objective and subjective criteria in reaching its social reality, it can often be substantially different from objective reality.

And this brings us back to South Seas and other speculative periods. In each case, the investor was aware of the soundness of the initial idea, watched the continual rise in prices, and saw how widespread the support for each concept was. He might certainly have questioned how realistic price levels were—whether they were overblown or whether, in fact, substantial gains still lay ahead. Because the facts were undoubtedly most difficult to evaluate, it is probable that social comparison processes played an important role in influencing the investor's own view of reality. Most often, it tilted it closer to the view of the crowd, which was distorted with visions of larger and larger profits.

Once the mind is accustomed to quick and fabulous gain, it becomes almost addictive. All that spring and summer of 1720 investors were looking for the "next South Sea Company" in the way modern ones often looked for the next Xerox or Polaroid. Companies were organized to buy ships to suppress pirates, to "erect saltworks in the Holy Land," to trade in human hair, to make soap (recently discovered), to provide poor workmen with watches, to import jackasses from Spain, to drain the bogs in Ireland, to pave the streets of London, and to build hospitals and homes for illegitimate children.

Some of the schemes tickled the fancy. Companies offered to extract oil from radishes and silver from lead, to create a wheel of perpetual motion and to make gold out of seawater. One even promised to bring up hellfire. It mattered little what the company actually proposed to do, for investors were in thrall to Le Bon's "images." All that was needed was a company with "concept," and wealth would follow automatically.

Among the most intriguing stories is that of the hard-working printer on Cornhill Street who grew envious watching the promoters in Exchange Alley coin money. He hatched his own scheme offering investors to participate in "a company for carrying on an undertaking of great advantage, but nobody to know what it is."[3] Capitalizing the mystery company at 5,000 shares priced at £100 each, he opened the doors of his office on Cornhill for subscriptions at 9 A.M., with crowds already waiting patiently outside. When he closed at 3 P.M., 1,000 shares were subscribed for with each investor putting down a deposit of £2. Pocketing this sum, no small amount in today's purchasing power, and not explaining what the funds would go for, he had the good sense to set off that evening for the Continent, never to be heard from again.

A considerable number of issues rose sharply in the aftermarkets, just as hot new issues rise today. Many investors believed they lived at the beginning of a major new age of advancement. Invention was coming to the forefront, so anything might be possible even if ideas appeared to be farfetched. Modern investors have paid just as happily, as we shall see in the next chapter, for the contemporary magic of electronics, pharmaceuticals, computers, and medical technology.

The price of the South Sea shares hovered around £1,000 in late July. This was the high-water mark of the bubble. It broke quickly and spectacularly. Part of the reason was the directors themselves; they were just too effective. Their substantial bribes, both in money and stock, to members of Parliament, cabinet ministers, and even to several of the King's favorite mistresses were effective in getting what they wanted. They did not at all like the numerous little companies springing up and diverting money away from the main bubble, and got Parliament to pass legislation outlawing most of them. After public discussion on the lack of substance of these companies, the Bubble Act was passed on July 12, 1720. The directors also launched a suit against four minor bubbles. They won it, but by so doing they aired all the worst abuses of the time. People increasingly wondered if the South Sea Company was really only a gigantic version of these smaller bubbles.

News poured in swiftly, and it was all bad. Investors' fears were reinforced by the collapse of the gigantic Mississippi Company in France. Rumor, now working against the company, reported that the king of Spain had no intention of increasing the company's trading privileges and, in fact, might restrict the limited ones granted to date.

In early August the stock began to decline. The directors, led by the chairman Sir John Blunt, secretly disposed of their shares, but the news became known fairly quickly. In August the stock dropped steadily and by September 2 it was down 30% to £700. A public meeting was called on September 8 to rekindle enthusiasm, but it was too late. By September 12th the stock was at £580. The directors, previously among the most celebrated figures in London, could no longer appear on the streets without having to run from crowds while dodging stones.

> We find that whole communities suddenly fix their minds upon one subject, and go mad in its pursuit; that millions of people become simultaneously impressed with one delusion and run after it. . . . Sober nations have all at once become desperate gamblers, and risked almost their existence upon the turn of a piece of paper. . . . Men, it has been well said, think in herds . . . they go mad in herds, while they only recover their senses slowly and one by one.[4]

So wrote Charles Mackay in 1852 in his book *Extraordinary*

Popular Delusions and the Madness of Crowds. He may have had the South Sea fiasco in mind when he wrote this, or he may have been prophesying about speculative manias yet to come. The point here is that "the madness of the crowd" does not end when the speculative enthusiasm turns sour. When the bubble bursts, when the "image of the magic lantern" changes, an almost inevitable reaction sets in and the crowd becomes as extreme in its panic as it had been in its euphoria. Again, caution and rationality are thrown to the winds in the headlong rush to sell. Just as the true value of the investment was overestimated on the way up, so is it ignored on the way down. Frightened investors caught up in the new social reality tried to sell at any price.* This was the scene in London in the autumn of 1720.

The desperation to get to Exchange Alley and sell became a stampede. Masses of people crowded every inch of the alley to the point of suffocation. Anxiety enveloped everyone. Some ran up and down adjoining streets aimlessly in stark terror. Nobody knew the full extent of the disaster and rumors circulated, each worse than the last. For those involved it was like watching a hundred-foot tidal wave approach, knowing that in a matter of minutes they and their world would be swept away.

With the public in the throes of a panic, the stock continued to plummet. By the end of September it was quoted at £129. Thousands were ruined, some committed suicide. Banks that held South Sea shares as collateral shut their doors, and even the Bank of England narrowly escaped being carried off with the rest.

The King, vacationing abroad, hurried back and summoned Parliament. The investigation that followed turned up widespread corruption, and eventually the directors were stripped of most of their estates and a number of government officials cast into the Tower. One parliamentarian proposed putting the directors in sacks, stitching the tops, and throwing

---

*Social reality, unlike reality based on objective criteria, can be subject to sudden and violent shifts. The writings of Mackay and LeBon, precursors of this theory, clearly show this.

them live into the Thames. Curiously enough, Sir John Blunt, the prime organizer of the company's machinations and among the most responsible for the ensuing disaster, was a deeply religious man who spoke out repeatedly against the thievery and corruption of the age and the greed of the wealthy. Do times ever change?

You, Too, Can Own a Swamp

We turn now to an episode somewhat closer to home: the Florida land boom of the 1920s. This differed from most land booms, which tend to be localized phenomena, in that it attracted buyers and speculators from all over the United States. It also satisfied the twin criteria or preconditions for a speculative mania. The mid-1920s was a time of considerable prosperity in the United States. We had emerged from World War I as the strongest nation on earth, with a prosperous and confident middle class. With no clouds on the horizon, there seemed to be no reason the good times should not last indefinitely. Secondly, the specific investment vehicle, real estate in Florida, represented good value at the outset. The rich had gone to Florida for years to soak up the sun in elegant resorts such as Palm Beach and St. Augustine. Shortly before World War I they were followed by northern manufacturers and prosperous midwestern farmers who began to winter there.

In the new age that was dawning after World War I, the middle and lower classes discovered Florida and the real migration began. Farmers, teachers, merchants, laborers, and clerks all trekked south, many of them in their own cars. They spent the winter touring the state and were often called "tin-canners" because they slept in their cars or tents along the road and lived on canned or packaged foods. It was like the promised land—or a reasonable approximation of it. The long, pleasant hours in the sun and the relaxed way of life led many people who had come for a vacation to think of settling there permanently, and owning their own home and property. Even if salaries were low and work hours long, times were good, and they would certainly find a way to make it all come true.

With such an influx of people and such a tide of confidence in the future, it was only natural that land prices, which were low in relation to other parts of the United States, should start to move up.

The beginnings of the boom were sound enough. Real estate projects at Palm Beach, Miami Beach, Coral Gables, and Davis Island were all prosperous and growing. Original purchasers now enjoyed sharply higher values for their properties, and tremendous stretches of undeveloped land were still available for purchase.

Florida's population increased 22% between 1923 and 1926 to 1,290,350, while bank deposits increased 275%. Housing was short, salaries were rising, and expectations high. As tourists returned for a second and third time, they began to buy heavily.

A lot purchased for $800 in the development of Miami Beach only a few years before was resold for $150,000 in 1924. A strip of land in Palm Beach worth $240,000 just prior to the war was sold for $800,000 in 1923. The same property was subdivided and sold for $1,500,000 in 1924. By 1925 it was claimed to be worth $4,000,000. A poor woman paid $25 for a piece of land near Miami in 1896 which was resold in 1925 for $150,000. The lesson of these windfall profits was not lost on people just arriving in Florida: buy the first piece of land you can get your hands on and don't be choosy about the price.

With the public appetite whetted, hundreds of developers sprang into action and new projects shot up everywhere. Most of the activity occurred in a hundred-mile stretch extending from Palm Beach to Coral Gables. Miami and Miami Beach, raised from swampland, were the center of the magnet. Excluding construction, $3 million in lots were sold in Miami in 1923, $8 million in 1924, and $12 million in 1925.

The developments were often laid out in splendiferous style, possibly best termed "early Cecil B. De Mille." Boca Raton's main highway, El Camino Real, was 20 lanes wide and ran the grand length of half a mile. The homes were to be situated on canals. Gondoliers were actually imported from Venice to sing mellifluous Italian melodies as they glided peacefully through the new paradise. "Near" paradise is more exact, for despite repeated and costly efforts, the water refused to blend with the heavenly scenario, obstinately staying a murky brown rather than the desired blue.

Heavy advertising was carried on in major newspapers across the country, and responses were excellent. Many developments sold out quickly, often in the first day. If anyone had bothered to check, he would have found that these advertisements bore only a tenuous relationship to the actual properties. Manhattan estates, a typical example, was billed as being less than a mile from the fast-growing, prosperous town of Nettie. Nettie, it turned out, was not a town at all, but an abandoned turpentine camp. Such evidence of fraud, even when revealed, seemed to have little effect on the buying mood of the public.

Some of the larger developments incorporated themselves as cities and sold their own municipal bonds. The "city" of Coral Gables contained 2,000 houses in various stages of construction, a business center, banks, churches, hotels, schools, and apartment houses. The famed orator William Jennings Bryan was hired to sit under an umbrella on a raft in a lagoon and extol the virtues of Coral Gables in his golden tones, at a purported $250 a talk. The oratory was followed by the performance of a celebrated dancer and culminated with the unleashing of a horde of hungry salesmen on the large enthusiastic crowd.

The real frenzy began in 1924 and continued through 1925 before the collapse the following year. Salesmen swarmed south to make their fortunes selling the new dream. Many had given up the stock market or other real estate dealings for this more lucrative venture. By 1925, Miami was in the grip of a gigantic land fever. An estimated 2,000 real estate offices lined its streets, and 25,000 agents worked out of them, a not inconsiderable number when the census listed the entire Miami population at 75,000. No one at the time seemed to be bothered by the ridiculously high ratio of salesmen to potential buyers. An idea of what the scene must have been like may be had by imagining one Sabrett hot-dog vendor for every three residents of New York City. Once again, the image had shaped its own reality.

Had any one been able to sit back and look objectively at what was going on (and as we have seen this is about the last thing persons in the grip of a speculative mania are able to do), they would have noticed many telltale signs and portents of disaster to come.

The city's utilities were overloaded, and the railroad placed an embargo on imperishable freight such as building materials in order to prevent famine. Steamship capacity was also strained, and restrictions were placed on types of cargos handled. The harbor was filled with shipping, and highways were clogged for hundreds of miles with cars bound southward. Miami Beach was so deluged with buyers that residents put signs on their front lawns, indicating their lots were not for sale. Transactions accelerated, as they always do toward the end of a mania. One man paid $3 million for a stretch of beach and resold it a week later for $12 million. That summer the *Miami News* printed a 504-page edition, almost entirely devoted to real estate ads, while the *Miami Herald* that year set a new record for the volume of newspaper advertising carried.

Only one final touch was required to make the giant speculative cauldron boil over—easy credit—and it was readily provided. When a transaction was closed, a buyer would make a 10% down payment on the lot. For this 10% payment he was given a "binder," an option on the selected lot which he could resell immediately. The terms normally required a first payment of 25% within thirty days.

Businessmen, speculators, and "tin-canners" wandered into the various offices and heard stories of the fabulous profits made from the salesmen called "binder-boys." People were encouraged to buy a number of binders as an investment. The real estate offices were so busy and the paperwork so backed up that the first payment need not be made for months. In the meantime, with prices going up, some binders could be sold at a profit, and the rest kept for nothing.

Although transportation to the more legitimate sites was available, buyers were encouraged not to see the property but instead to examine the large, beautifully detailed blueprints that showed the fanciful images of what was to be: houses, churches, schools, commercial buildings, parks, and excellent transportation facilities. Such wishful thinking disguised the fact that most lots were small, usually 50 by 100 feet, and many were under water.

The purchase of binders became increasingly speculative. Eventually, at least 90% of the buyers had no intention of living on the property. Many were quite aware that their dream lots lay in a swamp or in bottomless mud, but the frenzy was expected to continue and quick gains would be made before the first payment was required. This line of thinking, common to speculative manias, is aptly termed the "Greater Fool Theory." According to this theory, any price, no matter how out of line with historical values, can be justified if you believe that there is another buyer who will take the stock or the real estate off your hands for an even greater price. So a final deed might have six or more binders on it, with each holder making a profit.

Buyers were encouraged by the optimism exuding from a variety of sources. The *Saturday Evening Post*, America's most widely read magazine at the time, published favorable articles on Florida throughout the boom. Many well-known people, including J. C. Penney, the Ringling Brothers, T. Coleman duPont, and the famed speculator Jesse Livermore, endorsed the soundness of Florida land. Stock market expert Roger W. Babson, although he predicted the stock market's later demise, believed the land boom to be fundamentally sound. Financial experts expressed the opinion that Florida land was still quite undervalued relative to property in the rest of the nation. The boom, it seemed, was only just beginning. . . .

But as we know, the cauldron does not bubble cheerfully indefinitely, or usually even for very long. In this case, the euphoria began to disintegrate in 1926. In the spring and summer of that year, trading in binders started to slow, and fewer people appeared to be coming south. Too, the Better

Business Bureaus in some northern cities put out warnings about the sharp practices often carried out in Florida. Although the various Florida interests counterattacked furiously, the impact sank in.

Speculators began to take losses. An investor who bought some property in the summer of 1925 and refused an offer of $325,000 in November of the same year, with declining values was forced to settle for $50,000 in cash in April of 1926. By mid-1926 large-scale defaults were occurring on binders, as new buyers could not be found. Prices continued down. In some cases, land came back by default to the original owners with larger taxes and assessments than the money they had received and marred by partially completed structures and roads.

The coup de grâce was given by mother nature herself. The first major hurricane in 16 years ripped through Florida, uprooting trees, smashing buildings, and tossing large yachts onto the streets of Miami and Coral Gables. Almost 400 people were killed and over 6,000 injured. The worst devastation was in the major development areas. Although promoters continued to beat their drums, the tourist industry did not recover, and buyers stayed away. By 1927 most of the real estate offices in Miami were closed. In 1928, when it seemed possible that the land business might recover with an ebullient stock market and economy, the Almighty did not heed the prayers of the remaining binder-boys, for a second hurricane struck.

A journalist in 1928 describing his approach to Miami by car wrote:

> Dead subdivisions line the highway, their pompous names half obliterated on crumbling stucco gates. Lonely white . . . lights stand guard over miles of cement sidewalks, where grass and palmetto take the place of homes that were to be. . . . Whole sections of outlying subdivisions are composed of unoccupied houses, past which one speeds on broad thoroughfares as if traversing a city in the grip of death.[5]

Florida had more bank failures than any state in the nation in both 1928 and 1929. By 1929 bank clearings had dropped to under 15% of the 1925 level. The practice of incorporating real estate developments as separate cities resulted in widespread defaults, and only the strongest separately incorporated cities have survived. Even today they are struggling under heavy financial burdens, and in each city can be found partially completed structures, the untended graves of earlier dreams.

Looking back on the speculative periods we have just viewed, we can see how each of the last three manias was propelled far more by images of wealth fostered by tulip bulbs, the trade with the New World, and Florida land than by hard fact. The next crowd we shall view is that of 1927–1929. Contagion was again widespread and the dominant image was the wealth to be gained from buying blue-chip common stocks.

1929—Stocks Discount the Hereafter

The flapper era of rumrunners, bathtub gin, speakeasies, cool jazz, and "jazz babies," with short skirts and boyish bosoms, was also an excellent period for business. Although the twenties was not a period of outstanding technological achievement, economic activity, in spite of several setbacks, moved progressively higher as did real per capita income. Rising consumer spending increasingly flowed into new markets such as automobiles. By 1924 Henry Ford had produced his ten-millionth auto.* The first million took seven years, the last million, 132 working days.

In these prosperous times, business was almost a national religion. "The business of America is business,"[6] said President Coolidge, and business reached a peak of public esteem it has never regained. Salesmen were led in prayer meetings by clergy before dashing out with righteous conviction to sell insurance policies or automobiles. Many were also encouraged to study the Bible to come up with creative merchandising techniques.

Confidence, prosperity, abundant savings, and an intrigu-

---

*Model T's were selling at $290.

ing investment opportunity—the now familiar cast of characters to stage a speculative mania—were all present in the American economy by the end of 1927. A sociological survey of the time showed that a growing proportion of young American working men wanted to strike it rich quickly rather than struggle in the prescribed Horatio Alger fashion, and they were looking to the stock market to make their dreams come true.

The Dow* opened 1927 at 155, moving steadily higher with only minor setbacks that year and closed at 194, a solid 25% increase. Volume in the final months rose but not sharply. The year 1928 seems to be the clearest dividing line between value and fancy. With the improvement in business conditions, earnings and dividends were also moving up rapidly, so it could be argued that price rises were justified to this time. The public now came into the market with a vengeance, encouraged by the assuring statements they heard from the media and leading financiers about a depression-free economy and a "new era" of rising stock prices.

Credit was plentiful and cheap. In those days, margins were razor thin, often only 10 or 20% of the value of a stock was required. Many new margin accounts were opened, and brokerage loans soared, increasing over 45% that year to $6.44 billion.

January and February of 1928 were rather inauspicious; then in March the rise began in earnest. Stock prices soared, individual prices going up 5, 10, or even 15 or more points† in a single day. On Monday, March 12, Radio (RCA), a glamour stock of the period, opened at 120½ and closed up 18½ points. Trading that day broke every previous record (3,875,910 shares), and the tape fell behind by six minutes. The next day was even worse—Radio opened 21½ points above the previous close of 138½ before receding. On the 20th it rose 18 points. Volume in 1928 established new records with regularity. Four million shares changed hands on March 22. Over 85 million shares were exchanged for the month

---

*All references to the Dow are to the Dow Jones Industrial Average.
† A point is a market term for a dollar.

TABLE 3

	March 3 1928	Sept. 3 1929	July 8 1932
Air Reduction	60	216	32
Anaconda	54	162	4
Burroughs	31	73	7
J. I. Case	256	350	23
DuPont	98	215	22
General Electric	129	396	28
General Motors	140	182	8
Montgomery Ward	134	467	4
Radio Corporation	95	505	18
U.S. Steel	140	262	22
Westinghouse	92	313	16

Adjusted for stock splits and rights offerings following March 3, 1928.

versus 47 million in February. By September monthly volume had reached 90 million shares. The stock exchange, presaging 1969, had to be closed down several times to allow a catch-up in paperwork.

The country's interest now clearly centered on the stock market. As always, there were rumors of fantastic fortunes gained overnight. A broker's valet, acting on advice from his employer, made a quarter of a million dollars; a nurse taking tips from an appreciative patient made $30,000. The next 18 months were a speculator's paradise. A glance at Table 3 will give some idea of the gains made on representative blue-chip stocks before the roller coaster ride down.

The speculator on thin margin could reap many times these gains. If he bought Radio on 10% margin and invested $10,000 on March 3, 1928, his stock would have been worth $534,000 on September 3, 1929. If he had been even more aggressive, he could have bought additional stock as the market value of the original holding increased, greatly expanding his returns. The game is perilous, and a misjudgment brings disaster. The player must be convinced he won't slip. Each member of the crowd held this conviction, and reassured one another of the soundness of the strategy.

Stock prices danced further and further away from all benchmarks of fundamental value. One observer noted that stocks no longer fully valued only future prospects but also those of the hereafter. The effects of prices broadly and consistently moving higher can be mesmerizing. In John Kenneth Galbraith's words, "The tendency to look beyond the simple fact of increasing values to the reasons on which it depends greatly diminishes."[7]

The crowd, our friend Le Bon might say, was thinking in images. If investors thought Radio was fairly valued by fundamental yardsticks at $75 and it then soared to 150, 300, and 490, why should it not maintain its flight up? The true speculator believes that other investors do not see the absurdity of prices, and will continue to bid them higher. Again, the "Greater Fool Theory." For 18 months fantasy became reality.

The stock market possessed America, and the situation was ripe for mass exploitation. This was accomplished easily enough by introducing a few new wrinkles into the current game. One of the most widespread was pooling, which was specifically designed to take advantage of the public's desire for the quick kill. A group of wealthy people banded together pledging purchasing power, often totaling tens of millions of dollars, which would be run by a talented trader with an excellent feel for the market conditions. The "maestro" would stealthily accumulate a large position in the stock without disturbing the market. Then all hell broke loose. In order to attract the public, large amounts of stock would be traded back and forth among confederates in the pool through numerous brokers so that the activity could not be traced. This procedure was known as "wash sales," because no gains or losses were really made, the sales "washed out." But it looked impressive to the outsider. A tapewatcher would see 2,000 shares of General Motors trade at $155\frac{1}{4}$, a little later 3,000 at $155\frac{3}{4}$, and still later 10,000 at 157. The price was rising on increasing volume.

Often rumors were spread of impending mergers, and if corporate officers were involved, they might make exaggerated favorable statements. Watching the price movements and thinking something big was afoot, the public scrambled to get in, pushing prices up. The skilled operator at this point gently eased out of his position. By the time the truth was realized by the outsiders, the pool had sold out and profits were being divided. Although pooling bordered on being a form of confidence game, it was entirely legal at the time.

Curiously enough, the pool operators were held in awe by the public. Among the heroes was Jesse Livermore, the audacious speculator who had made huge fortunes; William C. Durant, a founder of General Motors; John Jacob Raskob; and the seven Fisher brothers, who had sold their company to General Motors for many millions. Rather than being frightened away, the public could not get enough of them. People caught up in the frenzy of the market concentrated on the "magic" wrought by the pool operators and turned a blind eye to the obvious fact that they were the intended victims. The tape was carefully scrutinized to determine whether a stock was being "taken in hand." If one got in early, quick profits would be made. Brokerage houses and tipsters also fed this desire, not only telling which stock would be "taken in hand" next, but at what hour. The credibility of such information may well be guessed.

The investment trust was another exploitation of the public's confidence in the rising market and of their faith in financial wheeler dealers. The idea was simple. The investment trust would sell its bonds and preferred and common stock to the public and invest the proceeds in the stock market and occasionally a portion in real estate and other assets. Such trusts were sponsored by highly successful men in the "know" on Wall Street, and there were few restrictions on what a trust could do. By buying into a trust, the public would get the experts to play the pools, and utilize "inside information" on their behalf. Further, the trusts provided extra leverage in a market already highly leveraged. The trust's bond-and preferred-share holders received fixed interest and dividend payments, while the common-share holder got all the "action" from any rise in the trust portfolio. Of course the common stock of the trust itself might be bought on margin. If one trust invested in the common stock of another trust, then the leverage increased geometrically. Often an investment of $1,000 could get a play of $10,000 or more by pyramiding of this sort. Of course we know now (or do we?) what so many people in 1928 seem to have forgotten: leverage works both ways.

The crowd loved the odds and bought heavily. Promoters made large profits by organizing the trusts, buying all the stock themselves, and then reselling it to the public at a higher price. A premium, often substantial, was willingly paid to be in the company of such high-powered shooters. Many trusts were organized by brokers which not only gave them commissions and fees but also a place to dispose of new underwritings which could not be sold elsewhere. One must shudder at the quality of merchandise that could not be disposed of at this time. Some 265 investment trusts were organized in 1929, and total trust assets were estimated to have exceeded $8 billion.

The Dow Jones Industrial Averages made a spectacular 48% gain in 1928, and many new records were set along the way for trading volume. The speculative fires were building. The first five months of 1929 saw little movement in the averages, although trading stayed high, but then the advance began again with a passion. Blue chips moved ahead 30%, 40%, 50%, or more in the next 95 days. In early September, the Dow stood at 381, up nearly 100% in 18 months.

As more speculators swarmed into the game, brokerage loans rose from $6,440 million at the end of 1928 to $8,525 million by October 1929. The Federal Reserve attempted to limit loans for speculation by increasing the interest rates on brokerage loans to 20%. The damper was temporary. The rate of 20% works out to only 1.67% a month, and the lessons of the recent past had led investors to expect gains of 10, 20, even 30% in a single month. Three hundred million shares were estimated to be carried on margin.

The stock market was now second only to baseball as the national pastime, and people from all walks of life studied the averages and swapped hot tips. Every warning about

TABLE 4 Price action of some blue-chip stocks on Black Tuesday.

	Low	Close	Net Decline on the Day
Air Reduction	100	120	25
Allied Chemical	204	210	35
American Machine & Foundry	175	175	23
Auburn Automobile	120	130	60
Brooklyn Union Gas	100	112	34
Burroughs	29	38	21
DuPont	82	116	34
Electric Auto Lite	50	50	45
General Electric	210	222	28
Purity Bakery	115	115	23
United Aircraft	40	41	19

Source: *New York Times*, October 30, 1929.

the growing instability of the situation was more than offset by the dozens of optimistic statements by such respected figures as Bernard Baruch.

Looking back now we can see many indications that ought to have signaled danger or at least caution to the participants. But it is characteristic of such periods of speculative fever that most people are firmly entrenched in the reality of the moment and can "rationally" explain away all the danger signs.

The first real market break occurred on October 3 with no particular warning. Stocks fell sharply particularly in the final hour. Big Steel was down 10; Air Reduction, 11$^3/_4$; American and Foreign Power, 19$^3/_4$; and American Water Works, 24$^1/_8$. Margin calls went out and the news made the front page. The market rallied, and by the tenth of the month was back to the mid-September level. On October 15, Professor Irving Fisher of Yale made the statement that was to immortalize him. "Stocks are now at what looks like a permanent high plateau."* Permanent in this case turned out to be two days, for on October 18 the market took a

---

*Many leading market figures had made similar statements, but they were not Yale professors.

savage pounding with the decline continuing into the half-session Saturday.

There is not space here to give a full account of the succession of panics which racked the market over the next several weeks and sent the averages plummeting. A glance at Tables 3 and 4 will show how dramatic the drop in prices actually was.

Of course there were moments in the general rush to sell securities at any price when it looked as if the tide was turning. At such times the mood of the crowd was ambiguous, torn between the panic to sell and the dim perception that if everybody attempted to do so then everything was lost.

On October 24, in the midst of a disastrous day of trading on high volume, a consortium of major banks hurriedly met at the office of J. P. Morgan to try to stop the tide, and a large pool of capital (estimates vary from $20 to $300 million) was pledged. Richard Whitney, the Morgan floor broker who was also the Exchange's vice-president (and at that time the acting president) was dispatched to the Exchange. The scene that followed was one of the most dramatic in the Big Board's history. Whitney, tall and aristocratic in bearing, calmly strode onto the floor, oblivious to the 1,000 brokers in roaring pandemonium around him. Walking to the U.S. Steel post, he placed an order for 10,000 shares at 205 (the bid then was several points lower). This action was repeated for various other blue-chip stocks. A cheer rose from the beleaguered brokers as they realized that the hoped for support from the powerful banks had finally arrived. Big orders began to appear and the market turned around. After being down as much as 33.5 points on the day the Dow closed only 6.38 points lower. Some 12.9 million shares had been traded, and the tape at times was over five hours late.

The strong support of the banks proved to be only a plug in the dike, however, and when the brokerage accounts were updated and new margin calls sent out, a horrendous liquidation of stocks followed. Black Tuesday, October 29, 1929, is the best-known financial date in history. The last illusions of millions of investors were knocked out with the

Exchange's opening bell at 10 A.M. An avalanche of sell orders hit the floor. Activity was so hectic that the containers used for orders proved too small, and wastepaper baskets were substituted instead. One exhausted broker put aside a waste-paper basket filled with orders while dealing with others and forgot to execute them entirely. Again bids vanished. The story is told of how a messenger boy put in an order to buy White Sewing Machine stock at $1.00 a share. The stock had declined from a high of 48 for the year to 11¹/₈ the day before and had earned $1.48 in its most recent quarter. Because of the complete lack of other bids, his order was filled, such was the level of the hysteria.

The Dow dropped 30.5 points (the equivalent of over 100 points with the Dow at 900) that day on a mammoth 16,410,000-share turnover. Investors now found that leverage to be a terrible two-edged sword whose blade ruthlessly hacked away slice after slice of their net worth, till nothing remained. An idea of the havoc may be gauged by the low and closing prices of some major blue chips. (See Table 4.)

Fourteen billion dollars of value were erased on Tuesday, the worst single day of the liquidation, but the market continued its descent until November 13, dropping from the close of 230.07 on October 29 to 198.69 on the November date. From the November lows the market gradually began to improve on light volume recovering 50% of its losses by April 1930. Prudent men who had stood aside unaffected by the madness began slowly to invest. But in June the horrendous bear market resumed again. Although less spec-tacular, the erosion in values was far more severe with the Dow touching a low of 41.22 on July 8, 1932. Many of the most cautious who had patiently waited for the return of solid value were wiped out. Had the clever messenger boy who bought White Sewing Machine at $1.00 on Black Tuesday held it to 1932, he would have seen its value decline by 75%.

Julius Caesar said, "Whom the Gods have chosen to destroy they first exalt." This proved all too true for some of the greats of this era. William Durant was found washing dishes in the late 1930s in a restaurant in New Jersey; Richard

Whitney, who became president of the New York Stock Exchange after his heroic moment on the floor, was later sent to Sing Sing prison for fraud. Mike Meehan, a renowned pool manager and one of the most successful floor traders of the day, was committed to a mental home; and Jesse Livermore, the greatest speculator of his day, shot himself in a New York hotel.

In this chapter we have seen how crowds of investors moved by recent events that created their own social reality were unable to learn the lessons of history. And as Santayana warns when this occurs, they were destined to repeat its mistakes. Rational omniscient investors, if such creatures exist at all, had little effect on the course of these events. Let us see if it is any different in our own times.

4

The Tulips
of the Sixties

Each wave of speculation has its own new concepts, or images as Le Bon would put it. Beguiling in their simplicity and seemingly foolproof, they dazzle myriads of investors simultaneously. Victor Hugo said nothing can stop an idea whose time has come. In the early 1960s the time had again come for a journey into fantasyland.

It had taken a very long time for investor confidence to recover from the holocaust of 1929–1932. The Dow Jones Industrial Average did not break through its 1929 high of 381.17 until November 1954, and by the end of 1954 it had crossed the 400 level. The market worked higher in 1955 and 1956 losing some of the gains in 1957. But in 1958 and 1959 it was up again sharply, and closed the year 1959 at 676.36.

Although the nation had suffered a sharp recession and high unemployment in 1957, the worst of the post-World War II period, business had moved up sharply thereafter, and there was widespread confidence in the "new economics" and the ability of the nation's economic advisors to keep the economy out of serious difficulties. This confidence was not to be dissipated for another 15 years.

As the decade of the fifties closed, the stock market again became the subject of widespread interest. Large profits had been made by people who picked up stocks at the distress levels of the 1930s and the 1940s. Gains of tenfold or more were not uncommon on blue-chip securities. By 1960 prices of many leading natural resource companies were up as much

as 25 times from their 1932 lows. Mutual fund sales were
strong, and investors were shown via charts that even if they
had purchased stocks at the top of the 1929 market, with
price appreciation and reinvested dividends, each dollar
invested then would have been worth many times more in
1960.*

An entire generation had grown up deprived of the
memorable experience of a final margin call followed by
insolvency. Confidence in the stock market had been fully
restored. I was part of a new wave of university-trained
investment professionals who were provided with theory of
stock valuation which we believed, if properly practiced, would
have prevented us from making the speculative errors of
the twenties and allowed us to take advantage of the severely
depressed price levels in the following two decades. And
so we, like so many well-meaning, intelligent, seemingly totally
rational experts of previous generations, marched confidently
on toward the next cataclysm, and it was not far away.

Electronic Bubbles

In the market of the early 1960s some of the most
spectacular gains were made by growth stocks, stocks whose
earnings and dividends grew at a faster and more stable
rate than the market as a whole, usually because they were
in rapidly growing industries that often involved technology.
IBM, Xerox, and Polaroid were examples as were Fairchild
Camera, Texas Instruments, and General Instruments with
the new technology of semiconductors.

At the same time, institutional ownership of stocks was
increasing, accompanied by rising public interest in the
market. With relatively few additional offerings of blue-chip
shares, fears were being expressed that a shortage of high-
quality investment stocks would develop. (The same fears

---

*Primarily the magic of compound interest. In *Rates of Return on Investments
on Common Stocks* (Lorie and Fisher, University of Chicago, 1964), the average
return on all stocks on the New York Stock Exchange was calculated to
have increased 10.8 times from 1929 to 1960 with reinvestment of dividends
excluding taxes. The Dow itself was only 62% higher.

had been expressed in the 1927–1929 market.) Smart investors were concentrating on finding new issues which would become "blue chips" because of their excellent growth records. Often such investment in solid young companies paid off. A purchase of discounter E. J. Korvette in the mid-1950s appreciated tenfold by 1961. The investor who bought a thousand shares of Control Data, a manufacturer of large-scale computers, when it was first issued at $1.00 in 1958, had stock valued at $121,000 in 1961. The acceleration of the U.S. space effort after the Sputnik launches in 1957 meant that tens of billions of dollars would be appropriated for the U.S. program in the ensuing years, with creative technological companies likely to benefit substantially. Once more we see both solid beginnings and excellent material for concept.

Intrigued with the gains made in new issues to date, a tremendous appetite for exciting new companies was fostered. The interesting feature of the early 1960s new issues market—and a link with speculative manias of the past—was that people were ready to buy almost anything: all that was required were one or two scientific Ph.D.'s who would promise to develop such items as iconoscopes, particle accelerators, photoelectric cells, or silicone semiconductors. The more esoteric the concept, the better the public liked it. Any company ending in "-onics" was almost automatically guaranteed an enthusiastic reception. Adler Electronics, Bogue Electronics, Nytronics, Bristol Dynamics (not "onics," but close) all were snapped up and commanded large premiums within a few months. (One is reminded here of the company established during the South Sea boom to extract oil from radishes—a product for which there was no known use. So, many investors in the early 1960s had not the slightest idea of how or to what end such technology was to be used.) Investors scrambled for such issues without the least idea of the company's fundamental situation. Promoters took advantage of the public's infatuation with technology to provide as much "merchandise" as possible.

Another spectacular growth area during the new issue boom was the more pedestrian one of bowling stocks. With the development of the automatic pinsetter, the sport became more profitable to the proprietor. There also seemed to be a growing public interest in the sport. So far, so good. But what happened in the marketplace bore little relation to this modest reality. Brunswick and AMF, principal manufacturers of the automatic pinsetters, became overnight glamour stocks. A flood of new issues came on the market representing bowling lane operators, pin and ball manufacturers, and even construction firms specializing in building new bowling alleys; all were greedily snapped up by the public. A few sane heads, including some people who had been in the business for some time, realized that there was indeed a finite limit to the future of the sport and that such overexpansion would come back to haunt everyone. The boom in bowling stocks continued merrily on despite the warnings.

Another phenomenon of this market was the rise of the Small Business Investment Companies (SBICs) authorized by an act of Congress in 1958. SBICs were encouraged by the federal government to invest in promising new companies; they were given both tax concessions and cheap federal loans, which had a leveraging effect on the money put into the company by private investors. The SBICs were the hatcheries from which the future new issues would come. They were in on the ground floor, normally having options on large blocks of stock in addition to making loans to the young companies. Through SBICs, investors would be getting a play on electronics, medical technology, bowling, and many other interesting sugarplums at bargain basement prices. And, of course, the SBICs were run by professionals.

According to *Forbes* magazine, between January and August 1961, 177 new SBICs were licensed, with almost 50 being publicly held.[1] Investors were frantically bidding up the prices of SBIC shares, and SBICs were just as hungrily buying the small companies they thought would be the next winners. In allowing investors a crack at the action earlier and being run by well-informed pros, the SBICs bore an interesting resemblance to the Investment Trusts of the 1928–29 market. Certainly investors regarded them in the same light.

The underwriters of new issues did of course operate

under some regulations, but many of the underwriting firms were one- or two-man organizations with a single secretary. At first, electronics were the favorites, but later the interest expanded to discount retailers, bowling, SBICs, and other areas. The countryside was scoured for companies that could be sold to the public. "Why go broke—go public" became the underwriter's rallying cry.

The promoter/underwriter had to properly package his merchandise. This meant that if it was remotely connected to technology, the company was given some sort of space-age name. Most buyers looked no further. Although a prospectus was issued few speculators examined it. It didn't matter if an electronics company had never made a profit, and likely never would. If the stock the speculator was getting at 5 was likely to open at 7 bid in public trading, who cared? With the small supply put on the market and the large public appetite, many stocks immediately opened at huge premiums, sometimes doubling or more. This sort of blind, almost willful ignorance of reasonable value is a danger signal in any market.

Not only did the promoter/underwriter earn an excellent underwriting fee, he often also took large positions in warrants at a nominal cost; and if the stock moved up sharply the underwriter made a second killing.

New issue prices were made to open artificially high by keeping the number of shares offered small, and carefully controlling the distribution. If a corporation wished to sell 200,000 shares and they could be placed easily, only 100,000 might be offered by a more unscrupulous underwriter. In a tight issue, price could be pushed much higher by telling a buyer he could have a given amount of stock only if he bought an additional prescribed amount at higher prices in the aftermarket. This procedure is illegal but is still followed among more unethical underwriting houses. (Widespread irregularities were found in an SEC study afterward.) Brokers kept their allotments until the issues opened at premiums, and hot stocks were distributed to relatives, privileged accounts, or people to whom favors were owed. Most investors either didn't know or didn't care about these goings-on. Images of wealth (perhaps more simply called greed) through new issues were too strong to be overcome by such plain truths.

For a while the public made tremendous profits in new issues and interest was exceptionally widespread. Again, as in the 1920s, the discussion of exciting issues, the money made, and the "hottest" underwriting houses dominated conversation.

One way of judging speculative manias is by the literature they produce, and in this period there was no lack of books offering advice to investors. One of the better known was written by a dancer, Nicholas Darvas, entitled *How I Made Two Million Dollars on the Stock Market*. An art market guide even put together an average of 500 painters and advertised that it was increasing much faster than the Dow.

New issues were the speculative overflow of the get-rich-quick attitude prevailing in the overall market in 1960 and 1961. Established growth companies were venerated and their price/earnings multiples soared. At their peaks in 1961, IBM traded at 81 times earnings, Polaroid at 164 times, and Xerox at 123 times. Blue chips, too, continued to trade at higher and higher multiples. The price/earnings ratio of the S&P 500 moved from 7.2 to 22.2 between 1949 and 1961.

The Dow closed near its peak of 735 for the year, but by year end speculative ardor for both new issues and glamour stocks had already begun to cool and both groups were trading well below their highs. In an antiinflationary move, the Kennedy administration forced the steel companies to roll back price increases in April of 1962, and the market interpreted the action as antibusiness. This was the trigger for already mounting bearish sentiment. More and more people were beginning to believe the lofty ratios for growth stocks, and even the Dow itself, were out of line with historical standards, and that the new issue game was merely another variation of the greater fool theory.

Prices fell on rising volume. The week of May 25 was the poorest for the market in over ten years with $30 billion in values lost, and on the 28th, the Dow declined almost 35 points, the worst day since October 29, 1929. At the close it stood at 576.93. A wave of anxiety and fear again swept through the boardrooms of America, shattering confidence and dreams. A question not thought about for years surfaced again: Was this the beginning of another 1929? The violent reaction also touched off panics in Europe.

In fact, it turned out not to be another 1929, but the credit for this belongs more to tighter regulations and higher legal margin requirements (70%) rather than to the wisdom of the speculators. Many individuals had circumvented the margin requirements by borrowing from banks to purchase the high-fliers and met the fate of their predecessors in 1929. In the midst of a day of particularly heavy, pessimistic trading, the market suddenly and inexplicably turned around. After being down by 23 points in the morning, the Dow soared to a gain of 28 points for the day.

TABLE 5

	Price When Issued		1961–62 High	1962 Low	% Decline from High
Electronics					
Adler Electronics	(April 1961)	8	24	$8^1/_2$	65
Bogue Electronics	(June 1955)	8	16	$2^1/_4$	86
Supronics	(April 1960)	$9^1/_2$	$13^3/_4$	$2^3/_4$	80
Universal Elec. Labs	(Nov. 1961)	4	18	$1^3/_8$	92
Bowling					
Bowl-Mor Corp.	(Jan. 1955)	3	51	$3^7/_8$	92
Fair Lanes Inc.	(Sept. 1959)	10	$12^3/_8$	$4^3/_4$	62
Major League Bowling	(Nov. 1960)	9	$14^1/_4$	$^5/_8$	96
Sports Arenas Inc.	(Nov. 1959)	4	$14^1/_2$	$1^1/_8$	94
SBICs					
Boston Capital	(Sept. 1960)	15	$28^7/_8$	$7^1/_8$	75
Electronics Capital Corp.	(June 1959)	10	$66^1/_2$	$8^3/_4$	87
Franklin Corp.	(June 1960) ·	10	25	$6^3/_4$	83
Greater Washington Industrial Investments	(April 1960)	10	$30^1/_2$	$4^7/_8$	84

Sources: S&P Industrial Manual, 1962–1963; S&P Financial Manual, 1962–1963.

The panic was over, but the crash had wiped out over $100 billion in paper values. While the averages recovered and went on to new highs, the crisis had broken the back of the new issue market. Like the "binder-boys" before them, most of the small promoters closed their doors. Gone were the big paper profits on their warrants, many of which were valueless. Gone also were the tremendous paper gains made by investors in new issues. All too often they turned into large losses. Table 5 shows the issue price, the 1961–1962 high, and the 1962 low of selected issues.

And what became of all those hot new issues in the ensuing years? An SEC study of 500 randomly selected issues underwritten in the late 1950s and early 1960s revealed that 12% had simply vanished, 43% had gone bankrupt, 25% existed and were operating at losses, and only 20% showed any profitability whatsoever. Of the 500, only 12 appeared to be highly promising. The odds of a big kill were far less than playing a single number in roulette, and possibly even somewhat less than purchasing the bubble companies in Exchange Alley in 1720.

The Rise and Fall of the Gunslinger

The speculative spirit, so often dormant for centuries, rested only briefly after 1962 before possessing the market again in the latter part of the decade. A glance at the years 1967–1970 shows that a number of time-honored fiduciary and accounting principles were abandoned in favor of a new "reality." The operative image of the times, to which so much was sacrificed, was performance. In this era, it meant the rapid turnover of stocks in pursuit of the quick kill. And at the vanguard of the revolution was a group of fast-moving, free-wheeling young men in their twenties and thirties who were out to conquer the market by the speed of their reactions and the sureness of their instincts. They were called the gunslingers.

Youth brought a new honesty to Wall Street. Stocks were not bought to be held forever. The difficulty of judgment was recognized, and errors were unashamedly acknowledged, and the gunslingers would buy or sell in the blink of an eye. If one liked a story, he bought a large block of stock, often researching it later; if he turned negative on a security or the market, stocks were just as quickly sold. Quick turnover led to exceptional results, and the rapid buying and selling of large blocks of stock by the gunslingers became known as "go-go" investing. Trading as a result mounted sharply, and portfolios were often turned over in their entirety several times or more in a single year. Value, according to the new rules of the game, was not to be found in the established blue chips preferred by their elders. The real gains were in the new issues, the growth stocks, and the concept stocks. The year 1962 was already ancient history.

For some time prior to 1967 public attention was increasingly riveted on the better-performing mutual funds. Gerald Tsai, the young Chinese whiz who chalked up an exceptional record managing the Fidelity Growth Fund, became the first go-go star. Buying or selling at the drop of a hat, Tsai increased the asset value of this fund almost 50% in 1965. Tsai left the Fidelity Group and set up his own Manhattan Fund hoping to raise $25 million and surprised himself by raising $247 million in his initial offering. Tsai's fund was up 40% in the exceptional 1967 market, more than double the Dow, but even this performance was dull next to some of the emerging new go-go managers. By 1968, when his fund was down 7% and ranked near the bottom, 299th out of 305 funds rated by Arthur Lipper, Tsai's luster had already dimmed considerably. A low ranking in mutual funds often meant the withdrawal of capital by investors, which was then transferred into the more successful funds. In the long run, Tsai's business acumen seemingly proved significantly better than his market capabilities, as he was able to sell his mutual fund complex to CNA for approximately $30 million in its stock.

The new breed was bruisingly competitive. It paid to be. Fred Alger, at 34, ran $300 million in 1968 and received a million a year in compensation. He was quoted as saying "I would rather be down 60% in a year, and be number one [among funds] than be up 60% and be number ten."

Fred Carr, 38, ran the Enterprise Fund, the nation's leading mutual fund in 1967, with an almost 118% gain, and the best-performing large fund in 1968 with close to a 45% increase. So impressed were investors with his performance that in 1968, $1.1 billion worth of the group's funds were sold, approximately one-sixth of mutual fund sales nationwide. Carr's management company, which was public and commanded a high premium, gave him a net worth at the time of $30 million.

Enterprise purchased small, thinly capitalized growth stocks. Carr's buying, followed by swarms of eager investors, pushed such stocks up, a self-fulfilling prophecy as long as nobody sold. Carr, however, did not view events in this light. Believing he was a traditional conservative long-term investor, Carr was bothered that people thought his funds were risky.

Some of the games the fund managers played bore a distinct resemblance to the operations of investment trusts in the 1920s. One of the brightest meteors in the performance sky was Fred Mates whose Mates Fund began operations in mid-1967. Mates had a highly developed social conscience and would not buy stocks of cigarette or armament companies, nor of companies that polluted the environment. Even so, his fund was for a time the wonder of the industry showing a gain of almost 154% in late 1968.

For all his social conscience, Mates followed some very borderline financial practices. Along with other funds, he purchased "letter stock." This stock is not registered with the SEC and cannot be sold publicly. The buyer gives the selling company a letter stating it will not attempt to register the stock for a specified time period, often several years or more. Because such an investment is extremely illiquid, a discount from market of 30% or more is usually given. In September 1968, the Mates Fund purchased 300,000 shares of Omega Equities, a small conglomerate, at $3.25 a share with the stock trading at $24—a tremendous discount even for letter stock. Mates then revalued the stock at $16, a one-third discount from the market, giving his fund an instant profit of almost 500%. Not to fault Mates alone, the practice of revaluing letter stock was fairly common in the industry at the time, and the records of other funds were also boosted by such machinations. Instant results was the name of the game.

The fact that so much of the gunslingers "performance" was achieved with mirrors and sleight of hand should cause us to wonder where all those prudent, rational investors had disappeared to. Anyone involved in the market should have known, even without the benefit of our historical review, that such practices as letter stock revaluation were very dangerous and would almost certainly end in disaster. Once again, the public either didn't know where such "perform- ance" came from or, worse, didn't care.

So much money flowed into the Mates fund that its bookkeeping snarled and it could not accept new business after mid-1968. Orders for $50 million, three times the asset value in early June, were turned away. Hundreds of angry letters flowed in and the switchboard was flooded with calls. Even bribes were offered to get shares in this money-making machine.

Pollution-free companies are not always pollution-free investment values. Omega Equities, which was 22% of the Mates portfolio, was suspended by the SEC from trading on December 20, 1968, and an investigation was begun. Mates revised the stock down to his cost of $3.25 a share, but with no market existing for it, he could not redeem his mutual fund shares. Investors who had so desperately wanted to get in six months earlier now wanted out but the door was bolted. It was all downhill from here. In early 1969, Omega resumed trading at $4.00. The Mates Fund asset value disintegrated, plummeting from $15.51 in late 1968 to under $4.00 at the end of 1970, where it stood close to the bottom of the Arthur Lipper Rankings.

Wealthy and more aggressive investors usually did not buy mutual funds; instead some received their kicks from hedge funds. Mutual funds are normally forbidden to borrow, short sell, or trade in commodities. A hedge fund, which is a limited investment partnership with ten to twenty shares normally ranging from $100,000 to $250,000, was free to do any of these. The hedge fund provided go-go action at its fastest, and it was the ideal instrument for the high-powered gunslingers of 1967 and 1968. Large investors flocked to them and by the end of 1968, hedge fund assets had grown to $1.3 billion. Entrance was not cheap: a 1 or 2% annual fee and 20% of the profits to the manager. A $10 million fund up 50% provided $1 million a year to the successful manager. If a "High Noon" atmosphere existed on Wall Street in these years, the quickest draws and the highest turnover were generated by this group. The entire portfolio could easily be turned over four or five times in a year.

Many of the gunslingers were encouraged to take extraordinary risks by the nature of the beast itself. It was a heads-I-win, tails-you-lose situation. A gamble that paid off gave the manager 20%. If he lost, it was the client's money. Besides, if he was too conservative, a more aggressive gunslinger might easily lure the customer away with a more impressive performance record. Excessive risk does not stay caged for long. In the 1969–1970 crash, the hedge funds as a group were devastated, and the battered partners drew out a good portion of the remaining capital. Many of the managers, accustomed to lavish living on their six-figure profits, suddenly found themselves without any source of income. Some of the smoking pistols were traded in for bartender aprons, shoehorns, or cabdriver medallions.

What kind of stocks attracted the gunslinger in his heyday? The most important common denominator as always was concept. The stock had to have "a story," one that excited the gunslinger and would excite the market. The conglomerates were one of the first manias to sweep the market beginning in 1964 or 1965. Investors were mesmerized with the tremendous earnings growth of Litton Industries, Ling-Temco-Vought, Walter Kidde, Teledyne, and a cast of dozens of others and bid these stocks up to extremely high multiples. Many of the most highly regarded companies appreciated five or tenfold in a few years.

Conglomerate executives talked of new free-form management philosophies and techniques to go with the swinging times. Deadwood was immediately cut away from acquired companies, marketing efforts were rejuvenated, and *voilà*, rapidly rising earnings resulted. Synergism (1 + 1 = 3) was mentioned often. A company that produced tennis racquets, fighter planes, and toilet paper would speak glowingly of its interlocking markets, which would allow it to pare costs and increase sales. The gunslingers, interested only in the "bottom line," loved the high-earnings streams of these companies, and the exciting concepts behind them.

The conglomerates gave them the rapid earnings growth they wanted, but it was done mostly by financial sleight of hand. In its essence, the game was played as follows:

International Dynamics is trading at 30 times earnings and acquires another company, Standard Broom, whose earnings are 50% of the acquirer's $1 million. International Dynamics pays ten times earnings for the acquired companies, some 30% more than it currently trades for on the market, and rather than paying cash pays for it in its stock at its current market value of $30 before the acquisition. The earnings are pooled; that is, the income of the two companies are added together and divided by the new number of shares outstanding. Table 6 demonstrates the effect of such pooling.

Because it commanded triple the P/E multiple of Standard Broom, International Dynamics increased its earnings per share 29% by the exchange. Only 16.7% more stock had to be issued to increase total earnings by 50%. If the market

TABLE 6

	International Dynamics before Merger	Standard Broom	International Dynamics after Acquiring Standard Broom
Net earnings	$1,000,000	$500,000	$1,500,000
Shares outstanding	1,000,000	Shares issued in Exchange 166,667	1,166,667
Earnings per share	$1.00		$1.29
P/E ratio	30		30
Price	30		38³/₄

keeps the same valuation on these earnings, the stock would rise to $38³/₄. To provide earnings growth in the following year, International Dynamics could, with its P/E multiple of 30, simply acquire another company with a low P/E multiple. It might then create an exciting earnings record accompanied by steadily rising stock prices (if the P/E multiple remains unchanged) such as the one shown below:

	Year 1	Year 2	Year 3
Earnings	$1.00	$1.29	$1.65
Price	30	38³/₄	49¹/₂

The process can continue for years with none of the companies acquired or International Dynamics itself increasing internal earnings one penny. Furthermore, the rate of earnings growth can be tailor-made by deciding what size companies to acquire in each period. If it continues to acquire low P/E ratio companies and maintains its multiple, the price of its shares will increase steadily. Nothing could be easier!

This example is simplified but provides the essentials of how the conglomerate game was played. The extent to which the concept was bought is shown by the price/earnings ratios of the various favorites in Table 7. The 1970 low prices again give us an idea of the tremendous drops that take place when disillusionment sets in.

James Ling of Ling-Temco-Vought was a particularly colorful conglomerater. Ling went public by selling the stock of his company from a booth at the Texas State Fair in the mid-1950s. At its pinnacle, Ling's corporation ranked among the country's top 15 industrial companies. To raise capital and get an even higher value for his stock in the late sixties, he decided to sell to the public a portion of three companies owned by the conglomerate: a pharmaceutical concern, a sporting goods company, and a meat packer. The subtle humor of the Exchange floor dubbed the companies Goof Ball, Golf Ball, and Meat Ball. Ling considered himself a high priest of finance. One year he urged his shareholders after reading his elaborately embossed report to present them to students as a model in understanding

TABLE 7. The "Glamours"—and 1929.

Thirty growth stocks lost 81% of their value in the 1969–1970 crash, just a shade under the drop in history's worst market break.

| | Stock Prices | | | |
	1967–68 High*	1970 Low	Extent of Decline	P/E Ratio at High
Computer Stocks				
Control Data	163	28	83%	54
Sperry Rand	65	18	72	28
Mohawk Data	111	18	84	285
University Computing	186	13	93	118
IBM	375	218	42	49
Data Processing Financial	92	6	94	38
Leasco Data	57	7	88	31
Levin Townsend	67	3	96	38
National Cash Register	81	29	64	39
Electronic Data Systems	162	24	85	352
Average decline of computer stocks			80	
Technology Stocks				
Polaroid	141	51	64	72
Xerox	115	65	43	50
Optical Scanning	146	16	89	200
Texas Instruments	140	61	57	46
Itek	172	17	90	71
Recognition Equipment	102	12	88	†
Fairchild Camera	102	18	82	443
EG&G	72	9	88	100
General Instruments	63	11	83	42
Kalvar	73	11	85	**
Average decline of technology stocks			77	
Conglomerate Stocks				
Litton Industries	104	15	86	57
Gulf & Western	66	9	87	24
Ling-Temco-Vought	135	7	95	47
Bangor Punta	61	5	93	24
Kidde	87	15	82	28
ATO	74	6	92	**
Teledyne	72	13	82	42
Northwest Industries	60	8	87	23
Textron	57	15	74	28
United Brands	58	12	80	44
Average Decline of Conglomerate Stocks			86	
Average Decline of All Stocks			81	
Average Price/Earnings Ratio				84

*Several stocks reached highs after 1968; in such cases, the post-1968 high is used. †Company had earnings deficit. ** In order to avoid distortion, the P/E ratios of Kalvar (1.216) and ATO (740) are omitted. Had they been included, the average P/E ratio would have been substantially higher.

Source: *Dun's Review*, January 1971. Reprinted with special permission. © 1971, Dun & Bradstreet Publications Corporation.

finance. Ironically he may have been right. The report is as good a starting point as any to study how the bubblemaker thralls his audience.

One of the most interesting performance concepts of this market was National Student Marketing, a company we met briefly in Chapter 1. A conglomerate, NSM dazzled both institutional and individual investors alike. So good a concept spinner was its president, tall, polished Cortes W. Randell, that the company's shares rose from $6 to $14 the first day it traded in April 1968, although the bloom was already fast fading from conglomerates at that time. It reached a high of $82 later that year and $143 in 1969. All in a bear market! In 1969, while investors were annihilating the P/E ratios of other conglomerates, NSM was trading at the astronomical multiple of 104 times earnings.

Randell surrounded himself with all the trappings of power: a Lear Jet named Snoopy, a suite in the Waldorf Towers, a 55-foot yacht that slept 12, and a $600,000 castle on the Potomac, which even included a mock dungeon, possibly for disbelievers. In addition, he had a net worth in NSM stock of $50 million. How did he do it? Randell dazzled Wall Street with an idea that was perfect for the time: the youth market. The company estimated that the disposable income of this market was $45 billion in the late 1960s. It projected that the key 18-to-24-year-old segment would grow from 11% to 25% of the population in the next seven years* and their income would rise to $72 billion by 1980. NSM had 600 students acting as part-time sales representatives on college campuses. He told analysts his company had a "lock" on this market, and to continue his expansion program he was acquiring only "core" companies (a wonderful Wall Street term meaning vital companies whose successful future cannot be doubted; I sometimes wonder if "rotten

* According to Andrew Tobias in *The Funny Money Game*, a book about the rise and fall of NSM, these population growth figures were highly exaggerated. In order for these percentages to be realized, 25 million 18- to 24-year-old immigrants were needed, or 100 million outside of this age group had to be disposed of. Apparently few outsiders checked these figures. Another indication of the "rationality" often found in markets.

to the core" might also apply all too often).

Randell preached youth, and through youth, earnings tripling annually. Investors took the bait and kept the stock at a tremendous price/earnings multiple. This allowed Randell to make his fast-paced acquisitions program using his stock to buy other companies. Some of his acquisitions only remotely dealt with the youth market: shirt making, housing, insurance and travel companies, as well as a sports jacket manufacturer. Randell's program was in fact a kind of acquisitions treadmill—he was spinning the wheels faster and faster in order to make his earnings projection come true. Randell could pay high prices for the companies he acquired, often 20 or 30 times earnings, double or triple what could be realized elsewhere, because his stock traded over 100 times earnings itself. Such is the power of "funny money." Most amazing of all was his ability to carry it off in the cold light of 1969, when all conglomerate tricks and "buzzwords" were completely discounted by a disillusioned and burnt Street.

Randell's secret was his extraordinary ability to romance Wall Street. Analysts were showered with attention, their sense of importance flattered by being called from the skyphone in his Lear jet and taken as guests to his castle or for a cruise on his yacht down the Potomac. Some of the believers were prestigious indeed: Morgan Guaranty, Donaldson Lufkin and Jenrette, the Harvard Endowment Fund, the General Electric Pension Fund, the Cornell Endowment Fund, and Gerald Tsai's Manhattan Fund (122,000 shares for $5 million) to name just a few. With such prestigious fellow investors, highly regarded lawyers (Covington and Burling) and auditors (Arthur Andersen), and Randell's dazzling visions, it was easy to overlook the signs of trouble.

In November 1969, Randell made a speech to the New York Society of Security Analysts stating that NSM's earnings in 1970 would triple to $2.00 a share. Other executives in the company objected, saying it could only be done with acquisitions which had not even been considered to date. As the stock was nearing its peak, a group of officers and directors sold almost $10 million of their own shares as letter stock to institutions at a 40% discount. Less than a week later Randell made another smaller sale. Like their South Sea counterparts 250 years earlier, they were getting out.

In the company's fiscal 1969 year (ended August 31) earnings were created entirely through ingenious accounting. One rule after another was stretched, all duly footnoted, of course, for those who had the bad taste to look. The biggest item was the consolidation into income of $3,750,000 in earnings from acquisitions not even consummated at the fiscal year end. Legally they were said to have been agreed to in principle. With middle-of-the-road accounting procedures the company would have taken a loss for the fiscal 1969 year. It did show a loss in the first quarter of the next year, and interestingly enough it was the announcement of this reverse in earnings, rather than the readily available evidence of corporate chicanery, in its annual report that sounded the death knell for this company. The bubble broke as quickly as and more severely than the South Sea Company itself. From a high of $143 on December 22, 1969, it was down to $3.50 in July 1970.

Another group of stocks that caught the enthusiastic attention of the gunslingers was the franchisers. Fast food chains, particularly fried chicken outlets, were expanding at a terrific rate. One analyst wryly noted that with the completion of current expansion programs every man, woman, and child in the country would have to eat a pound and a half of chicken a day to justify the present prices. Nursing homes were also a heavily exploited area. With increasing federal money going into health care for the aged, many gunslingers naturally concluded that chains of nursing homes were the way to riches and big positions were taken in them. One of the favorites, Four Season Nursing Homes, got up to over a hundred times earnings and turned a handsome profit for the institutional holders before going bankrupt. Accounting again!

The earnings growth of many of the concept stocks of this market were put together by creative accounting* but few bothered to analyze statements thoroughly. The new

---

*I will discuss this further in Chapter 12.

generation had the "feel" for this market and were proved right as the prices of their choices shot up. Images exercised a stronger influence over investors than facts or rational analysis.

The ending of this mania was similar to all the others. Greater and greater risks were taken, but no matter how large the odds appeared to be against them, investors seemed to win most of the time. Professionals and amateurs alike appeared drunk with the incredible gains that had been made in less than two years. Articles appeared by senior Wall Street figures condoning the current speculation and rationalizing why it should continue. One young money manager exuberantly told *Forbes* at the peak, "It's going up, up, up; we're going to get accustomed to higher and higher price-earnings ratios." *Forbes* added prophetically, "While the ups can be exhilarating, the downs can be terrifying."[2]

The break that followed was the most severe since 1929. The Dow fell from 985.21 on December 2, 1968, to 631.16 on May 26, 1970, some 35%. But this was not where the real damage was done. The devastation was in the concept stocks of the gunslingers. (See Table 7.)

Many of the more famous gunslingers ended up on Boot Hill. Some of the money men I knew who had made five- or tenfold or more on their personal portfolios lost even their original investments. If they were lucky enough to hold their jobs, they were often finished with investing for themselves.

The Common Characteristics of the Manias

The most surprising thing about speculation is its remarkable similarity from period to period. Similarity in the conditions necessary to breed the manias, in the abandonment of prudent principles, and in the infatuation with concepts. Most important, there is a tremendous similarity in the attitudes of the market participants. In each case—tulipmania in seventeenth century Holland, the South Sea Bubble in eighteenth century England, the "new era" market of the twenties, and the go-go years of 1967–1970—the bulk of people in the market were intoxicated with the idea of wealth and the ease with which it could be procured. The image was so simple. One merely had to own a tulip bulb or land in Florida or a computer leasing company share to build a fortune. There is even a remarkable similarity in owning exciting "concept" companies in 1720, 1929, 1962, and 1967–1968.* Each mania created its own social reality far removed from past standards of value. Caution was tossed aside by many, and justifications were made about why things were really different "this time."

In each market excessively risky actions were justified as prudent, and those who did not go along were pushed aside. A young gunslinger at the height of the go-go euphoria of 1967–1968 was interviewed on TV and discussed his aggressive investment "strategies." When the name of Benjamin Graham, whose measured approach emphasizing full evaluation of risks and conservative pricing formulas, came up, the money manager said "the trouble with old Ben is that he just does not understand this market."

He was right. Benjamin Graham could not, for it violated all his investment standards. Shortly it came crashing down, carrying most of the go-go crowd with it.

In every era, once the crowd begins to realize the excesses of the boom, there is a scramble to escape, resulting in panic which most often carried values far below the point from which the manias began. Perhaps the most curious fact of all is that the sharp percentage drops from each highwater mark were so similar—on the order of 90%. (See Table 8.)

Our history lesson, then, has shown us that speculative bubbles are not simply relegated to the realm of the past; and the examples of recent history—all too recent for comfort—would indicate that any theory or hypothesis which assumes consistently rational, prudent behavior on the part

---

* John Kenneth Galbraith, for one, noted that the concept of glamour stocks in the 1967–1968 market perfectly duplicated the market of the late 1920s, with even the industries to an "extraordinary extent being the same." The mutual fund boom was the counterpart of the investment trust, with the public in both cases paying homage to the brilliance of their managements. Galbraith concluded "Financial genius is a rising stock market."[3]

TABLE 8. Market favorites of different eras.

	High Price	Low	Price Decline from High, %
Holland, 1637			
Semper Augustus (tulip bulb)	5,500 fl.*	50 fl.	99
England, 1720			
South Sea Company	£1,050	£129	88
1929–1932			
Air Reduction	223	31	86
Burroughs	97	6$^1/_4$	94
Case	467	17	96
General Electric	201	8$^1/_2$	96
General Motors	115	7$^5/_8$	94
Montgomery Ward	158	3$^1/_2$	98
1961–1962			
AMF	63$^3/_8$	10	84
Automatic Canteen	45$^5/_8$	9$^3/_4$	79
Brunswick	74$^7/_8$	13$^1/_8$	82
Lionel	37$^7/_8$	4$^1/_2$	88
Texas Instruments	207	49	76
Transitron	42$^3/_8$	6$^1/_4$	85
1967–1970			
ITEK	172	17	90
Leasco Data Processing	57	7	88
Ling-Temco-Vought	135	7	95
Litton Industries	104	15	86
National Student Marketing	143	3$^1/_2$	98
University Computing	186	13	87

*Florins

of investors is simply building on sand. The academic explanation of professional investment performance is gravely flawed because its hypothetical assumptions simply do not apply to the cases just touched on. For all its usefulness in focusing attention on the difficulties in beating the market, the efficient market hypothesis does not satisfactorily explain why investors do not outperform the market. In the next section we will analyze the irrationality we have viewed in the market in an attempt to formulate a better explanation.

Part III

Groupthink on Wall Street

5

A Poisonous Competitive Environment

What Is Groupthink?

In each of the speculative manias we visited in the previous chapters we noted how difficult it was to step aside from the almost irresistible movement of the crowd. The majority of investors could not do so, even though most knew better, and were presently sucked into the vortex of the market whirlpool.

But interesting and useful as the study of the crowd has been, we know that the crowd and crowd behavior are not the major forces in today's marketplace. Rather, the market is now dominated by professional investment organizations, which, unlike the large masses of investors we viewed previously, are normally small, cohesive, and well-trained groups of decision makers. Yet, strangely enough, some of the symptoms of psychological crowds, so carefully recorded by Gustave Le Bon, also seem to apply to these groups.

Although a great deal of work in social psychology has been done on group dynamics in laboratories, it is only in the last few years that the evidence of thousands of experiments has been synthesized·and has evolved into a far-reaching new hypothesis on group behavior. One of the most important contributors to this work has been Irving Janis, Professor of Psychology at Yale.

In *Victims of Groupthink*, Janis writes that extensive social science literature indicates that the most frequent behavior of individuals in groups shows "instances of mindless conformity and collective misjudgment of serious risks which are collectively laughed off in a clubby atmosphere of relaxed conviviality." [1]

The mindless conformity and the excessive risk taking that Janis describes in smaller groups are precisely the major symptoms that Le Bon pinpoints in larger crowds. Curiously enough, these symptoms, and the relaxed, chummy atmosphere often found in cohesive group decision making were also found to a significant degree in each of the speculative bubbles we previously viewed. Large good-natured crowds gathered in Exchange Alley and benignly convinced each other of the bright future of "South Seas" while overlooking the risks as prices boomed ever higher. The same thing occurred in the boardrooms of 1929, 1962, and 1967–1968.

Janis notes that the abandonment of past standards and excessive risk taking are forms of temporary group derangement, which may also often affect groups of decision-making executives. With smaller groups of decision makers, there is an additional factor which may often lead to unanimity of opinion—the pressures of superiors and colleagues within the organization. Often the leader does not intentionally try to bring the group around to his viewpoint and may be very sincere in trying to foster open discussion and encourage honest dissenting opinions. Group members are not sycophants and usually do not fear to speak their minds. Still, restraints which the leader may unintentionally reinforce exist to prevent members from fully assessing the suggested course and from expressing doubts when the majority of the group appears to have reached agreement.[2] Thus, the subtle pressures of superiors and colleagues within an organization can often make it easy to follow what appears to outsiders to be an insane course of action.

Janis defines groupthink as· a "mode of thinking that people engage in when they are deeply involved in a cohesive in-group, when the members striving for unanimity override their motivation to realistically approve alternative courses of action. . . . Groupthink refers to a deterioration of mental efficiency [and reality testing] . . . that results from in-group pressures."[3]

The closer knit decision makers are and the more they are in tune with each other's thinking, the greater the danger that critical independent evaluation so necessary for proper decisions will be replaced by concurrence-seeking tendencies. Repeatedly, faulty decision making is the usual product of this process.

In *Victims of Groupthink,* Janis is not writing about conformity pressures in street gangs or groups of elementary school children; he is discussing major policy-making decisions at the highest level. The Kennedy brain trust and the ill-fated Bay of Pigs invasion; the belief among policymakers in the Truman administration in 1950 that China would never enter the Korean war; the confidence of Admiral Husband E. Kimmel, commander of the Pacific Fleet in 1941, and his staff, that the Japanese would not dare, and could not in any event, launch an aerial attack on Pearl Harbor. In each case, competent policy makers were lured away from objective decision making by subtle pressures in spite of the fact that a significant amount of contradictory information was available.

Closely knit organizations are not always affected by groupthink, although all may on occasion display its symptoms—an extremely cohesive decision making group and repeatedly defective decision making. As Janis comments,

> When the conditions specified by these two criteria are met, according to the groupthink hypothesis there is a better-than-chance likelihood that one of the causes of the defective decision making was a strong concurrence-seeking tendency, which is the motivation that gives rise to all the symptoms of groupthink.

> The concept of groupthink pinpoints an entirely different source of trouble, residing neither in the individual or the organizational setting. Over and beyond all the familiar sources of human error is a powerful source of defective judgement that arises in cohesive groups—the concurrence-seeking tendency, which fosters over-optimism, lack of vigilance and sloganistic thinking.[4]

Whether the group is composed of national policy makers, investment professionals, or military planners this type of thinking repeatedly results in defective decisions.

In summing up his findings, Janis indicated that he believed the prominent symptoms of groupthink were clearly present in a substantial number of all miscalculated executive decisions, regardless of the field of endeavor. To borrow his words, "Every executive who participates in group decisions is potentially susceptible to groupthink."[5]

Janis's hypothesis may appear to be somewhat radical to those who examine it for the first time, even though, as noted earlier, it is constructed on the findings of many thousands of psychological experiments concerning the dynamic interactions between individuals and groups. We do know from the striking similarities in the aberrations of market crowds that there must be some parallel psychological force at work in each case. But does the Janis hypothesis, supported by Le Bon's observations of crowd action, have any validity in explaining current market behavior? More specifically, can it help explain how groups of professional decision makers actually operate? Can it explain for example why professionals liquidate securities rapidly at market bottoms rather than buying, even when their valuation methods indicate prices are at the lowest levels in many years, or why favorite institutional stocks usually do worse than the market, or why professionals as a group do not outperform the averages?

In order to answer these questions, we must look closely at the actual operating environment of today's professionals to see if there are indeed compelling pressures on them which lead to conformity in decision making. If there are, we can trace through the factors causing such conformity in more detail and then examine the outcome.

A Gun at the Money Manager's Temple

Anyone familiar with the stock market today might well assume that the tremendous competitive pressures which characterize its operations are simply part of the game, a natural force in the financial environment. And yet things have not always been this way. For the major part of American financial history, preservation of capital and not its appreciation was the most important criterion of investment management. In 1830 Justice Samuel Putnam of the Massachusetts Supreme Court rendered the decision that served as the critical guideline for management of money for over 130 years. He said in part,

> All that can be required of a trustee to invest is that he conduct himself faithfully and exercise a source of discretion. He is to observe how men of prudence and intelligence manage their own affairs, not in regard to speculation but in regard to the permanent disposition of their funds, considering the probable income as well as the probable safety of the capital to be invested.

Thus was born the famous "prudent man rule" defining the responsibilities of a trustee handling funds for others; it was the cornerstone of American fiduciary practice until well into the 1960s. It made money management a gentleman's profession, respected, dignified, and relaxed. Prior to 1945, with a few brief exceptions, inflation was not a serious problem in this country. The prudent man might well have stayed primarily in bonds and preferred shares, with possibly small amounts of carefully chosen common stocks and revenue-producing real estate. Decisions could be made after long and careful deliberation. All in all, little stress was required to fulfill the trustees' obligations.

The continual devaluation of the dollar in the post-war economy made preservation of capital a far harder problem to cope with. The conservative policies that worked so well for the prudent man up to this time now failed miserably. By being conservative and investing primarily in fixed income securities, "prudent men" were often reducing clients portfolios in terms of real purchasing power. And sophisticated institutional clients increasingly noted the change, as witnessed by McGeorge Bundy's statement made in the 1966 Ford Foundation Annual Report, urging college trustees to be more aggressive.

Other investors, too, encouraged more venturesome investment policies. By the early 1960s, as we have already seen, the general public was becoming increasingly interested in mutual funds that were making above-average capital gains. Money poured into the successful funds such as Ivest, Dreyfus, Fidelity Capital, and Manhattan.

By the middle of the 1960s, large flows of pension fund money were also shifting to the more successful money managers. Performance, as we have seen, was the focal point of the 1967–1970 market, and the results were disastrous. Yet, remarkably, the phoenix that soared out of the 1970 crash, larger and more alluring than ever, was again performance. Pension funds, various institutions, wealthy individuals, and the general public placed even more emphasis on measuring the short-term results of money managers. Numerous professional consulting firms sprang up to measure the performance of money managers and advise clients on a fee basis which to choose.

Money managers normally receive a fee for supervising assets. The business usually has high fixed and low variable costs. This is one important motive for the rising tide of competitive spirit among Wall Street professionals. Salaries, office expense, research, and communication costs tend to change far less dramatically than the flow of business itself. Thus, once the breakeven point has been passed, new business will increase profitability rapidly, and conversely as accounts are lost, the effect flows swiftly to the "bottom line." Because of the economics of money management, Fred Alger's apparently paradoxical statement, "I would rather be down 60% in a year and be number 1, than be up 60% and be number 10" makes eminently sound business sense. Given the rules of the game, Alger would likely still wind up with more money under management in the former case.

Theoretically, the performance of money management firms should be judged over a full market cycle or a minimum of five years.* Theorists in security analysis caution that it may take considerable time for investments to work out properly. In too short a time span, sheer luck or fads that burn out quickly may result in by far the best performance.

*Some consultants believe a decade or more.

We have already seen how a variety of investments, from tulip bulbs to "bubble companies" to conglomerates, made their proponents appear to be genuises for a year or two before they and their sponsors were swept into oblivion. The conscientious consulting firms also warn clients when choosing an investment advisor of the necessity of allowing an adequate time span to measure their record. All the same, this advice is mainly discarded. Money managers are constantly pressured by clients for relative performance results in much shorter time periods. One leading money manager noted that what he termed the "12–24 rule" was widely followed. A manager who does 12% worse than the S&P 500 for 24 months is fired.[6] Because money management can be highly profitable, it is also very competitive. Clients change their investment advisor frequently. One survey of 297 pension funds in late 1974 indicated that 55 or 19% had changed at least one money manager during the year.[7]

Pension funds are the largest and most rapidly growing source of investment funds. Corporate executives control most of this large flow of funds. Many corporate treasurers regard money management as similar to a corporate profit center. It has been estimated that a 1% improvement in the performance of pension fund money under management reduces the mandatory annual contribution by the employee by 25%, thus providing a healthy boost to corporate profits.[8] In order to contribute less to employee pension plans, whose requirements are continually rising, corporations want higher performance from their money managers. According to *Business Week* in one survey in mid-1973, 25 of 40 corporations demanded performance.[9] Many asked their managers to outdo the S&P 500 by 25% or more. The money manager was expected to meet his goals every quarter and every year. In a growing corporation these goals tended to increase constantly. The portfolio manager who could not meet these standards was dismissed as was, in some cases, the corporate executive in charge of selecting the manager. This emphasis on immediate results, which appears to have permeated the thinking of a significant number of corporate officers, led them into the fallacy of believing that the stock market could be "budgeted" or programmed to provide a steadily growing and predictable stream of capital gains which would reduce their "bottom line" contributions to pension funds. They were to be cruelly disappointed.

The pressures on the investment manager to perform—not biannually but annually, semiannually, and often quarterly—have been rising at a geometric rate and have concerned many sophisticated professionals. As Roger Kennedy, chief financial officer of the Ford Foundation, noted in a recent article, "Let us admit that performance measurement in the hands of nervous men, can make them more nervous. The new emphasis upon market valuation and upon the passage of time, implicit in performance measurement, can become overemphasis."[10]

Money managers are not in small part responsible for the performance dilemma. As a group, they successfully merchandised the concept of significantly superior returns through superior management.

Recently, a thoughtful money manager expressed his doubts. "The selling job in this business has been dreadful. . . . The bad selling especially in the late 1960s, when independent money managers were trying to woo money away from the banks, also included a tendency to make lavish and unachievable promises, and downplay the fact that some years might be better than others."[11] The money managers, in short, were playing right into the hands of the corporate officers who were trying to "budget" the market.

The ultimate responsibility of portfolio managers for the present situation might be debated, but the outcome cannot. Many operate as though a client's gun was constantly pointed at their temples. Every move is closely observed, and it is extremely dangerous to make the wrong one. The client can become edgy if he sees the professional holding stocks that are currently falling but which the manager believes represent excellent value. It is equally dangerous not to buy rising popular favorites that the money manager considers overpriced. The pressures in either case can become severe, particularly if the manager is not performing as well as the current market.

Our professional likened the experience to "a Chinese water torture. The way it happens is very subtle. . . . For the fourth quarter in a row they'll say, 'tell me again your feelings about the mobile home stocks. Do you still have your convictions? *The damn things are so unsightly* along the roads' . . . I finally cleared out the whole bunch because I got so damned tired of defending them." He believed they were good values, but the "constant badgering" got to him and he gave in.[12]

Another manager was subjected to the same sort of pressure about Burlington Industries. Every time the stock went down a couple of points, his client called him, and he had to reaffirm his reasoning. Finally, in frustration, he sold the stock, only to watch it double in price rapidly. He noted sadly that this type of capitulation was usually made just at the time when the appreciation prospects were best for a stock.[13]

A portfolio manager of independent mind who adopts a course of action contrary to prevailing market opinion is often subjected to sharp client pressure. Robert Kirby of Capital Guardian refused to buy the rapidly growing high-multiple companies in early 1973 when they were performing well and were close to their all-time highs.

Instead, he followed a more conservative, value-oriented approach not in vogue at the time, which resulted in below-average results. Although he had thoroughly explained his investment philosophy beforehand, he lost a number of clients and acquired less new business. One pension administrator said mockingly of his policy, "Capital Guardian was like an airline pilot in a power dive, hands frozen on the stick; the name of the game is to be where it's at."[14] Had Kirby been "where it's at," he would have immolated his client's portfolio in the next 18 months. Human nature being what it is, the pension fund manager probably neglected to credit Kirby for his wise conservatism when the market turned.

Unfortunately, the pressures of survival make it difficult for many to show the independence of a Kirby. Chase Manhattan, which had followed a conservative, value-oriented approach similar to Capital Guardian's, was under severe pressure from its large institutional clients to abandon this approach and adapt the growth-stock philosophy that was working so well for Morgan Guaranty, its archrival. Chase finally succumbed in late 1972 and started heavily buying the high-multiple growth stocks near their highs and selling sound lower-multiple companies ignored by the market. It did so just in time, as a consultant put it, "to run smack into the swinging door." The stocks it sold began to move up sharply while the upper-tier stocks collapsed. In the words of a former client, the bank "saw the light, just as it went out." [15]

One of the most insidious outcomes of the need to perform is the investment manager's attempt to avoid any action displeasing to the client. An investment policy that might ultimately prove highly successful but is not currently in vogue is approached with great diffidence. The client's short market time span and the numerous monthly and quarterly assessments form a treacherous obstacle course he may have to move through before his judgment is vindicated. One money manager, discussing the tremendous pressures clients can bring, said: "I've been worn down. Like a lot of other people in this business who make their own decisions, I have much less conviction than I used to. I fight the loss, but it is happening." [16] This money manager believed his loss of conviction resulted in poorer performance for his clients because of an increased fear of making mistakes.

The lack of conviction under client pressure constantly recurs. In early 1973 a prominent manager correctly concluded that the high flyers were vastly overpriced, so he sold them and then considered investing the cash proceeds in the high-yielding bonds available at the time. He had not sold at the absolute top, and his client put him under extreme pressure because selling made his quarterly performance lag behind the market. The manager discussed the idea of investing in bonds with his colleagues, but, in his words: "We decided against them. We figured . . . if the market goes up in the next few months, and we don't go up as much in this account, we'll really be in trouble." A bank research director, commenting on this decision, was convinced that many other money managers failed to switch from stocks to high-yielding bonds for the identical reason. "Everyone was afraid," he laments. "If a guy did, say, 15% (with appreciation) in bonds, and Morgan did 20% in stocks on a market rally, he might lose the account."[17]

Such pressures work both ways, and may result in excessive conservatism. At the bottom of the most recent market slide, one prominent investment-advisory mutual fund complex, partially as a response to client fears, recommended to its investment-advisory clients that they sell 50% of their stock holdings at the lowest relative values seen in decades. At the time, the firm found client reaction to this policy to be quite favorable. The policy was perfectly suited to assuage fears during a period of market collapse, but it was 180 degrees away from meeting the clients' best interests.

The problem, in short, is obvious but difficult to correct. The constant threat of outright dismissal or the removal of a portion of the money under management by unsatisfied clients can often strongly influence decisions. The clients' time span in judging results is frequently far too short. The resulting pressure on the money manager forces a reorientation of his policies, if not his thinking. Such pressures can shorten the manager's own time frame, with disastrous consequences. Decisions, which could prove to be the best overall, are frequently not made. But instead, the decision is the one that is the most expedient at the time. The money manager may be forced to be conservative when he should be aggressive, or bold when he should be cautious. Clients who are themselves very often swayed by current market opinion pressure money managers to conform, leading to wide unanimity of action.

When the client applies substantial force on the manager to follow the current market norms, he acts like the patient diagnosing himself and demanding that the doctor concur or be dismissed. Most doctors have an abundance of patients and can afford to lose one, so they can be entirely objective. The money manager with a relatively small number of clients, each of whom pays a substantial fee, very often finds he cannot be so independent. Repeatedly, because he is behind in the performance game, even if it is only for a few quarters or a year, he will be forced to throw a long, desperate touchdown pass. The results more often than not will be disastrous.

The current whims of the market can thus directly be forced onto the money manager by his clients. If the crowd is optimistic, strong forces are applied on the money manager to comply. Likewise, if it is selling with abandon and the money manager refuses to go along, or perhaps even goes against the trend, the penalties can be severe.

The chain of conformity can prove to be long. Sometimes the corporate executives who are administering pension funds are in agreement with the money manager's deviation from popular opinion, but are themselves forced by their superiors in the hierarchy to conform. The corporate executive overseeing one account that dismissed Kirby told him, "I think I agree with your philosophy. You're probably right. But I'm going to be fired myself if I don't make a change fast." [18]

Several years ago Benjamin Graham, the respected dean of financial analysts who we met briefly in Chapter 1, was invited to participate in a conference of money managers. The conversations at the conference disturbed him. One young manager told him, "Relative performance is all that matters to me. If the market collapses and my funds collapse less that's okay with me. I've done my job."

Graham admonished him:

> That concerns me, doesn't it concern you? . . . I was shocked by what I heard at this meeting. I could not comprehend how the management of money by institutions had degenerated from the standpoint of sound investment to this rat race of trying to get the highest possible return in the shortest period of time. Those men gave me the impression of being prisoners of their own operations rather than controlling them. . . . They are promising performance on the upside and the downside that is not practical to achieve. [19]

Charles Ellis, a financial author who attended the conference, likened Graham's dialogue to that of Socrates addressing the Athenian youth.

The search for short-term performance results in a signiti-
cant convergence of policy. Most money managers focus on
the stocks they think the crowd will choose next. The following
passage by John Maynard Keynes so accurately describes
the contemporary problem that one could believe it was
written in 1972 and not in 1935.

> Professional investment may be likened to those newspaper
> competitions in which the competitors have to pick out the
> six prettiest faces from a hundred photographs, the prize being
> awarded to the competitor whose choice most nearly corre-
> sponds to the average preferences of the competitors as a whole;
> so that each competitor has to pick, not those faces which he
> himself finds prettiest, but those which he thinks likeliest to
> catch the fancy of the other competitors, all of whom are looking
> at the problem from the same point of view. It is not a case
> of choosing those which, to the best of one's judgment, are
> really the prettiest, nor even those which average opinion
> genuinely thinks the prettiest. We have reached the third degree
> where we devote our intelligences to anticipating what average
> opinion expects the average opinion to be. And there are some,
> I believe, who practice the fourth, the fifth and higher degrees.[20]

Can anyone consistently win such a competition? Where
quarter-to-quarter performance is the criterion, fundamental
analysis must for the most part be abandoned, whether
consciously or unconsciously. Investment becomes a matter
of attempting to guess near-term market fluctuation. As we
have seen, there is an impressive amount of academic statistical
evidence that says this cannot be done. In discussing the
syndrome, a money manager said: "It suggests that the way
to succeed in this business is to have men whose chief ability
is doing the 40-yard dash to the trading room to yell "get
out—Oppenheimer is taking it off its buy list." The result
becomes speculation, not investment.

Markets have always had a manic-depressive quality to
them, and whatever the direction in which they are currently
moving, investors expect the "sophisticated professionals" to
lead the charge. In a rising market many funds will buy
the favorites, to display their acumen. In a falling market
the pressure is even more intense to sell the losers. When

a former favorite receives a sharp jolt, there is a strong
tendency to get rid of it, often disregarding the price. Even
worse than not picking the winners is to show a large position
in a stock that has broken badly. If a fund manager has
sold a previous pet near its low in the quarter in which
it collapsed, it may not matter. The report shows only that
he has liquidated his position. Rather than having "egg on
his face," some shareholders might believe the manager was
astute and "bailed out" early. With an investment manager's
income and career dependent on results, this behavior by
some, if not many, is not surprising.

The quest for performance can lead to convergence in
an extremely narrow group of current market favorites. Just
how narrow this group can sometimes be is remarkable, as
the tables in Chapters 7 and 9 indicate. Many money managers
who would like to venture out are forced by economic dictates
to stay within this defensive perimeter. Keynes saw the
problem and observed, "Worldly wisdom teaches that it is
better for reputation to fail conventionally than to succeed
unconventionally."[21]

It is always dangerous to stray outside the circle of wagons.
A money manager who does and proves wrong for any period
of time will probably be handed his head by irate clients.
Even if he is right, his results may be attributed to chance,
though they are soundly based on accepted fundamental
principles. Warren Buffet, a leading disciple of Benjamin
Graham, clearly describes the often impossible pressure the
professional has to bear. "It's like Babe Ruth at bat with
50,000 fans and the club owner yelling, 'Swing you bum!'
and some guy is trying to pitch him an intentional walk.
They know if they don't take a swing at the next pitch the
guy will say, 'turn in your uniform.' "

Very often the consensus that a great number of professionals converge toward is not arrived at intentionally or
even consciously. Indeed, portfolio managers can point to
the fact that they spent a good portion of their large
commission dollars to buy the best independent research
available. The bulk of professionally managed investment
funds flow into securities analyzed in-depth and recommend-

ed by research brokerage houses. To understand more of the performance syndrome, we shall next look at the role of the institutional analyst. How good is his advice, and how "independent" is it?

Institutional Research—The Great White Hope

The first research firms dealing exclusively with institutions made their appearance in the Wall Street of the mid-1950s. They provided professional investors with a new and much needed service previously unavailable on a continuing basis. Until then, most research consisted of short reports, often not more than a page or two, recommending a particular security. Since the report was a merchandising tool to generate business, there usually was no follow-up. The analyst blithely moved on to the next recommendation and then the next.

In contrast the institutional research house provided continued coverage and updates on a variety of companies and industries, so the money manager was always kept current on developments and outlook. The institutional manager could spend his brokerage dollars far more effectively, for in exchange he was getting intensive analysis from security analysts who knew their companies and industries extremely well and were in constant communication with their managements. Adequate information, the key to fundamental analysis, was now available for decision making.

In 1957 institutional research was welcomed by no less an authority than Bernard Baruch, who said: "The emergence of this new profession of disinterested and careful investment analysts, who have no allegiance and alliances and whose only job is to judge a security on its merits, is one of the most constructive and helpful developments of the last half-century."

With the rapid growth in both size and numbers of mutual funds and other institutional holders of stock, there was now an avid market for such research. Significant numbers of institutional research operations were formed; some were entirely new while others developed as departments within large brokerage firms that increased their research budgets substantially. The market for professional research continued to expand through the 1960s as numerous smaller banks and other financial institutions began to enter investment management. Having little or no research of their own, they relied on that supplied by the institutional research firms.

By the early 1960s the climate was ripe for institutional "boutiques." Highly regarded analysts "spun off" to set up their own firms, providing detailed research in the areas where they had reputations of expertise. To improve the quality of the research effort, Wall Street offered alluring salaries and attracted many of the brightest MBAs from Harvard, Wharton, Columbia, Stanford, and other distinguished business schools.

The product turned out was impressive. Often well-written, thoroughly researched, and flawlessly reasoned institutional research at its best appeared to add a scientific dimension to the investment business not heretofore seen. Intensive coverage of many major industries was made available to the professional money manager by numerous in-depth research organizations, which also offered detailed work on a fair number of promising growth situations. Tremendous enthusiasm was generated for this major new concept.

Trends in the nature of stock market trading—such as the growth of stock holdings by institutions and their rising volume of turnover—also favored the new vogue of institutional research. Since the cost of executing a 10,000- or even a 50,000- or 100,000-share order is really little more than that for several hundred shares, the brokerage firms were anxious to attract such large, profitable business. By the end of the sixties orders for 100,000 shares or more occurred fairly frequently while at the beginning of the decade a 10,000-share order was a rarity. Such economies of scale swelled the budgets for the brokerage research departments.

Like money management, institutional brokerage research is a high-fixed-cost business. Competent analysts usually command high salaries and additional incentives. Too, the supporting costs of salesmen, offices, trading departments, research assistants, travel, and communications might triple or quadruple the overall operations budget. Again, as in money management, because there are few incremental costs other than commissions, profitability soars once the breakeven point is passed.

Because the rewards could be extremely high, the competition to provide the institutions with the research excellence they desired was ferocious. To the victors in this tournament went high salaries and commissions, often reaching six figures, and tremendous returns on firm capital. The less skillful often took heavy losses because of the high fixed costs of maintaining the business.

What Went Wrong?

The dreams of Camelot of the early 1960s have almost entirely faded. Rather than greeting it with enthusiasm, many money managers today look at institutional research with cynicism. The following discussion, taken from the *Wall Street Transcript* in late September 1974 is fairly typical of the thoughts of a good number of managers.

> *Money Manager A:* You pick the top [research] house on the street and the second top house on the street all during the 60's. They all built tremendous reputations, research-in-depth, but they killed their clients.
>
> *Money Manager B:* They're all the same. They sit at the same lunches, they all get excited at the same time.
>
> *Money Manager A:* And it's so logical what happens downtown too. If you get a stock that suddenly starts moving, and one head of research gets his guy, "Hey! Go out and see the company," and then another head of research, and then all of a sudden, all these guys are putting out reports after the stock has had its move.[22]

Christopher Elias in *Fleecing the Lambs* writes: "At best analysts are poor investigators of fact . . . executives often seem to the analysts just as formidable as their Wall Street bosses. At meetings between analysts and corporate executives the hard questions are seldom asked, and managements are rarely grilled as they might be by a skeptical newspaper or magazine reporter."[23] Mr. Elias is, of course, a reporter.

The attack on analysts' capabilities also comes from academia. In his highly readable book, *A Random Walk Down Wall Street,* Burton Malkiel, a Princeton economics professor, and now a member of the Board of Economic Advisors, writes: "The overall performance of analysts in many respects reflects the limits of their abilities." He adds a few pages later, "Many analysts . . . too lazy to make their own earnings projections . . . prefer to copy forecasts of other analysts or to swallow the ones released by corporate management without even chewing."[24] As an analyst, I have to say "ouch!"

This is but a tiny sampling of the criticism leveled against researchers in recent years. The critics argue that in spite of the high salaries paid to top institutional analysts, the extensive support from assistants, statisticians, and consulting services, and the eagerness with which corporate executives open their doors to them (if not batter down the analyst's door to present their cases), professional research has failed, very often badly. As we shall see shortly, extensive lists of favored stocks of the 1971–1972 market, most of which had wide research sponsorship, did far worse than the market averages. If measured by the fact that clients have not made money overall by utilizing institutional research, one would be forced to conclude that it had failed in its primary goal. The failure here, as in the complementary interlocking case of the money manager, seems largely due to the pressures of the operating environment which produce conformity, conscious or otherwise, of professional opinion.

At the end of 1971 there were about a dozen brokerage institutional research firms that covered a wide range of industries, and there were another 40 firms providing more specialized or regional coverage. In addition, 10 to 20 primarily retail firms had separate institutional departments. Almost to a man, institutional analysts stress "excellence of research." When a new analyst comes to the Street from a business school, he is more than likely well trained in fundamental analysis and, with apologies to Mr. Elias, imbued with the desire to do hard investigative work. Undoubtedly, he has made a thorough study of Graham and Dodd or other excellent writers on fundamental techniques. He is encouraged by his colleagues to be independent, analytical, thorough, and accurate. He is told only his best and most completely researched ideas should be presented. He is advised to stay away from concepts and fads, and is cautioned to stand clear of the herd. He is warned of the danger of becoming emotionally involved in his work and of the crucial need to maintain objective analytical detachment. Research ideas are to be the end product of creative, critical, and individualistic thinking. They should be the best ideas that highly competent people can conceive after the most rigorous investigative effort.

And here we have the problem. What do we really mean by "best"? The professional research firm is totally dependent for its existence on institutional commissions. The institutions in turn will buy only the "best" research, that of outstanding quality.

Here again, perhaps in a more subtle manner, we have a case of the patient prescribing his own treatment. Institutional money managers, by directing large flows of commission dollars for the research they favor, make the primary determination of what the "best" research is. The institutional research house is thus often absolutely bound to its major client's tastes in securities. A Wall Street researcher knows intuitively the answer to Bishop Berkeley's dilemma: If a tree falls in a forest and nobody hears it, it doesn't make any noise. If a recommendation, although analytically excellent, is made outside the range of current institutional acceptance, it is of no consequence. In a brokerage house, competitive pressures very often inextricably fuse the marketing and analytical functions. The range of choice becomes extremely limited.

At any time, there are always market favorites. Some have been popular for years, and a score of new concepts that the market believes are destined for phenomenal growth arise with each new cycle. As we have discussed, there is a significant concentration of institutional buying interest in these favorites, in some cases because of compliance pressures, in others because of conviction.* The preference of the institutional buyers is instrumental in shaping the research effort.

The research director and the analyst are under constant pressure from the salesmen and senior partners for "excellent" ideas. One would like "excellent" ideas to mean the recommendation that will work out best for a client overall. From an analytical viewpoint, a well-managed good company may present extraordinary value because it is out of vogue at the current time and thus trading very cheaply. This might be an excellent investment over a period of years. Even if it is still out of vogue six months or a year later or perhaps longer, eventually the projected return is more than enough to justify the wait.

An institutional research firm that adamantly steers away from the stocks currently popular, believing them to be overpriced, while recommending stocks that buyers are not now interested in, may well not generate enough commission to sustain itself, even if it is proved right eventually. The prospect of being "dead right" is understandably not terribly appealing to many. As in the case of the money manager, it is very risky for the research firm to take a highly independent stance. All the economic pressures that result in a convergence of opinion among great numbers of money managers operate in a similar manner in research houses.

The heyday of the research firms ended when the ground rules of the market changed. The rapid turnover in institutional portfolios began to decline after the halcyon 1967–1969 period. Beginning in the spring of 1971, negotiated rates†

*Situational pressures force many people to conform to popular thinking even when privately disagreeing. Psychologists call this common behavioral pattern compliance. A good example was the money managers in the last section who were forced to buy the high flyers. On the other hand large numbers of professionals conform to popular thinking willingly, if not enthusiastically. This conviction, as we shall discuss in the next chapter, is often caused by groupthink.

†The institution could negotiate the amount of commission paid. At first this was for only large blocks of stock, but by 1975 it applied to all trades. The competitive effect has been to reduce commissions on orders sometimes drastically.

came into effect, which reduced the size of a commission received on an order. The commission dollars available for institutional research were being squeezed at a time when inflationary pressures resulted in research firm costs moving rapidly higher. Institutions systematically reduced the number of research firms they would deal with, concentrating their shrinking research dollars on the "best" research houses to keep them in business. Beginning in 1972, research firms began to close their doors; by 1975 the trickle of closings had become a flood.

An *Institutional Investor* article in early 1972 found that "almost to a man heads of [research] firms tell you that they are competing harder for business and will certainly be among the ones that last."[25] In these circumstances one can see the compelling pressure for researchers to choose the photograph, in the Keynes's analogy, that they think the institutional judges will pick. These pressures, already severe in the good times of early 1972, increased markedly in the declining market of 1973 and 1974 as volume dried up.

It is worth noting that job insecurity is a way of life among analysts. In May of 1974 a spokesman for the New York Society of Security Analysts, by far the largest in the country, indicated that 15 to 20% of its membership did not hold regular jobs.[26] These estimates were probably quite conservative, as many former analysts may have allowed their memberships in the Society to lapse.

Job insecurity becomes far worse at the higher level of director of research. An article in *Institutional Investor* magazine in the fall of 1973 estimated that the average research director for New York brokerage houses held his job for only about two years. Nationally, the life expectancy of research directors was still short, under five years.[27] In this environment we can see how conformity may be the road to survival for many analysts and research directors alike.

The consensus we have been observing in the field of security analysis seems to prevail at almost every level in the operation. To sum up, there is often broad conformity among analysts, on the state of the current market "climate." More specifically, a large proportion of analysts following each major industry have similar viewpoints on its outlook as they do on which stocks within the industry should be bought and which avoided. (Sell recommendations, for reasons of corporate diplomacy and good relations, are usually rare and couched in the most circumspect terms.) There is also a narrow convergence of opinion about what the exciting new concepts are in each market, as we saw previously in the phenomena of bowling, franchise, and computer leasing stocks. Finally there is fairly wide consensus among analysts about which stocks are the "hottest" within this group.

But what if the portfolio manager paid no attention to the interpretive musings of his friend the analyst? What if he said, in effect, "Cool it, Fred. Just let me see your figures"? At the heart of the security analyst's operation, the nuts and bolts of his profession, is the earnings report. Almost all of his buy and sell recommendations, his advice on hot stocks and booming industries, are based on projected future streams of earnings, which he predicts according to the time-honored principles of fundamental analysis. And here again, in the hard figures themselves, we find a remarkable convergence from analyst to analyst.

In Chapter 10 we shall examine the factors which make such earnings forecasts extraordinarily difficult, not to say impossible. No matter how knowledgeable an analyst may be, the unpredictable flow of political and economic events in a dynamic environment often wreaks havoc on his figures.

Now, suppose you were to have a contest to see who could guess the number of jelly beans in a large glass jar (and for all its sophistication, security analysis isn't really such a different game). You would expect to get a considerable range in the estimates, from a few hundred on the low end up to several thousand. Now consider the fact that estimates of earnings compiled by reputable research houses on favored stocks usually fall within a very narrow range, with usually little more than 5% deviation from the average.* The actual

*The remarkable conformity in earnings estimates that has always existed among analysts is shown both by an examination of the estimates published in the *Standard & Poor's Estimator* over a period of time and by observing

reported earnings often turn out to be far outside these parameters.

What we are seeing here is a fairly basic pattern of human behavior: The more difficult the decision to be made, the more dangerous it is to err, and the fewer the objective guidelines, the greater the tendency toward conformity.† There is strength in numbers, the researchers seem to say, consciously or unconsciously. With all those indians out there, it would just be foolish to wander too far from the circle of wagons.

Such consensus would be a constructive force in the marketplace if it made clients both happy and rich by pointing to good investment values. All too often, however, the course of action arrived at by professional consensus is 180° wrong, and the clients' portfolios suffer accordingly.

A Limit to Critical Thinking

As Chapter 10 will discuss in some detail, precise sales and earnings measurements some years ahead or even 12 months in advance are often impossible. They depend on too many assumptions about market growth, operating financial and economic conditions, that, as recent history has repeatedly shown, cannot be made with a high degree of confidence, given the rapid and unpredictable flow of modern political and economic events. Although the analyst is highly knowledgeable about a company or industry, in a dynamic and quickly changing economic environment there is a good chance that his precise recommendations and estimates may turn out to be wrong. And, if his course of action deviates too far away from current thinking, even if later developments

---

the estimates of research houses for widely followed institutional favorites. It is true that some companies and some industries do have far better "visibility" of immediate earnings prospects, and these estimates should legitimately converge. In utilities, for example, earnings estimates months out can very often be forecasted accurately within a range of 5%. However, in other industries the operating conditions are far harder to assess particularly in difficult periods. Still the striking conformity exists.

†The social comparison processes discussed in Chapter 3 play a major role in eliciting this behavior.

do prove him right, in the shortened time span of today's market he may be out of a job well before this happens.

We see then that the research department in an institutional brokerage house operates under tremendous constraints, which tend to significantly limit the critical thinking that can be done. Very frequently, "excellence of research" seemingly breaks down into two important categories. The first is to provide coverage of the new "concepts"—smaller companies such as Leasco Data Processing—that are of paramount interest to the institutional buyers at the time. Each research house, of course, has somewhat different merchandise in its stall, but the merchandise is similar enough so that the buyer interested in such concepts will at least stop and examine the goods.

Secondly, the coverage of major established companies— the IBMs and Eastman Kodaks—varies from firm to firm but concentrates on those large companies in which institutions express current interest. That overall research coverage changes with changing market conditions is axiomatic on Wall Street. In late 1970 and early 1971, computer peripheral analysts were sought by many houses as the prices of Telex, Memorex, and Mohawk Data moved sharply higher. In late 1973 and early 1974, during the first stages of the energy crisis, many more houses were looking for energy analysts. In early 1975, with the rising strength in chemicals stocks, chemicals analysts were a more favored group. In each case, far more ads appeared in *The Wall Street Journal* and *The New York Times*, and more interest was indicated by "headhunters" for these analysts than for analysts covering other industries that were less appealing to the institutions.

Under such conditions, excellence of research too often becomes the effort to convince clients that an analyst covering the favored stock is one of the "Street experts" who knows it in detail and thus deserves their commissions rather than the effort to critically appraise whether the stock should or should not be followed. Many professionals refer to this as "maintenance research." Each research house tries to convince the client institution that its knowledge is the most "in depth" in the favored area. The information is abundant but safe because the competition is doing the same work. Detailed analysis of quarterly earnings reports and in-depth industry reviews that quantify large amounts of "safe" information (often from government reports) are examples of this approach.

Sometimes the amount of "safe" information an expert is supposed to have may border on the absurd. One institutional client asked an analyst how many holes there were in a steam iron. The analyst so queried commented, "Maybe if I didn't have to spend so much of my time counting holes in a steam iron, I'd be able to get back to finding stocks that go up."[28]

Much expertise today seems to consist of more detailed conventional wisdom. If an analyst is considered an expert, his product is far more readily marketable. The *Institutional Investor* has helped the process along by naming an "All American Research Team," each year selected by a wide number of institutions. (Each analyst is portrayed in a football uniform with the company's name on his jersey.) To make the team is a tremendous boost to the analyst's career as well as to his brokerage house. Institutional salesmen almost all tell their accounts the number of "All Americans" working for their firms, and institutions use such lists themselves to make sure they are using the Street experts.

The subtitle of the article naming the 1974 team, "1974: The Year Stock Picks Didn't Matter So Much," underlines the importance of "maintenance research" to the institutions. The article goes on to say that of course analysts who saved clients money by getting them out early were appreciated. "But the more significant point was that when an analyst had something special to offer—such as solid statistics or company knowledge—institutions in many cases were willing to overlook his mistakes in making stock recommendations per se."[29] The brokerage house that placed 13 people, the second highest number of members on the team in 1974, had by its own admission a disastrous research record that year, following a disastrous record in 1973.

Once the mantle of "expert" is acquired, it becomes a sort of protective armor and separates its owner from the most important function of a security analyst, the evaluation of securities. The expert can and does make monumental judgmental errors, but most often he does not lose his credibility.

Social psychologists note that people tend to expose themselves more readily to information that they agree with. If the expert's views are reasonably close to those of his clients and of other experts, even if he is wrong, he is unlikely to suffer repercussions. If, however, the expert takes a dramatically opposite point of view and proves wrong, he may lose his credibility as an expert—another strong shove toward conformity and away from the bold imaginative thinking that is supposed to characterize institutional research.

In many cases, for the sake of its very survival, institutional research has been driven to recommending to money managers the stocks that they are themselves pressured to buy. "Safe" or maintenance research may be the best answer for survival in today's competitive milieu, but often the important independent critical thinking necessary to avoid mistakes or to seek out areas of outstanding opportunity is sacrificed by the very convergence to accepted opinion. Such research is disarmingly parallel to the Roman soothsayers' practice of dissecting the entrails of a chicken before a battle, and predicting victory, thereby bolstering the morale of the legions.

In this chapter we have seen how strongly the pressures of conformity work on professionals. These pressures always pushing in the direction of currently popular trends tie in closely with what we learned in Chapters 3 and 4 about the conformity and irrationality of investor behavior in markets of the past.

6

A Flourishing Environment for Groupthink

In Chapter 5 we looked at the often crushing economic forces on both money managers and institutional researchers which lead to a convergence of opinion. To what degree, we may ask, do Wall Street professionals understand this situation? Some Wall Streeters, quite consciously aware, accept the problems and cynically work within their framework. One investment partner with a "gentlemanly" old firm regularly encouraged if not instructed his analysts and money managers to play the popular favorites. When they did not work out, he cleaned house, scapegoating his underlings and promising his clients better things in the future, only to begin the process again. Like Sir Douglas Haig, the British commander on the Western Front in World War I, he knew a certain number of casualties were necessary for the continuation of the game—"normal wastage," as Haig termed it. Both the investment partner and Haig, of course, stayed well clear of the front lines. Such practices are not rare on Wall Street. Judging by the rapid turnover of analysts and money managers, "normal wastage" has always been an accepted way of life for part of the Street. Knowing cynics exist in the investment field, but I doubt that their proportion is very much different from that found in other professions or businesses.

A second group of professionals, probably a very small minority, are influenced only minimally by the pressures of conformity. A third and larger group of professionals, aware to some degree of the tremendous forces leading to convergence of opinion, make an honest compromise with the situation they face. Often, however, the pressures are so strong and the personal peril so great that they give in against their better judgment.

A fourth category probably encompasses a significant portion of Wall Street professionals. These people sincerely believe the opinions of the majority to be correct. We have some evidence on the prevalence of groupthink obtained through extensive confidential polls taken among Wall Street professionals concerning favorite stocks and industries. Such recommendations, which we will examine in detail in Chapter 7, have fared consistently worse than the market.

The professionals in these surveys were under no external pressure to conform to prevalent thinking, since their identity was kept secret. Yet, they picked the popular favorites. These ideas and concepts were appealing if not exciting to them. They had watched the prices of favored stocks and industries increase, and the rise appeared to be backed by eminently good reasoning. They were convinced that the appreciation would continue. The pressures to consensus described in the last chapter were not important in the sampling, if the professionals were aware of them at all. The only pressure was the subtle, perhaps unconscious, one of knowing what the other professionals were thinking. The professionals polled were totally cognizant of the "expert" thinking, and were themselves privately and sincerely enthusiastic about it.

The Global Village

In Chapter 5 we saw how the pressures of clients, often mirroring the market crowd, play an important role in influencing professional decisions. Other more subtle influences on professional decision making also cause the professional to deviate from important independent thinking when it is most needed.

To begin with, professionals are literally inundated by

a cornucopian flow of information and opinions. Information is available in *The Wall Street Journal* and the financial sections of other major dailies, in scores of financial publications, and in the *Wall Street Transcript,* which is crammed with brokerage house reports and opinions (one recent issue alone had comments or analysis on 347 companies). Each week the various financial publications present interviews with highly regarded analysts and money managers who give detailed views of companies, industries, and the market. Professionals regularly receive information, both solicited and unsolicited, from hundreds of corporations. Money managers get a tremendous flow of information and opinions from the institutional brokerage houses hoping to land large commissions. A major institutional research firm might put out a dozen or more information releases a week. Multiplied by the number of firms existing in the field, the flow of information is staggering. Money managers and analysts are constantly exchanging information. Communication by telephone, at lunches, and in professional meetings takes up a substantial portion of the professional's working day.

This tremendous informational flow through almost instantaneous communications results in wide awareness of what other people are thinking. Here, indeed, is Marshall McLuhan's "global village." Almost nothing of any importance occurs without everyone very quickly being apprised of it. We all know or can find out almost immediately how many people attended Disney World last month, how a new line of Kodak cameras is doing, or whether Eli Lilly will have to withdraw a new drug from the market because of problems with the Food and Drug Administration. We know or can find out the opinions on the market and on individual securities of scores of influential money managers and analysts, the portfolio composition of most large institutions, and what stocks they have been buying or selling recently.

Does the knowledge of what other professionals outside the organization are doing affect the decisions inside the firm? I would expect at this point an almost unanimous chorus of no's from professionals, but the question of influence is tricky. Social psychologists have long noted the importance of what they call reference groups. Reference groups are simply collections of people with whom we tend to identify most. A professional money manager might, for example, have high regard for numerous colleagues who he knows either personally or by reputation as being successful. Their views on market strategy and individual stocks would most often be of fundamental interest to him. He might also like to know the opinions of other analysts and money managers buying or selling stocks he has an interest in. By contrast, he would probably pay little or no heed to the views he might by chance hear expressed by a single unsophisticated investor.

Social psychologists have found experimentally that reference groups are effective in both changing and creating attitudes. If a money manager found that a large number of colleagues he respected were recommending or buying the Oil Service group, they made a logical case for so doing, and the stocks were rising, it is likely to have some effect on his thinking, as would their disillusionment with the drug stocks or their negativity toward the market as a whole. Because often there is a large and conflicting body of information available about the market, the economy, and individual securities, a money manager may be uncertain about the proper course of action. Under these circumstances he is likely to compare his reactions to those of other professionals he respects.

In social psychology an extensive body of experimental evidence has been accumulated on the communication of information. Findings have repeatedly confirmed that the more the communicator has in common with his audience, the more highly regarded his expertise, and the greater his credibility, the more likely he is to influence opinion change. Several years ago Morgan Guaranty Trust was the leading institutional buyer of large growth companies (such as McDonald's, Disney, Avon, American Home Products, and Xerox) and had gained a considerable reputation for the astuteness of its selections. Money managers and analysts who concentrated on such stocks watched Morgan's actions carefully, and its policies were frequently discussed in financial publications and by professional investors. Any comments made by Morgan's money managers or analysts about changes in strategy or favorite stocks would undoubtedly influence other investors.

Research on communications has also found that if a communication is not directed at a "target," if instead it is overheard accidentally, it is even more effective in affecting opinion change. (The reader will remember the key role rumor played in the various boom and panic cycles of history.) A tremendous amount of such stray information is heard on the Street. Wall Street can be a gossip's paradise.

The opinions of "All Stars" and other analysts working for well-regarded institutional research houses carry a good deal of weight in the market. If a number of them move in concert, the influence is much stronger.

Just how much weight might be judged from the following examples. In June 1974, one prominent research firm pulled (rescinded) its buy recommendation on McDonald's and advised long-term holders to begin gradually selling their positions. The result was dramatic. The stock was the most active trader on the New York Stock Exchange, declining $6^3/4$ points. A large part of the selling that day had to be attributable to individuals and organizations that did not receive the news directly. In early October 1971, a widely respected analyst with one of Wall Street's prime research houses withdrew his buy recommendation on Disney (as it turned out, for incorrect reasons). The prestige of the communicator resulted in the stock's falling 15 points shortly thereafter, before eventually more than doubling.

In the environment of the global village, an investment organization is always influenced (and, at times of stress, markedly so) by the opinions and positions of respected nonaffiliated colleagues. Negative communications from respected sources in a rapidly falling market can be tremendously effective in influencing opinion. Chapters 7 and 9 will provide concrete examples which appear to support these statements. No investment firm can entirely isolate itself from these tendencies.

Money managers and analysts frequently pride themselves

on their independence of thinking and might well deny such influences. Yet there is little question that the great majority are vitally interested in the opinions and actions of important counterparts in other firms, and what they learn from such sources inevitably colors their independent opinion.

Evidence of Group Conformity

Within any organization there must, of course, be differences among prevailing opinions. What happens, then, when the group's majority opinion varies widely from that of the individual? A number of famous social psychology experiments have examined the influence the opinion of the group has on decisions made by an individual. Dr. Solomon Asch devised an experiment in which each subject in a group was asked to pick which of three lines on a card was the same size as the single line on a second card. The lines were of such disparate lengths (as Figure 4 shows) that there should have been no difficulty in immediately choosing the one of the proper length. Of the eight people who participated in each group, seven were confederates of the experimenter and one was a naive subject.

Figure 4. Asch experiment cards.

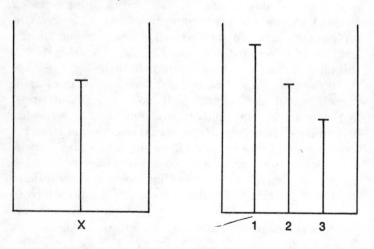

The experiment was designed so that in each series of comparisons six of the confederates would answer before the naive subject. Asch reasoned beforehand that in such a clear-cut choice, people would rely on their own perceptions and not be influenced by the majority opinion.

In the first series of tests, the confederates and the naive subjects made the correct choice. The same was true on the second. But suddenly in test 3 all confederates called out line 1 as being closest in length to line X. All confederates continued to call out the identical wrong answer in subsequent series. Asch found that the subjects in this clear-cut situation conformed about 35% of the time. Of the 50 subjects, 74% made at least one error. In the control group, where no intentional errors were made by the confederates, the error rate of subjects was only 5%. The pressure of the group opinion increased by tenfold the number of individuals who made errors![1] The experiment has been duplicated many times with similar results.

The Asch experiment demonstrates the pressures of compliance. Most subjects did not believe when questioned afterward that the group was right but went along in any event.* There was no penalty for noncompliance other than standing out from the group with whom the subject was only briefly associated during the experiment and which he would not see again. Still, a large number went along with the majority opinion. In the stock market, then, it should not be too surprising that so many professionals knowingly comply with their organization's or clients' opinions, even if they believe them wrong, because the stakes—livelihood and professional reputation—are infinitely higher.

Another interesting experiment illustrating conformity under conditions of greater uncertainty was performed using the autokinetic light phenomenon. The experiment was originally performed by Muzafer Sherif in 1935. A tiny pinpoint of light in a completely darkened room, although stationary, has the appearance of movement when beamed for a few seconds. Subjects were asked to estimate as accurately

*A few said they did, but psychologists are skeptical of these answers.

Figure 5.   Convergence of opinion in light movement experiment.

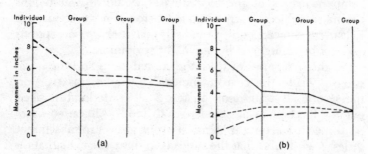

as possible how far they believed the light had moved. Since they were unaware of the autokinetic effect, they believed the light had actually moved. There were no reference points in the darkened room by which to measure movement, and the individual measurements of the viewers differed widely, varying from several inches to one of 80 feet (the latter subject believed he was in a gymnasium, when actually he was in a small room).

Most subjects, if left alone, would arrive at an individual median after 100 trials. This median estimate was anywhere from under 1 to over 8 inches, as the column on the extreme left in each of the two charts of Figure 5 shows. Subjects were then put into a room with either one or two other subjects who had also previously measured the movement alone, and three successive series of a hundred trials were run. Figure 5(a) shows the convergence of opinion with one other person; Figure 5(b) with a three-person group. In the three-person group, all guesses had converged at slightly over 2 inches, from individual medians that varied from under an inch to almost 8 inches for two of the subjects separately.[2]

As psychologist William Samuels noted in reviewing evidence in autokinetic light studies,

> The majority of subjects in such studies indicate little awareness that their perceptions have been manipulated by the estimates of others, for they maintain that they had previously made their own estimates *before the other spoke.* The influence process,

then, may be a rather subtle phenomenon. Partners who are well liked, who have high status, who are reputed to be competent on the judgment task, or who merely exude self-confidence when announcing their estimates, are all especially effective in influencing a subject's personal norm of movement.[3]

Samuels' remarks seem particularly pertinent to the investment scene. The institutional investor, often operating under varying conditions of uncertainty—not unlike the subjects in the darkened room—is affected by influential opinions of persons both within and outside his firm and, as in the case of the autokinesis experiments, his opinion often converges to their viewpoint without his conscious awareness of the process.

A substantial body of experimental findings has been accumulated on positive and negative reinforcement of opinions. An acceptance of certain behavior frequently leads to a repetition of the rewarded behavior while rejection usually results in a reduction of the disapproved of behavior. The more an action is encouraged and the greater the rewards for performing it, psychologists note, the more likely it will be repeated. The converse is also true. Reinforcement can then apply a powerful, and often subconscious, tilt to the decision maker's thinking.

Within the investment framework, decisions or concepts of professionals attuned to the thinking of superiors and colleagues are often respected and complimented. The analyst may never be asked to produce the salable reports desired by his institutional research director or salesmen. The banner of research excellence and critical thinking will continue to float loftily over the research department. However, his "best" research ideas may be dismissed as not marketable or may be commented upon negatively, while an idea that the analyst considered quite mediocre but merchandisable may be praised as an example of excellent critical thinking.

A money manager who purchases quite risky securities that are appreciating steadily in a rising market may be commended for his "bold realism." For both the analyst and the manager, the "proper" behavior may hold out the possibility of increased pay and status. With the chronic high insecurity of jobs in the industry, "improper behavior" is very dangerous. Often the people holding the power of reward or demotion are not consciously attempting to manipulate opinion; they believe they are acting objectively. They themselves are caught up in the process of groupthink, and accept popular but extremely dangerous courses of action uncritically.

Professional investment ranks are filled with individuals who enjoy competition and have a high desire to succeed. The need-for-achievement (or n-Ach) score of a person is a widely used measure of this motive. Upper-level business executives and salesmen tend to score high in n-Ach. There is not much difference in this score among comparable executives in the United States and a communist country like Poland. People do not readily admit to a high desire to achieve because it is often considered a social taboo. David McClelland, the author of *The Achieving Society*,[4] writes: "It requires special measurement techniques to identify the presence of n-Ach and other such motives. Thus what people say and believe is not very closely related to their hidden 'motives,' which seem to affect a person's 'style of life' more than his political, religious, and social attitudes."[5]

The characteristic of the high n-Ach scorer most pertinent to our discussion is his need to have concrete and continuous feedback of his success in order to measure his progress or lack of it. In the stock market, such feedback of success very often comes to both the analyst and money manager by determining how their ideas and decisions are accepted by their superiors, their colleagues, and their clients, and by how their recommended stocks perform in the current market. These criteria, as we shall find later, are usually closely synchronized. Such feedback is available continually. The loner who chooses a sound but unpopular course will not get much positive feedback. Most likely he will have to endure continued negative feedback from his superiors or colleagues, confirmed by current market action. His career survival itself may be jeopardized. The conflict between ideal standards and the need for positive feedback is often won by the latter, with the professional having only limited awareness of the battle.

Management psychologists have long been aware of the influence on the individual of his superior and his colleagues in the corporate setting. Harold Leavitt writes in *Managerial Psychology:*

> Some as yet undefined psychological characteristics of our culture seem to be making people increasingly interdependent for social and egoistic need satisfaction. . . . One observer has called us an increasingly "other-directed" people—people who need others not only for bread and warmth but for justifying our presence and for providing us with standards to live by. *The young executive finds it hard to separate good work from his boss's approval of it.* [Italics mine.] [6]

In the uncertain, high-pressured environment of modern professional investment, this inability "to separate good work" from the "boss's approval" seems to run through almost all levels of the firm.

A disturbing experiment demonstrating just how natural it is to comply with authority was performed by Stanley Milgram at Yale in 1960. Volunteers were recruited and paid for participating in what they were told was a learning study. There were two subjects in each trial, a "teacher" and a "student." The experimenter, dressed in a white lab coat, was also present with the "teacher." The "teacher" was asked to administer progressively stronger electric shocks to the "student" for incorrect answers to word-pairing questions. Although the selection appeared to be random, the actual subject of the experiment was the "teacher." The "student," always a 50-year-old man who supposedly had a heart condition, was actually a confederate of the experimenter. The shocks were to range from 15 to 450 volts, and were to increase progressively with each mistake made by the "student." The "teacher" was always given a 45-volt sample shock, normally strong enough to produce discomfort. Thirty shocks were available in stages clearly marked "slight shock," "extreme shock," and "danger severe shock." The "student" (actually an actor) pretended to receive shocks although, in reality, none were given. At 150 volts he responded with cries and begged to be unstrapped and taken out of the chair, refusing to continue. He jerked convulsively and screamed in agony at 300 volts, would frantically bang the wall at 330 volts, and slumped over with total lack of response at 450 volts. Although the experience was harrowing for the "teacher," and fears were often expressed about "killing the man," astonishingly over 60% of the participants continued the experiments to the maximum of 450 volts. The only pressure to do so was the presence of the "scientist," who instructed the "teacher" to go on. Nothing prevented the "teacher" from walking out at any time. The experiment has often been repeated with similar results.

Milgram was upset by his own findings and commented in part:

> With numbing regularity good people were seen to knuckle under the demands of authority and perform actions that were callous and severe. Men who are in everyday life responsible and decent were reduced by the trappings of authority, by the control of their perceptions and by the uncritical acceptance of the experimenter's definition of the situation, into performing harsh acts.[7]

The desire to achieve and the severe nature of economic pressures on the Street reinforce the natural tendency to comply with authority. Analysts and money managers are accused of "leaning to the wind" much of the time, with considerable truth. It may be impossible not to do so. The research director who tells his analyst grimly, "we don't think you're flexible enough," when he refuses to sell a good security at a market bottom, puts tremendous pressure on him to comply and may even change his thinking. The money manager may show lack of "creativity" by not buying companies that are "in style" but overpriced. The winds of authority are powerful, and most professional investors, like most people, do not attempt to defy them. As Harold Leavitt found when he asked each of 75 middle-management executives what they really thought was the basis on which they were most carefully judged by their superiors, "a very large number put conformity to the superior's standards at the top of the list."[8]

It is not merely compliance with the wishes of a superior or a group that results in the unanimity of thinking. In studies on groups it has been found that the more an individual likes a group, the more the group will influence his private opinion. To quote Kiesler and Kiesler in *Conformity*, "The more attractive the group for the individual, the greater the influence the group is able to exert on him. *In short, the greater the attraction the greater the private acceptance. . . ; this seems to be as solid an empirical generalization as one can arrive at in social psychology.*"[9] [Italics mine.] Attractiveness of the group is measured by such things as the prestige of affiliation, the importance attached to the position held, the friends within the group, the respect for the abilities of the members, the status and respect that one holds within the group, and the positive feedback one gets from well-received ideas.

All groups, on Wall Street and elsewhere, develop norms. One source defines a norm as "a standard of behavioral expectation shared by all members of a group; it is against these norms that the group member can gauge the appropriateness of his feelings, and by which his behavior and the behavior of others can be evaluated."[10] We saw (in Figure 5b) the formation of group norms in the autokinetic experiments where the judgments of individual members all converged.

An investment committee will have a series of norms or attitudes, which may be called "current policy." The committee's views on economic conditions and the course of the market, its attitude toward various industries and companies, and the degree of optimism or pessimism at the moment are all shared to some extent. The more important the group is to the individual, the greater the likelihood that each professional himself believes the policy to be correct. He is not simply complying, as in the case of the Asch experiment

(Figure 4), but he has internalized the committee policies so that they are now his own, as in the case of the autokinetic studies.

Often in cooperation with, or under the influence of, the leader, the group is a powerful force in bestowing awards of prestige and status to money managers and analysts whose "excellence" of thinking is in accordance with group criteria, and in applying sanctions where it is not.

Psychologists have performed experiments to demonstrate that under stress we choose to affiliate more with other people. The greater the anxiety and stress, the greater is the need for affiliation. We also choose to affiliate with other people under stress. Undoubtedly the stock market is among the most uncertain and anxiety-producing areas of endeavor. Nothing is assured, neither the best of intellect nor of research, nor are the most intensive efforts guaranteed to produce the desired results, for they very frequently wind up with remarkable failures. In such circumstances there should be little wonder that the need for affiliation both within the organization and with expert opinion on the outside is particularly strong.

Both uncertainty and heightening stress result in individuals taking a position closer to that of the group, strengthening both the cohesiveness of the group and the commonality of its thinking. In the investment business, where crucial decisions must be made in the most difficult and uncertain circumstances, the investment committee is an important source of reassurance and clarification. A highly cohesive, high-status group can serve both to reduce the anxieties of its members and to increase their self-esteem. In such a setting, it is particularly difficult for a member to take an unpopular independent course.

The factors normally abetting the social comparison processes—limited and difficult-to-define objective information, major uncertainty, and anxiety-producing situations—are all abundantly present in the investment environment. Social psychologists have further subdivided social comparison processes into comparative and reflected appraisal. Comparative appraisal involves measuring one's own position against that of other people whose opinion one values. In seeking information, the individual need not interact with this reference group. In reflected appraisal, one acquires information through the group's response to one's opinion. In the investment scene, these two processes most often interact, and not surprisingly, bring the individual's opinion closer to that of the group.

The psychological findings do not refute the necessity of company policy. A standardization of policy is required to keep the company viable and arrive at its goals. Widely divergent and inconsistent approaches to investment strategy would result in chaos and cause the firm to lose its credibility. The investment group can also be quite constructive in finding errors and providing members with new information and appraisals of complex situations. The problem we are concerned with is the excessive conformity in high-status, high-cohesive groups, where consensus is encouraged and opposition is only an exercise of going through the motions. Each individual participating in such decisions believes his own doubts are perhaps overplayed, and he settles for comfortable, friendly unanimity. It is under such conditions, without the presence of strong devil's advocates constantly contesting and challenging courses of action with no risk to themselves, that the dangers of groupthink and the resulting errors in policy are the greatest.

Pressures to Conform Within the Organization

Groupthink, of course, can strike anywhere. The executive committee of a shoe-manufacturing concern may at times face much the same sort of pressures as a group of institutional investment analysts. But the efforts of groupthink on Wall Street do seem to be particularly obvious (once you know what you are looking for) and particularly disastrous. Why should this be so?

One clue is given by the results of the Asch and the autokinetic light experiments. In the Asch experiment, the tendency toward conformity, while pronounced, is much less than in the light experiment, because the experiment deals with a more easily measured reality. Anyone looking at those lines can see plainly that line X approximates line 2 and not line 1 or line 3. It is more difficult to change or manipulate an opinion founded on solid, measurable reality. The auto-kinetic light experiment is much more ambiguous. Almost everyone looking at the stationary light in the darkened room has the impression that it moves; how much is anyone's guess.

So it is with the stock market. We are dealing with a "reality" that is extremely ambiguous. The facts, such as they are, can be but dimly perceived (see Chapter 10) and are, in any case, constantly changing. Opinions are also constantly changing on Wall Street—one's own and those of one's colleagues. Wall Street does not censure sudden, radical changes in opinion. Quite the contrary, great pressure is placed on other professionals, as already noted, to join in. In short, the marketplace is a highly subjective, highly psychological setting, and in such circumstances, it should not be at all surprising to find a marked tendency toward compliance or groupthink.

Committees and groups are undeniably integral to many tasks, but where independent thinking is crucial, as in the stock market, they can be most destructive without proper safeguards. William Whyte, Jr., articulately poses the difficulties in *The Organization Man:*

> Here is one activity where committee expertise is an obstacle. In a committee which must produce something, the members must feel a strong impulse towards consensus. But if the something is to be a map of an unknown country, there can hardly be consensus on anything except the most obvious. Something bold and imaginative is by its nature divisive, and the bigger the committee, the more people are likely to be offended.[11]

Again we view the crucial dilemma of modern investment practice. The best is almost by definition controversial, for it is most often not in style. The economic and psychological battles that must be fought almost on a daily basis take their toll. In the end, very few truly independent thinkers survive.

It is also interesting to see what happens to the brave

(or foolhardy) few who take an openly deviant stance against the opinions of cohesive groups and push their cases with vigor. Unfortunately, the same fate appears to be in store for most dissenters, be they grade school children or national policy makers at the cabinet level. A large number of laboratory experiments have studied the effect of deviance. In one experiment, nonconformists were never chosen for the pleasant tasks assigned to the groups, but were consistently chosen for the unpleasant ones.[12] In another, the group was required to choose a member to receive electric shocks, and naturally it chose the deviant.[13]

Groups may apply sanctions to members who deviate beyond their prescribed boundaries of acceptable behavior (the group norms). Such sanctions can be gentle and meant primarily as a warning if the deviation is mild, or quite harsh if the deviator has slipped too far out of line.

Irving Janis, in *Victims of Groupthink,* describes the pressures placed on senior administration officials to conform to the escalation decisions on Vietnam in the late 1960s.

> We learn from Thomson* that during the Johnson Administration everyone in the hierarchy, including every senior official, was subjected to conformist pressures, which took the form of making those who openly questioned the escalation policy the butt of an ominous epithet: "I am afraid he's losing his effectiveness." This "effectiveness trap"—the threat of being branded a "has been" and losing access to the seats of power—inclines its victims to suppress or tone down their criticisms. In a more subtle way, it makes any member who starts to voice his misgivings ready to retreat to a seemingly acquiescent position in the presence of quizzical facial expressions and crisp retorts from perturbed associates and superiors.[14]

Other dissenters were "domesticated," allowed to speak out but only within narrowly defined limits, never challenging basic assumptions, and always keeping the discussion "in house." As Janis continues: "The domesticated dissenter repeatedly gets the message that there is only a very small

---

*Historian James Thomson, Jr., was a member of McGeorge Bundy's White House staff.

piece of critical territory he can tread safely and still remain a member in good standing."[15]

Many variations of the "effectiveness trap" are played on Wall Street. Effectiveness, of course, is the same as "excellence of research" or superior ability attributed to a money manager. It appears highly intangible and thus liable to become what the superiors and colleagues judge it to mean at that particular moment.

We have reviewed the tremendous pressures causing convergence of opinion among both money managers and researchers so that their thinking parallels current market directions and fashions. Excellent or "effective" work must then also parallel the market. Opinions may be voiced within limits, but one should not "make waves."

The pressures of leadership and group can blend together in the "effectiveness trap" to actually make the professional perceive things differently. He thus honestly believes that the reality he is observing has changed. The human brain has sometimes been likened to a large-scale computer because of the amounts of information with which it is constantly bombarded. Although such analogies have to be used cautiously, it is true we are constantly fed millions of bits of facts from our sensory organs, only a portion of which can be acted upon. Realms of information we do not focus on may escape our conscious attention altogether. A person can walk along a crowded street for years and never notice a store, although passing it almost daily, or drive along a road repeatedly without noticing much detail, because neither has any bearing on his activities.

Psychologists have observed that cognitive shaping of events involves varying amounts of distortion or nonverticality. Witnesses to a sudden violent crime or accident may come up with quite disparate descriptions of the criminal in the first case or of the circumstances in the second.

The process of selective perception of information is extremely complex. It may, as experiments have shown, cause us under some circumstances to be hyperalert to information that is positive to our viewpoints, while filtering out information that is negative or disturbing. In situations of panic or danger we may accentuate all negative information received.

Writing in *The American Economic Review,* H. A. Simon made very clear the problems in perception faced by the business decision maker:

> The decision-maker's information about his environment is much less than an approximation to the real environment. The term "approximation" implies that the subjective world of the decision-maker resembles the external environment closely, but lacks, perhaps, some fineness of detail. In actual fact, the perceived world is fantastically different from the "real" world. The differences involve both omissions and distortions, and arise in both perception and inference. The sins of omission in perception are more important than the sins of commission. The decision-maker's model of the world encompasses only a minute fraction of all the relevant characteristics of the real environment, and his inferences extract only a minute fraction of all the information that is present even in his model.[16]

And in discussing how people only selectively perceive certain information from the mass available, Simon goes on:

> In fact, the filtering is not merely a passive selection of some part of a presented whole but an active process involving attention to a very small part of the whole and exclusion, from the outset, of almost all that is not within the scope of attention.

Alexis and Wilson in *Organizational Decision Making* sum up clearly the interactions of groups and superiors in perceptual processes.

> In psychology it is becoming increasingly clear that "believing is not seeing." People "see" what they want to see . . . . *In summary, the information gathering function is not a sequence of purely mechanical, routine physiological processes. Personalities and social needs are intricately woven into how people see things."*[17] [Italics mine.]

It is the "nonpassive" process of selective filtering which is terribly important in understanding how individuals can be influenced by the market action and group pressures into adopting similar opinions. The accentuation of certain facts and the downplaying of others by investment committees, which is confirmed by current market action, often has a powerful effect on the individual's own thinking.

Social perception for investors, as for everyone else, is not a constant unchanging process. The perceptual focus can vary markedly for both individuals and committees. The members of the organization can reinforce each other's changing focus, in turn reinforced by the change in opinion of many outside experts and investment groups.

Investment decisions depend on thousands of constantly changing, often contradictory, facts which must be observed and weighted. At times, the information is so extensive and inconsistent that, like the psychological ink-blot test, the subject may see almost any pattern he chooses in the amorphous shapes. Thus only minor changes in the professional's perceptual-cognitive processes might upset the ginger balance favoring any one course of action. We have reviewed the effects of psychological experiments where even the mildest influence from a group or a leader strongly influenced the subject's decision about seemingly obvious situations. In the investment situation, which is so frequently anything but clear and where the economic and psychological pressures are so intense, there is a much wider field of play in which to channel decisions more into line with group thinking. Only slightly more emphasis on certain facts, and a slight deemphasis of a few others, is all that may be required. And this is often done without the professional's realization. Thus, the individual who has changed his opinion may very likely think he has reached the new road critically and independently.

A study of professional decision making should provide a constant repetition of this phenomenon. An oil analyst I knew at the height of the 1973 oil embargo argued forcefully that the energy shortage, even if the embargo were lifted, would devastate American industry. His views fitted in snugly with those of his superiors and colleagues, who were frightened badly at the time, and he moved up careerwise. I disagreed with him, but could not shake his conviction. With a rising market only 15 months later, he decided that

American industry might somehow survive after all. I suspect a genuine opinion change, but again one fitting in well with his firm's new beliefs.

A money manager I once worked with provided me with a classic example of perceptual change. At the 1974 market bottom he was convinced, as were many of his colleagues, that Honeywell was headed for extinction. Market conditions, reinforced by his colleagues' views, appeared to be distorting his judgment, and even when he was presented with conclusive statistical refutation, he remained unconvinced and sold the stock heavily. Less than five months later, in a rising market, he forgot his concern for the company's finances and concentrating on other fundamentals, he bought the stock at double the price he had sold it at previously. I wish this was an exception, but it appears, as we shall see shortly, that this is closer to the rule.

In both the oil embargo and the Honeywell examples, the individuals were influenced far more in their reactions by the process of groupthink than by direct pressures of clients. Let us now look at some evidence of how widespread groupthink may actually be.

7

The Ascendancy of Groupthink

    In Chapters 5 and 6 a hypothesis was presented to explain the apparent paradox of highly trained professional investors and their poor performance in the market. The intense competition of the marketplace forces some professionals to knowingly abandon investment fundamentals and shorten their time span, which results in their purchasing or recommending concept and other currently popular stocks in order to survive. We also examined the groupthink hypothesis, which states that highly cohesive groups will often develop dangerously incorrect homogeneity in their views. Shared illusions on the proper course of action are reaffirmed continually by outside experts and influential investment organizations with whom the decision maker is in constant communication.

    According to the groupthink hypothesis, the apparent consensus, without the heavy buffeting of serious critical evaluation, can produce and encourage undue optimism and promote excessive risk taking in a rising market. Pertinent warnings of potential dangers are dismissed through collective rationalizations. Usually there are no strong and persistent arguments within the firm against the major course of action. Each member holds back any serious doubts, and opposing discussion is not prolonged or heated enough to make "waves" that could possibly change the direction. Such a syndrome should very often lead to serious investment errors. Investment decision makers do not comply out of fear but because most members of their organization sincerely believe the committee's policies and decisions are correct and that their own reservations are overstated.

Groupthink may account for a significant portion of all professional investment errors. It may also explain why professionals have not outperformed the markets, even in periods in the past when competitive pressures were substantially lower than they are today. The hypothesis also helps to explain why smaller banks and other financial institutions not as directly affected by performance pressures also do not outperform the averages. Next, let us move on to some empirical evidence.

Investment Forecasts Made by a Large Sample of Experts

In order to examine the process of groupthink on an empirical basis, we require the confidential recommendations of investment professionals over a period of time. These recommendations would then be compared to the appropriate market average. The recommendations must be secret so that it can be established that the professionals were not simply going along to please clients, superiors, and colleagues (compliance).

If the groupthink hypothesis were valid, a wide cross section of professionals would choose the same stocks (those favored by the market and many investment organizations) on their own when surveyed secretly. Groupthink would apply only if such selections were faulty fairly often.* Although no work of this type exists on the decisions in individual firms, there are a number of confidential surveys of professional investor opinions by which to test the hypothesis. Such samples are valuable in measuring the results of professional judgments because they take the ideas "at the margin," so to speak. In the surveys the professionals recommend what

---

*It is certainly in line with statistical probability that the faulty decision-making processes described by groupthink may on occasion generate good decisions. However, poor decisions should be the outcome far more often if the hypothesis has validity.

they consider to be their "best" ideas. The constraints of superiors, client pressure, or market liquidity, plus tax considerations are not limiting their decisions. These restrictions often do not allow the optimum restructuring of the portfolio. The portfolios measured by the EMH theorists are usually very large, often 100 to 200 or more stocks, so even though new favorites are chosen and old ones abandoned, the net effect of the decision making may be small and the results may not vary much from the market.

It is crucial to both EMH and the groupthink-compliance hypothesis to eliminate all distorting variables and measure the record of professional decision making as accurately as possible. The direct measurement of wide samples of the best ideas of professionals and the examination of how they have done eliminates the exogenous variables present when the performance of the entire portfolio is measured. We have a much clearer picture of what the "best" ideas actually are and how they subsequently perform. All of the following stock selections were widely held by institutions at the time of the recommendations. It seems almost certain that a disproportionately large amount of new institutional funds flowed into these stocks.

We looked in Chapter 1 at the results of the February 1970 Institutional Conference, where the favorite choice of 2,000 professionals for the best-performing stock that year was National Student Marketing, then trading at a gravity-defying P/E ratio of 104 times earnings.

While looking back with 20–20 hindsight is as dangerous in the market as it is for military and political historians, there can be little doubt that the price paid for NSM stock indicated excessive risk taking and inadequate investigation of the company or even its published material.*

Such an investigation would have resulted in avoidance of the stock. The question is not whether all the necessary information was available at the time. Of course it was not,

*Andrew Tobias, a young vice-president of National Student Marketing, gave some excellent insights into the machinations of the company during this period in *The Funny Money Game*, cited in Chapter 4.

but a reconstruction of events indicates there was certainly enough information available to seriously question the exorbitant price paid, a price that was excessively high even if the earnings estimates were legitimate. The excessive risk taking and lack of serious questioning fits in well with the groupthink hypothesis. A number of very prestigious foundations and financial institutions purchased a block of 320,000 shares close to the all-time high in December 1969. The knowledge that so many other sophisticated investors were also buying it probably strengthened the conviction of each organization that its own decision was correct.

We also looked at the results of the 1972 conference where the airlines were picked in March as the group with the outstanding appreciation potential that year and then dropped 50% for the balance of the year while the S&P 500 registered a 9% gain. In the 1973 conference the industry was voted as one to avoid. The favorite two stocks at the 1972 conference were IBM and Pan American airlines. If equal amounts of both had been purchased at the time, investors would have shown a loss of 16.4% for the remainder of the year and a total loss of 45.5% by December 31, 1973. By comparison, the S&P 500 declined 9% for the same 21 months.

Although opinions were markedly wrong in these cases, they are unacceptably small samples. The surveys conducted by *Institutional Investor,* referred to earlier in Chapter 1, give us a broader base. In the weeks before Thanksgiving 1971, more than 150 money managers representing a wide range of financial institutions in 27 states were asked to pick the five stocks they expected to show the best gains in 1972. Although 400 companies were mentioned, the magazine article states: "the fact remains the stocks in the Top Ten received unusually broad support from institutional investors." [1] Some of the money managers owned the stocks already, while others would buy them by the beginning of the year. The ten favorites and their subsequent performance relative to the S&P 500, assuming each stock had been purchased on January 1, 1972, are shown in Table 9.

This table clearly shows the favorites performing worse

TABLE 9. The 1972 top ten.

Company	Price		% Change to	Price	% Change 1/1/72 to
	1/1/72	12/31/72	12/31/72	12/31/73	12/31/73
IBM	269¼	321⅝	19.5	246¾	−8.4
TWA	41	42⅛	2.7	15⅞	−61.3
First Nat'l City Corp.	46½	76½	64.5	45¾	−1.6
Bausch & Lomb	88½	27¼	−69.2	37¾	−57.3
FNMA	24¾	20	−19.2	16¾	−32.3
United Artists	12	9¼	−22.9	7½	−37.5
Levitz	39⅝	26⅞	−32.2	3⅝	−90.9
Teleprompter	29	33¼	14.7	3⅞	−86.6
Burroughs	152¾	217¼	42.2	208⅜	36.4
Ford	70½	79⅝	12.9	40½	−42.6
Average change			+1.3		−38.2
S&P 500 (without div.)	102.9	118.1	+15.6	97.6	−4.6

All companies adjusted for stock splits.

than the market, both on the way up and on the way down. These results have not been adjusted for dividends, but since most stocks in this group are low yielders, an adjustment for dividends would make the comparisons even worse.

These stocks were genuinely favored by professionals, and large amounts of new institutional funds flowed into them. Vickers Associates, which surveys the holdings of almost 1,000 investment companies, primarily mutual funds, in the United States and Canada, indicated that at year-end 1971, these companies owned 29% each of FNMA and TWA, 24% of Bausch and Lomb and Levitz, 10% of Burroughs, 8% of Ford, and 5% of IBM.[2] Investment companies represent only about 15% of total institutional stock holdings. Because the survey sampled a wide range of professional investors, including bank trust departments and insurance and pension fund management, all of whom favored these stocks, it is very likely that total institutional holdings were substantially higher.

The 1972 *Institutional Investor's* survey named 50 other companies that were "runners up" after the top ten. These are listed in Table 10 together with their performance for both 1972 and 1973 relative to the S&P 500 index. Even the far broader sample performed significantly worse than the market.

Let us move on to 1973. Once again the *Institutional Investor* magazine conducted a wide survey in its January 1973 issue. This time, 160 money managers were interviewed, representing a broad assortment of financial institutions: banks, insurance companies, mutual funds, and other types of investment organizations. As in 1972, each money manager picked his five favorite issues. Although 450 stocks were named in all, 10 received major support, and 26 others fairly wide support.

First let's look at the top ten choices (Table 11).

The record speaks for itself: 27 runners up were listed in the poll. The results of these stocks compared with the market averages are given in Table 12.

The evidence appears to support the groupthink hypothesis. The selections were made secretly, and so expressed the real opinions of the money managers. The surveys were broad,

TABLE 10. The 50 runners up 1972.

Company	Price 1/1/72	Price 12/31/72	% Change	Price 12/31/73	% Change from 1/1/72
AMF	48 1/4	55 3/8	14.8	20 3/4	−57.0
Amerada Hess	41 3/4	44 7/8	7.5	38 1/8	−8.7
American Airlines	40 3/4	25 1/8	−38.3	8 5/8	−78.8
American Medicorp	20	11 1/2	−42.5	4	−80.0
Arcata National	19 3/8	13 7/8	−28.4	7 1/2	−61.3
Auto-Train	39 3/4	16 3/8	−58.8	15 3/8	−61.3
Bandag	54 1/2	70	28.4	26 1/8	−52.1
Brunswick	37 1/8	37 1/4	0.3	14 1/2	−60.9
Carrier	47 1/4	28	−40.7	11 7/8	−74.9
Centex	32 3/4	27 3/4	−15.3	11 5/8	−64.5
Chrysler	28 5/8	41	43.2	15 5/8	−45.4
Colonial Penn Group	64 1/4	63 3/4	−0.8	57 3/8	−10.7
Computing & Software	24	15	−37.5	3 1/8	−87.0
Comsat	64 1/2	64	−0.8	38 1/2	−40.3
Control Data	45 5/8	60 3/8	32.3	33 5/8	−26.3
Eastman Kodak	97 1/4	148 3/8	52.6	116	19.3
First Charter Financial	27 7/8	29 5/8	6.3	14 1/2	−48.0
Foxboro	36 1/2	29	−20.5	45 1/2	24.7
The Franklin Mint	19	23 1/2	23.7	14	−26.3
General Electric	62 5/8	72 7/8	16.4	63	0.6
General Motors	80 1/2	81 1/8	0.8	46 1/8	−42.7
General Telephone & Elec.	42 1/2	30 1/8	−29.1	25	−41.2
Hilton Hotels	54 7/8	43 1/8	−21.4	17 3/8	−68.3
Horizon	44	14 1/2	−67.0	4 3/4	−89.2

Hycel	23¾	10⅞	−54.2	2¼	−90.5
ITT	58⅜	60¼	3.2	26⅜	−54.8
Jim Walter	37	30⅞	−16.6	13¾	−62.8
Kennecott Copper	24⅜	23¾	−2.6	44¼	81.5
Walter Kidde	31⅝	29¼	−7.5	15⅛	−52.2
Kinney National Service	31¼	37	18.4	10	−68.0
Mattel	27¼	14¼	−47.7	2½	−90.8
New Process	59¾	21⅝	−63.8	8½	−85.8
Northwest Industries	33¾	30¾	−8.9	17⅝	−47.8
Pennzoil Offshore Gas Oper.	10	9½	−5.0	9¾	−2.5
Polaroid	89	126⅛	41.7	69⅞	−21.5
RCA	37⅛	38⅞	4.7	18½	−50.2
Saxon	20½	13⅜	−34.8	3½	−82.9
Seaboard Coast Line RR	57⅝	47⅜	−17.8	31⅞	−44.7
Skyline	53⅞	32⅜	−39.9	11	−79.6
Sony	18¼	49¾	172.6	30	64.4
Specialty Restaurants	28½	23⅞	−16.2	4½	−84.2
Standard Oil (New Jersey)	73¾	87½	18.6	94⅛	27.6
Syntex	83	80⅜	−0.8	114⅞	38.4
Tesoro Petroleum	38½	38⅞	1.0	48¼	25.3
Tool Research & Engineering	36⅜	44⅝	22.7	15	−58.8
Tropicana Products	62	56¾	−8.5	20¼	−67.3
Unionamerica Mortgage & Eq. Tr.	28⅜	26¾	−5.7	12⅜	−56.4
U.S. Industries	23⅞	20⅛	−15.7	8⅛	−66.0
Western Union International	43¾	48½	10.9	14⅛	−67.7
Westinghouse Electric	45⅞	43	−6.3	25⅜	−44.7
Average Change			−4.7		−42.5
S&P 500 (without dividends)	102.1	118.1	+15.6	97.6	−4.5

All companies adjusted for stock splits.

TABLE 11. The 1973 top ten.

Company	Price 1/1/73	Price 12/31/73	% Change	Price 12/31/74	% Change from 1/1/73
IBM	$321\frac{5}{8}$	$246\frac{3}{4}$	−23.3	168	−47.8
Polaroid	$126\frac{1}{8}$	$69\frac{7}{8}$	−44.6	$18\frac{5}{8}$	−85.2
ITT	$60\frac{1}{4}$	$26\frac{3}{8}$	−56.2	$14\frac{3}{4}$	−75.5
Teleprompter	$33\frac{1}{4}$	$3\frac{7}{8}$	−88.3	$1\frac{1}{2}$	−95.5
Eastman Kodak	$148\frac{3}{8}$	116	−21.8	$62\frac{7}{8}$	−57.6
Gillette	$63\frac{7}{8}$	$35\frac{7}{8}$	−43.8	$25\frac{3}{8}$	−60.3
McDonald's	$76\frac{1}{4}$	57	−25.2	$29\frac{3}{8}$	−61.5
Motorola	$65\frac{1}{2}$	$49\frac{1}{4}$	−24.8	$34\frac{1}{8}$	−47.9
Digital Equipment	$91\frac{3}{4}$	$101\frac{7}{8}$	11.0	$50\frac{3}{4}$	−44.7
Levitz Furniture	$26\frac{7}{8}$	$3\frac{5}{8}$	−86.5	$1\frac{3}{4}$	−93.5
Average Change			−40.4		−67.0
S&P 500 (without div.)	118.1	97.6	−17.4	68.6	−41.9

All companies adjusted for stock splits.

TABLE 12. The 27 runners up 1973.

Company	Price 1/1/73	Price 12/31/73	% Change	Price 12/31/74	% Change from 1/1/73
Amerada Hess	44⁷/₈	38¹/₈	-15.0	15³/₄	-64.9
American Broadcasting Co.	38¹/₈	23¹/₄	-39.0	13¹/₄	-65.2
American Medicorp	11¹/₂	4	-65.2	2	-82.6
Atlantic Richfield	77³/₄	108³/₄	39.9	90³/₄	16.7
Bentley Laboratories	38¹/₈	15³/₄	-58.7	12¹/₂	-67.2
Brunswick	37¹/₄	14¹/₂	-61.1	9	-75.8
Burroughs	108⁵/₈	104¹/₈	-4.1	75¹/₂	-30.5
Colonial Penn Group	63³/₄	57³/₈	-10.0	24³/₄	-61.2
Damon	61	38¹/₄	-37.3	11	-82.0
Deere	45³/₄	50¹/₂	10.4	42⁵/₈	-6.8
Delta Air Lines	65	40	-38.5	29¹/₄	-55.0
Walt Disney Productions	118³/₄	47¹/₄	-60.2	21³/₈	-81.9
FNMA	20	16³/₄	-16.3	18³/₈	-8.1
Flying Tiger	41¹/₂	20	-51.8	7¹/₄	-82.4
General Electric	72⁷/₈	63	-13.6	33³/₈	-54.2
General Motors	81¹/₈	46¹/₈	-43.1	30³/₈	-62.1
J. Ray McDermott	69¹/₂	107	54.0	80¹/₄	15.5
Philip Morris	59¹/₈	57³/₈	-3.0	48	-18.8
RCA	38⁷/₈	18¹/₂	-52.4	10³/₄	-72.3
Sperry Rand	48¹/₄	44¹/₄	-8.1	27³/₈	-43.1
Syntex	41¹/₄	57³/₈	39.5	39³/₈	-4.5
Texaco	37¹/₂	29³/₈	-21.7	20⁷/₈	-44.3
Trans World Airlines	42¹/₈	15⁷/₈	-62.3	5¹/₄	-87.5
Travelers	38⁷/₈	33¹/₈	-13.8	19³/₄	-49.2
Tropicana Products	56³/₄	20¹/₄	-64.3	14¹/₄	-74.9
Western Union	48¹/₂	14¹/₈	-70.9	9	-81.4
Average Change			-25.6		-50.9
S&P 500 (without div.)	118.1	97.6	-17.4	68.6	-41.9

All companies adjusted for stock splits.

and when the stocks were favored the institutional holdings appeared to be high. Thus there seems to be little question that the consensus on the chosen favorites was genuine, but in each case the consensus was wrong and sometimes very markedly so. The pressures to consensus, then, might well have ruled out the independent, critical thinking necessary to have avoided the mistakes. Strong reinforcement of opinion within the investment organization, by numerous outside authorities and by large numbers of similar investment firms, made the incorrect decision-making route appear to be the proper one.

In the cases we have shown it seems that the greater the unanimity of opinion, the greater the possibility of poor results. The top selections in both 1972 and 1973 fared far worse than the S&P 500, and the top picks (National Student Marketing in 1970; the airlines stocks; and the two top individual choices in 1972—IBM and Pan Am), fared worst of all.

The evidence dramatically contradicts the EMH line of reasoning, whereby professional investor selections should be no better and no worse than the market while appearing to corroborate the groupthink hypothesis. EMH would have us believe that professionals are instrumental in keeping prices in line with value. Evidence of such repeated error, as we have just seen, places a severe strain on the credibility of this hypothesis.

The measurements I have included are the only ones I have been able to locate to the present time. To further test for groupthink, it is important to accumulate additional broad confidential surveys of institutional choices and compare them to actual results over time.

The Herd Mania into Concept Stocks

In Chapter 4 we saw how many institutional investors went into concept stocks and their frequently treacherous performance after a short period of widespread popularity. The groupthink hypothesis can be further explored by studying this phenomenon.

After the disastrous experience with "concept" stocks in the 1969–1970 market, money managers went through a catharsis. Large numbers of "post-mortems" were held in which the faulty decisions that led to tremendous blunders in the "go-go" markets of 1967–1968 were dissected by the managers themselves.

An article by Peter Landau at the time seemed to capture the prevailing mood particularly well:

> A trust officer of a major bank widely praised for his "advanced" investment practices in times past, said: "I am ashamed, demoralized, embarrassed and disheartened to have lost this money for my customers." A competitor put it considerably more bluntly: "We have been kicked in a vital place, and it still hurts; it will be a long time before men are able to stand up straight again.[3]

Money managers indicated they would not repeat the critical mistakes of attempting to overperform, loading up with thinly traded stocks, buying "stories" before they were carefully researched, and buying "concept stocks." Landau noted that all these views had been stated before and added: "Never? Perhaps Gilbert and Sullivan's 'hardly ever' would be more precise. For the fact is that there is frequently a quite perceptible difference between what people say they are going to do and what actually happens when the chips are down—or the market is up." Landau further commented that when "the going gets good, the good concepts get going."[4] What is remarkable is that when the article was published in October 1970, the professionals' sparks of interest in new concepts were already being fanned vigorously, and a roaring speculative inferno would break out in a matter of months.

The risks of being overaggressive, so clearly understood by everyone in the fall of 1970, had seemingly vanished by the spring of 1971. As the new favorites soared in price, they were recommended by numerous research houses and approved by increasing numbers of investment committees. This reinforced the conviction of many professional investors that their decisions to buy the new concept stocks had been prudently made. The aggressiveness of the risk

TABLE 13. Twenty favorites of the 1971–1972 market.

Company	Price 3/31/72	Price 12/31/72	9 Months % Change	Price 12/31/73	21 Months % Change	Price 12/31/74	33 Months % Change
Bausch & Lomb	110½	27¼	−75.4	37¾	−65.8	21⅜	−80.7
Best Prod.	56½	61	8.0	9⅜	−83.4	2⅝	−95.3
BioMedical Science*	58	78	34.5	42½	−26.7	13	−77.6
H&R Block	26⅜	16⅝	−37.0	10¾	−59.2	10⅞	−58.8
Comsat	62¼	64	2.8	38½	−38.2	28⅜	−54.4
Damon	58⅜	61	4.5	38¼	−34.5	11	−81.2
Duplan	18½	13⅜	−27.7	3½	−81.1	1⅛	−93.9
Equity Funding†	40	36¾	−8.1	0	−100.0	0	−100.0
FNMA	22	20	−9.1	16¾	−23.9	18⅜	−16.5
House of Fabrics	23¼	9⅝	−58.6	7½	−67.7	3⅝	−84.4
Levitz	49¾	26⅞	−46.0	3⅝	−92.7	1¾	−96.5
Magic Chef	52⅝	20¼	−61.5	5⅝	−89.3	3⅜	−93.6
Memorex	29¾	16⅜	−31.0	4⅞	−79.5	1½	−93.7
MGIC	56¾	95¾	68.7	32⅞	−42.1	9⅜	−83.5
New Process	56⅞	21½	−62.2	8½	−85.1	3⅞	−93.2
Penn. Life	36¾	9⅜	−74.5	2⅛	−94.2	1⅝	−95.6
Sperry & Hutch.	49¼	29⅞	−40.4	33¾	−31.5	27	−45.2
Teleprompter	36¾	33¼	−8.6	3⅞	−89.3	1½	−95.8
Telex	12	5¾	−5.0	2⅝	−78.1	2½	−79.2
Tropicana	88½	56¾	−35.9	20¼	−77.1	14¼	−83.9
Average % change			−25.5		−69.0		−80.1
S&P 500 (without div.)	107.2	118.05	+10.5	97.55	−9.0	68.6	−36.0
Value Line Composite (without div.)	122.11	114.05	−6.6	73.64	−39.5	49.0	−59.9

Adjusted for stock splits.
*BioMedical halted on 10/11/73.
†Equity Funding suspended at 14⅜ on 3/27/73, eventually bankrupt.

taking and the underestimation of the danger was truly remarkable.

Through 1971 and most of 1972, concepts again were widely played, sponsored by leading institutional brokerage houses and heavily accumulated by institutional investors. Table 13 lists 20 of the favorite institutional concepts of the period.

While I would be the last to argue that Table 13 is an all-inclusive list of such stocks, I think it is a pretty representative one. Each of the stocks generated significant institutional interest, large numbers of research reports, and extensive institutional buying. Teleprompter, Levitz, Bausch and Lomb, and Federal National Mortgage were in the top ten favorites in the *Institutional Investor's* contest in 1972 or 1973.

For the 21 months ending December 1973, the average decline of this group was 69% from their price at March 31, 1972, almost eight times as much as the decline in the S&P 500. Even the more speculative Value Line Index* fared better. It declined 6.6% for the nine months and 40% for the 21 months.

The excellence of the concepts at the time was apparent at a glance. Levitz Furniture had a unique marketing approach, combining its warehouses and showrooms under the same roof. Prices were low, and buyers could take the furniture home with them rather than having to wait for normal delivery. The company was expanding rapidly and earnings were soaring. Bausch and Lomb with its "soft contact lens," so much easier for the new wearer to adapt to, was expected to tremendously expand the market for contact lenses and coin money in the process, as was Teleprompter with its strong and rapidly growing position in Cable TV. The exorbitant prices paid for the exciting prospects of such companies exactly paralleled the overvaluations of 1967–1968 or, for that matter, the "bubble companies" in 1720. Under the influence of groupthink and the pressures of compliance,

---

*It is unweighted and includes 1,634 stocks from various exchanges as well as the over-the-counter market. If adjusted for dividends, the favorites' performance would be substantially poorer.

the identical mistakes were repeated in the shortest time span in market history. The bulk of professional investors probably believed their actions to be prudent. It is extraordinary how quickly the "greed" motive, institutions' desire to improve performance in a rising market, replaced the "fear" of overexposure in stocks, which was prevalent only months before.

All the conditions necessary for groupthink to operate most effectively were present. Research houses marketed the concepts, with many reports. Each research firm vied to have the most in-depth expertise of the concept, few questioning the basic direction. Professional investment firms received constant assurance, not only from research experts but also from other decision makers with similar goals, that they were on the right path. This vote of confidence was accompanied by the tremendous influence of rising stock prices themselves and excited clients' acceptance of the course.

The Top 50

For some time the research department of Kidder Peabody has been compiling a list of the 50 stocks with the highest price/earnings multiples on the New York Stock Exchange. The more investors like a company, the higher the multiple they will pay for current earnings. The P/E ratios* are figured by calculating the most recent 12-month earnings available at the time. Institutions are usually concentrated heavily in these stocks, as we shall see in detail in Chapter 8. The analysis of how this group has performed, when compared to the S&P 500, thus provides another illuminating measure of determining how institutional thinking has fared over a period of time. In compiling the list, Kidder Peabody does not include gold mining shares or shares of companies with only nominal profits. As new companies are favored and their P/Es increase, they replace companies whose P/Es have fallen. Because the list has been compiled monthly since December 1972, we can measure how the 50 most favored

*P/E multiples or P/E ratios will at times be shortened to P/E.

TABLE 14. Percent change in Kidder Peabody "Top 50" 1973 to 1975.

Performance Period	Top 50 at			S&P 500 (without div.)
	12/31/72	12/31/73	12/31/74	
12/31/72–12/31/73	−26.79%	—	—	−17.4%
12/31/72–12/31/74	−54.52	—	—	−41.9
12/31/72–12/31/75	−43.5	—	—	−33.6
12/31/73–12/31/74	—	−33.1	—	−17.28
12/31/73–12/31/75	—	−17.28	—	−7.5
12/31/74–12/31/75	—	—	+22.2	+31.5

Adjusted for stock splits.

stocks in any period since that time have done relative to the market.

Table 14 shows that the stocks with the highest P/E ratios chosen as favorites at year's end in 1972, 1973, and 1974 subsequently performed significantly worse than the market averages.

Market Performance of Popular and Unpopular Stocks

The evidence in Table 14 is not terribly convincing because the measurement period is far too short and high P/Es were out of favor during this period. However, there is further statistical evidence on the market performance of popular and unpopular stocks over long periods which appears to support the groupthink-compliance hypothesis at the expense of EMH. The first study we shall look at is by Paul F. Miller, Jr. Miller (Drexel) took the data on the Standard & Poor's Compustat computer·tapes for all companies with over $150 million in sales in a given year.* The number of such companies increased from 110 in 1948 to 334 in 1964.

P/E multiples were computed by using calendar or fiscal year earnings† and the year-end stock price. The companies

---

*All fiscal years in the study ended between September 30 and January 31. All companies studied had positive earnings.

†A bias may exist in these findings. Some of the companies in the high P/E group may be there because they have only nominal earnings. This

(footnote continued on next page)

TABLE 15. Average price increase per year, 1948–1964.

P/E Quintile	Price Increase, %
1 (highest P/E)	7.7
2	9.2
3	12.0
4	12.8
5 (lowest P/E)	18.4

Source: Drexel & Company Inc., Philadelphia, *Monthly Review*.

were divided into five quintiles according to their P/Es. The results are given in Table 15. The findings are rather striking. The companies that investors believed to be the best according to the P/E multiples they were given actually had the worst average of subsequent performance. The performance record varies inversely with the level of the P/E multiple. The findings are completely uniform. The second most popular quintile had the second worst overall results and, conversely, the second most unpopular quintile had the second best results.*

Miller also found the lowest quintile (lowest P/Es) did best in performance in 12 of the next 17 years. The stocks in the top P/E quintile did the best in only one year and performed the worst in 8. The odds of better performance the next year in buying the stocks in the bottom quintile were thus 12 times better than buying stocks in the highest quintile.

Francis Nicholson made a later study of 189 companies in 18 industries for the 1937–1962 period.[5] In this study he grouped the stocks into quintiles by P/Es as did Miller, and measured the average annual appreciation. He further examined how the various P/E groups did after periods of two to seven years. The findings are provided in Table 16. In this more exhaustive study, varying the time periods, the findings strongly and continually favored the lower P/E

---

bias has been eliminated in several other extensive surveys made thereafter, and the bottom multiples still significantly outperformed the top. The bottom quintile also markedly outperformed the other three quintiles of the Miller study not as affected by such possible bias. The overall effect on the study, then, appears to be quite small.

TABLE 16. Annual earnings related to mean prices.

Grouped According to Quintiles in Each Year 1937–1962 Inclusive	Average Price Appreciation Percentages						
	After 1 yr.	2 yr.	3 yr.	4 yr.	5 yr.	6 yr.	7 yr.
A. Lowest P/E ratios	16	34	55	76	98	125	149
B. Next higher	9	22	34	48	65	82	100
C. Next higher	7	18	30	43	60	77	96
D. Next higher	6	14	24	35	50	65	83
E. Highest P/E ratios	3	11	21	31	46	65	84

Source: *Financial Analysts Journal*, January–February 1968.

multiples. The bottom quintile performed over five times as well as the top, after one year. This discrepancy was reduced with longer holding periods, but the bottom 20% still performed almost twice as well as the top quintile after seven years.

Nicholson further analyzed these results, using the fixed P/E multiples in Table 17. By this method, the performance of low over the high P/E groups is clearly more pronounced than when the groupings are made simply by quintiles. A number of other studies provided similar results.*

Finally a study made by Drexel, Harriman & Ripley tested the 30 stocks in the Dow Jones Industrial Average itself. The study measured the results of holding the ten lowest-multiple stocks in the average for consecutive five-year periods between 1937 and 1962 against holding the ten highest

---

*William Breen made a study eliminating companies with nominal earnings, and measured total return (dividends and capital appreciation) of a sample of stocks from the Compustat tapes between 1953 and 1960. His findings confirmed the better performance of the low P/E ratio stocks. He also found that a sample of stocks which had the lowest P/Es in their industries subsequently performed far better than the market.[6] Francis Nicholson in an earlier test (which eliminated companies with nominal earnings) measured the performance of high and low price/earnings multiple stocks in the chemicals industry between 1937 and 1954.[7] The results strongly favored the low P/E ratio stocks. James McWilliams used a sample of 900 stocks from the S&P Compustat tapes in the 1953–1964 period and found corroboration of the better performance of low P/E stocks. McWilliams further demonstrated that, while stocks having the highest individual appreciation in any given year appeared to be randomly distributed, those with the greatest declines were in the high P/E ratio group.[8]

TABLE 17. Annual earnings related to mean prices.

Grouped Each Year 1937–1962 Inclusive, by Fixed Ranges	Number of Cases Averaged	Average Price Appreciation Percentages						
		After 1 yr.	2 yr.	3 yr.	4 yr.	5 yr.	6 yr.	7 yr.
A. 10 times or less	1672 to 1582	13	31	51	71	90	110	131
B. 10 to 12 times	662 to 525	8	19	31	41	53	68	87
C. 12 to 15 times	872 to 606	6	15	24	36	52	70	88
D. 15 to 20 times	773 to 457	4	11	18	26	40	55	75
E. Over 20 times	581 to 277	2	4	10	17	32	54	71

Source: *Financial Analysts Journal*, January–February 1968.

TABLE 18. Average annual percentage gain or loss, 1937–1962.

Period	Ten Low Multiplier Issues	Ten High Multiplier Issues	30 DJIA Stocks
1937–42	−2.2	−10.0	−6.3
1943–47	17.3	8.3	14.9
1948–52	16.4	4.6	9.9
1953–57	20.9	10.0	13.7
1958–62	10.2	−3.3	3.6

Source: Drexel & Company Inc., *Monthly Review.*

multiples. The P/Es at the beginning of each time span determined the stocks chosen in each group. The results are illustrated in Table 18.

The results corroborate the Miller and Nicholson findings. The low multiples did better than the high multiples in every five-year period. Drexel and Company further calculated the results of investing $10,000 in each of the high- and low-multiple groups in June 1936, and switching each year into the higher P/Es in the former case and the lower P/Es in the latter. The $10,000 in the lowest P/Es would have grown to $66,866 by mid-1962. The $10,000 in the highest multiples, those normally with the "best visibility," would have increased to only $25,437. If $10,000 had been invested in the Dow Jones Average itself in 1937, it would have grown to $35,600 by June 1962.

TABLE 19

Holding Period	S&P 425, % change	Stock Purchased December 31, Year of Deficit, % change	Stock Purchased December 31, Year After Deficit, % change
1	12.1	23.2	25.4
2	25.5	47.9	49.6
3	38.1	78.9	100.0
4	52.0	116.9	127.1
5	69.3	159.7	158.1

Source: Marine Midland Bank, November 1968.

There is one final piece of important evidence we should view, that of the subsequent price performance of companies reporting deficits in a given year. Investors usually shun stocks that report deficits. As a result, such stocks have outperformed the S&P 425* with regularity, as a study (Table 19) prepared by the Marine Midland Bank indicates for the 1948–1967 period.† The study indicates the average performance of the S&P 425 for holding periods of from one to five years and compares it with the results of the deficit companies from the group. If the stocks with deficits had been purchased one year after the deficit occurred, they would have increased an average of 25.4% for the year and 158.1% for the five-year period, compared to 12.1% and 69.3%, respectively, for the S&P 425.

The consistency of the previous findings is truly remarkable. Over almost every period measured, the stocks that were considered to have the best prospects, according to the P/E multiples they were given, have done significantly worse than the stocks with the worst outlook, using the same criteria. These results confirm the findings of the inferior performance of selected samples of growth and concept stocks presented previously. They also explain why the usual professional preference for such stocks has resulted in the inferior professional performance that was indicated in Chapter 1.

Viewed in the light of the groupthink-compliance hypothesis, these results make eminent sense. Investors over-rate the prospects of "good" companies and just as steadily underrate the prospects of companies considered to have unfavorable outlooks. Many believe that the favorites will continue to rise. They are reinforced by most opinions around them and do not take adequate cognizance of the risks. Others

*The S&P 500 is comprised of the 425 S&P industrials together with 25 railroads and 50 utilities.
†A bias probably exists in this table, since only surviving companies are selected. If insolvent companies were also included, the comparisons of the deficit companies might be less striking. Because of the rarity of insolvencies among major companies, however, it does not appear that the differences would be significant.

comply because of economic pressures. The reasoning is reversed for the low P/E groups.

It is also interesting to note how quickly the self-correcting process begins. The evidence available (see Tables 15, 16, 17, and 19) suggests that it very often commences within a year.

The extensive evidence of the consistently better performance of the low P/E ratio stocks is precisely the sort of relationship that is ruled out by the efficient market hypothesis. Rational investors seeing the superior results over time of low P/Es should pounce on this group because of the better rewards it offers and, similarly, avoid the higher P/Es, until no discernible pattern of better performance by any group exists. But this clearly hasn't happened, which means the odds of beating the market may be better than these theorists believe. We will explore this possibility in the final section of the book. Next we shall view one of the more fascinating manifestations of the groupthink-compliance syndrome—the two-tier market of 1972 and 1973.

Note: A just-completed computer study updating the high/low P/E results for the mid-1967–1976 period for companies on the New York Stock Exchange is found in the Appendix to this book.

8

The Amazing
Two-Tier Market

The repetition of the concept mania was not the major institutional error of the 1971–1973 period. Even more startling were the tremendous excesses of the two-tier market. While the market has always valued rapidly growing companies with excellent prospects at significantly higher P/E multiples than companies with stodgier records and outlooks, the divergence had never become as marked as in this market cycle.

The Market's Aristocracy

There are approximately 3,000 stocks listed on various stock exchanges in this country and thousands more traded over the counter with some frequency. By March 1973 the average stock (not weighted for numbers of shares outstanding) on the New York Stock Exchange had dropped approximately 50% from its high of late 1968. On the American Stock Exchange, according to the *Indicator Digest's* unweighted index of 1,200 stocks, stocks were down about 80% over the same period.[1] While no comprehensive index exists covering all the thousands of companies trading over the counter, there is little doubt from the large numbers trading at P/E multiples of 3, 4, and 5 that the declines were even more severe.*

---

*Over 8,000 companies are traded over the counter, according to a recent New York Stock Exchange survey of investor stockholdings.

The nonpareil feature of the market at this time was that while most stocks were well under their 1968 highs and many were beginning to drop precipitously lower as the 1973–1974 market break gained momentum a small group of companies was flourishing. Unlike the great mass of stocks, this limited aristocracy was trading higher than in 1968. A survey compiled by Wiesenberger Services indicates that a group of 21 stocks most favored by institutions advanced 90% between December 1968 and April of 1973.[2] The market seemed to be going in two directions at once.

The small group of aristocrats were known by such names as the "nifty fifty," the "vestal virgins," the "high flyers," the "sacred cows," or the "religion stocks." Whatever name they were called by, there was little question that they were prospering. These were the elite among United States industry, the large, well-financed, and rapidly growing companies with excellent records. As a group they were experiencing well above average, if not dramatic, sales and earnings expansion.

An excellent article, "How the Terrible Two-Tier Market Came to Wall Street," describing these events appeared in *Fortune* in mid-1973.[3] Frequency distributions were run that showed the percentage of stocks trading at various multiples in each market upswing and decline since 1948 for a sample of 382 large, well-known companies. The P/E multiples tended to move up and down in unison with the prevailing optimism or pessimism of the time. In 1948, when stocks were completely out of favor, the median multiple was 5.8. In the euphoria of the 1961 bull market, the median was 19.4. At the end of the first quarter of 1973 the median was 11.5, the lowest since 1957. While most stocks were trading at moderate prices, the high P/E upper tier was relatively larger than it had been in any previous cycle. *Fortune* summarized its findings as follows:

> What can be said with certainty is that there has been no comparable situation in recent history . . . .in a pattern not otherwise seen during the twenty-six years under examination; 128 stocks had a P/E under 10, and 34 had a P/E above 30. Moreover, because the stocks in the upper tier were so highly valued by the market, they absorbed a far greater

proportion of investment dollars than the number of companies represented there would indicate.[4]

A wider sample was taken by the Security Pacific National Bank for the January 1971 to July 31, 1973, period. It divided the S&P 500 Index into three categories: basic, moderate, and high growth. The basic industries had declined 8.5%, the moderate growth had increased 4.4%, and the high growth had leaped 67.5%, clearly showing where the market preference was. The S&P itself was up 17.3%, indicating how important the relatively few growth companies with large capitalizations were to the index.[5]

Reginald Jones, the chairman of General Electric, examined the S&P 425 industrials between 1965 and the end of 1972 and found that 18 companies with an average multiple of 47 accounted for the entire $111 billion growth in the index in this period.[6]

The dichotomy existing in the marketplace in the first half of 1973 provided one of the strangest phenomena in market history. A raging bull market existed for perhaps 50 to 70 companies, while a methodical destruction in values was continuing for 98% of all public companies. Although many companies were trading at five times earnings or less, the median multiple of Kidder Peabody's top fifty at the end of March 1973 was still 48.4. P/E multiples in the stratosphere existed for some. International Flavor and Fragrances was at 76, McDonald's at 71, Baxter Labs at 67, Disney at 67, and Avon at 62.

The dichotomy was easily enough explained. Since 1959, individuals had been net sellers of securities, while institutions had been increasing their holdings substantially. According to SEC figures, institutional holdings almost doubled between 1965 and 1972, from $196.9 billion to $387 billion.[7] By 1972, institutions were estimated to own 45% of all stock traded on the big board.* As money was being withdrawn by the

---

* James J. Needham, then chairman of the New York Stock Exchange, told Senator Bentsen's committee on the study of financial markets that the figure was 30%, excluding bank trust department holdings. Including these holdings and those of other smaller institutions, he believed the figure would probably total 45%. By now, almost four years later, it is probably somewhat closer to 50%.

general public—the bulk from the bottom tier, which accounted for such a large percentage of total companies—institutions were progressively concentrating more narrowly in the upper tier with their large flows of new funds. Pension funds alone purchased $7.6 billion of new stocks in 1972. Overall, they purchased $23.3 billion of securities and sold $15.7 billion that year.[8] It is likely that with the significantly better performance of the upper tier, a fair proportion of all new institutional money and money taken out by selling other securities was directed into the upper tier.

The outflow of funds from the lower tier and the continued concentration of institutional funds in a favored few stocks produced striking discrepancies in value. A reporter for the *Financial Times* in London wrote that the market value of Avon Products exceeded that of the entire United States steel industry. (Some readers will recall here the situation that existed during the South Sea Bubble when the South Sea stock had a value greater than all the cash in Europe.) This comparison was made when Avon's growth rate was slowing down to less than 15% from 20%, a significant decrease, and the steel industry was enjoying an excellent year and improving prospects. The reporter observed: "The real problem must be a market with such a haywire sense of values."[9]

The situation was not unique. McDonald's, the hamburger empire, had a book value (the value of its assets less liabilities) of $200 million and a market value (the value of all shares outstanding multiplied by the market price) of $2.1 billion at the end of 1972. Coca-Cola had a book value of $800 million and a market value of $7.1 billion. To show the disparity, consider that U.S. Steel had a book value of $3.6 billion at the time, and a market value of $2.2 billion. McDonald's and U.S. Steel were about equally valued in the market. This valuation in effect meant each dollar invested in McDonald's was expected to earn 17 times similar dollar amounts invested in U.S. Steel over a period of time, and a dollar invested in Coca-Cola would earn 15 times more. This phenomenon occurred repeatedly. At its high, Levitz Furniture had a market value significantly more than double that of Goodrich which was both far larger and more profitable at the time.

By the spring of 1973, the concentration of institutional buying in a relative handful of stocks alarmed government industry and investment officials, and the Senate Committee of Finance subsequently formed a subcommittee chaired by Senator Lloyd Bentsen of Texas to investigate the matter.

The danger was real. In mid-1973, the inability of many ordinary companies to raise capital was particularly alarming. So ominous did it seem that a committee was formed of the presidents of over 600 public companies, representing 1.4 million employees and 2.3 million shareholders. Over two-thirds of the companies were listed on the New York or American Stock Exchange.

The prime economic function of a capital market is to allocate capital to companies that have proved their capability of using it profitably. But in 1973, thousands of companies with good financial records but with low P/Es for their stock found themselves barred from the equity markets on anything but prohibitive terms. If a stock sells at five times earnings, the issuance of new stock at this level gives the new shareholder a 20% aftertax return on his purchase price, since he is only paying $5.00 for each dollar of earnings. Allowing the normal corporate tax rate of about 50%, this would require a pretax return of 40%. There are precious few investments that will yield 40% with any assurance over a period of time. Money can either be borrowed (often at prohibitive rates or terms dangerous to the financial well-being of the company) or the expansion program can be postponed. Economists have estimated between $25,000 and $30,000 of new capital investment is required to create a new job. Thus, fears arose about the potentially serious and negative economic consequences of the "two-tier" market. The low P/E multiples most companies traded at also made them vulnerable to takeover by companies with better P/Es, thus increasing the risk of industry concentration.

The situation concerned major leaders in both finance and industry. James J. Needham, chairman of the New York Stock Exchange, said: "It is certainly pertinent to inquire why the large institutions persist in tightening their concentration on a few favored stocks, while ignoring hundreds of other choice investment opportunities."[10] James Roche, the former chairman of General Motors, in his address to the Securities Industry Association in 1973, warned: "This situation may be reassuring to the companies favored by the institutions, but it by no means satisfied the needs of the nation. . . . Our system cannot flourish solely on the basis of the health and strength of 75 glamour companies."[11] General Electric's chairman, Reginald H. Jones, expressed concern about whether the "industrial backbone" of the American economy could any longer attract equity capital.[12]

Whether or not the effects were destructive to the capital markets, another important question had to be asked. Did the move to the upper tier make good sense for the client who, after all, must be the primary responsibility of the fiduciary? We shall look at this subject next.

The Stampede into the Upper Tier

Although the upper-tier stocks had long been favored by many professional investors, the cult of the "one decision" stocks, as they were increasingly called, became almost obsessional by late 1972 and early 1973. The rationale of the "one decision" stocks was compellingly simple. A relatively few large companies with superb sales and proven earnings records over long-time periods could control their own fate. They were so well managed, had such excellent prospects well secured in rapidly growing markets through technology, highly regarded product lines, or unparalleled marketing organizations, and were so financially strong that continuing profitable growth could be expected well into the future. Avon, IBM, Xerox, Polaroid, McDonald's, and International Flavors and Fragrances were examples of such stocks. The "visibility" of their futures was so assured they need never be sold. Well, of course they would fluctuate; any sharp declines were simply opportunities to buy more on better terms. This was the repeatedly stated justification for their purchase.

The percentage of the one-decision stocks institutionally held was immense and growing. At the end of 1972, the ten largest banks and the mutual funds alone owned about 42% of Polaroid, 37% of Xerox, 38% of Avon, and 45% of Walt Disney. When other banks and institutional investors were counted, the concentration was significantly higher.[13]

In the Senate Finance Subcommittee hearings, a number of major banks involved in top-tier stocks defended their purchases. With assets of $27.2 billion under administration in 1972, the trust department of Morgan Guaranty was the largest in the nation. It was also one of the most successful, and its success was largely based on the one-decision stock approach. Morgan had no doubt that its method was correct. Samuel Callaway, the head of its trust division, told the Bentsen committee: "Blaming the two-tier market on investors is like blaming a rainstorm on the people who put up their umbrellas."[14] Quintin U. Ford, the head of the investment division of Bankers Trust, told the committee: "These high price/earnings ratios are reflective of increased investor recognition and awareness of those relatively few companies having greater ability to control their destiny and cope with the inflationary environment. Perhaps other investors are saying as we, with a portion of our funds, that these stocks in the current environment of a controlled economy represent the best investment."[15] George M. Lingua in charge of trust operations for New York's Citibank* said:

> We respectfully submit that it has not been the large institutional investors, not the large bank trustee managers of pension funds, who have caused this erosion of confidence in the future prospects for some of our basic industries. . . . In placing our primary investment emphasis on large, growing, technology advanced or consumer oriented companies in the so-called "top-tier," we have been trying to exercise our best judgment in carrying out our fiduciary responsibilities for the beneficiaries of these long-term capital funds.[16]

The chairman of the investment policy division of one

_____
*Now Citicorp.

of the largest investment advisory firms, writing in the *Financial Analysts Journal* in late 1972, stated very similar views:

> The [high quality, large growth] companies seem particularly well situated to prosper in the face of the major problems expected to characterize the years ahead. . . . All things considered, including participation in promising product areas—they offer relatively well defined prospects for superior earnings growth over the longer term. In contrast, major uncertainties cloud the future of many of the traditional "blue chip" companies. Since the relative advantage of [these companies] appears to have increased in recent years, it would be reasonable to expect an upward tendency in relative valuations.[17]

The author writes that he realizes these stocks may involve large risk and that some may be "substantially" overpriced. Further, he warns that in a major bear market, such stocks, because of the high P/Es, are terribly vulnerable. He also notes the danger of changed investment styles. Still, he advocates this course.

The growth companies had the highest earnings visibility. Their future profit growth seemed both rapid and assured. This was the common theme running through the thinking of the institutions advocating these stocks. Because of their proven competitive strengths, they could sail smoothly through the operating vagaries of the increasingly inflationary environment, improving their earnings consistently quarter by quarter while most companies floundered. As one money manager phrased it, "The rewards of the top-tier companies stand out like a beacon in the night."

Roger Kennedy, the chief finance officer of the Ford Foundation, may have summed it up well: "I would like to suggest the somewhat unorthodox view that stocks in the top tier of the two-tier market are now being used by many as substitutes for bonds. They are comforting to investors who have been trained to prefer stocks to bonds but are not willing to accept general equity risks. . . . They may buy a bond or a top-tier stock for the same psychological reasons."[18] High-tier stocks are far riskier than bonds in the degree of safety of principal provided in a short time

TABLE 20. The leading institutional investors.*

Institution	Investment portfolio at 12/31/72 ($ billions)
Morgan Guaranty Trust	$27.2
Bankers Trust	19.9
Prudential Insurance	18.3
First National City Bank	17.2
U.S. Trust of New York	17.0
Metropolitan Life Insurance	16.5
Manufacturers Hanover Trust	10.9
Mellon National Bank & Trust	10.5
Investors Diversified Services	9.7
Chase Manhattan Bank	9.2

*Based on data from Money Market Directories, Inc.
†Excludes real estate investments.
Source: *Business Week*, June 2, 1973. © 1973 by McGraw-Hill, Inc. Reprinted by special permission.

span. If such mistaken thinking existed widely, as Kennedy suggested, it might well indicate the presence of groupthink.

Whatever the reasoning, the institutional concentration on these stocks was tremendous. Morgan, Bankers Trust, First National City, the Chase Manhattan, all of whom strenuously defended this course, controlled $73.5 billion in trust assets at the end of 1972, as Table 20 indicates. The bank trust departments managed over 80% of the private pension fund money of some 30 million Americans. Of all these funds, 46% of the money was run by the New York City banks alone. Because of large new inflows of funds, pension fund assets grew at a 13% rate annually between 1966 and 1972. However, the percentage going into common stock increased at a 20% compound rate from $39.5 billion in 1966 to $115.2 billion in 1972, as stock holdings were expanded from 54 to 73% of total pension fund assets. With the prevalent thinking of leading bank trust departments favoring the upper-tier stocks, it was likely that a tremendous amount of pension dollars went into those stocks, both from new monies and from sales of bottom-tier stocks. In fact, one study of pension funds indicated that although fund stockholdings had risen dramatically between 1966 and 1970, the number of different stocks held decreased by 17%.[19]

Bank trust departments also administered $403 billion for 1,200,000 nonpension accounts at the end of 1972.[20] While the turnover here was much less and the diversity of holdings many times larger than for pension funds, much of the investment of new funds went into the favored "top tier," while bottom-tier stocks were sold.

With the strong pressure on mutual funds to perform in this period and the better results in the top tier, many mutual funds bought these stocks. Together the funds sometimes held as much as 20% of a company's total stock outstanding. Other institutions also followed this pattern, and institutional research coverage was by far the most intensive in the top tier.

Because of its tremendous size and its increasingly larger share of pension fund money, Morgan was, in *Fortune*'s words, "the player that everybody in the game watches. Its influence clearly extends beyond the sums it manages."[21] For years Morgan had been an aggressive top-tier investor. As a result of the huge flow of new investment money it received, about $1 billion a year, Morgan needed to invest in larger companies. Its normal criterion at the time was to choose companies with a minimum of $500 million in both revenues and market value. The number of companies that met this criterion was small, probably under 300.

Morgan Guaranty's position in many stocks was astounding. At the end of 1972 it held $2.1 billion of IBM, $1.1 billion of Eastman Kodak, $600 million of Xerox and Sears Roebuck, $473 million of Disney, and $432 million of Polaroid. It was difficult to switch course if a company it liked proved disappointing, and it would take substantial time to do so. Morgan seemed forced, of necessity, to accept the one-decision concept. It apparently had nowhere else to go. If it bought large cyclical companies, the size of its positions would prevent it from selling them when necessary. And, if it bought a large number of smaller companies, its research department would have to be expanded geometrically to cover them (a very costly alternative) while its results for clients might vary dramatically. So Morgan bought the one-decision stocks. And how it bought! In 1972, of about $1 billion in investment funds, $650 million went into seven top-tier favorites and another $150 million into eight others. Professor Roy A. Schotland of the Georgetown Law School calculated that Morgan alone in 1972 accounted for over 20% of the trading in 7 stocks, 10% in 28 stocks, and over 5% in 45 stocks, all on the New York Stock Exchange.[22]

Other bank trust departments and institutional investors also were imbued with the one-decision spirit, which they thought gave them better results and at the same time allowed them to move into and out of large blocks at will. In the first quarter of 1973, institutions purchased almost $15 billion of new stocks while selling $11.6 billion. A good portion of this money flowed from the lower to the upper tier, pushing the tiers further and further apart. If all roads once led to Rome, they now seemingly converged on the narrow strip that housed Disneyland, McDonald's, Polaroid, Xerox, and their illustrious relatives.

Samuel Callaway of Morgan, an appropriate spokesman in this case, believed the two-tier phenomenon to be the result of sound investment policy. He told Senator Bentsen's subcommittee in February 1974 that he had not "seen any evidence that would lead me to conclude that beneficiaries are endangered by the prevailing strategies of institutional pension fund managers."[23] He thought the *Fortune* article entitled "How the Terrible Two-Tier Market Came to Wall Street" was "the new demonology of the stock market."[24] In September 1973, *Barron's* editor, Alan Abelson, summarized the opposing view:

> We've had a de facto two-tier market for months now: one tier consisting of half a hundred big "growth" stocks and their loyal institutional admirers, the other made up of the thousands of hum-drum issues and just-plain-folk investors. . . . A section of the market [should be] officially set aside for the exclusive use of the big players and their chosen playthings, more or less like an African game preserve, if only in the interest of public safety. For sure as shooting, should the institutional gamesmen tire of the sport, many an innocent might be trampled

in the resulting stampede. We're still convinced that one major excess of this bull market—the institutional herding into a relatively few stocks—has yet to be remedied.[25]

Was the Two-Tier Market a Manifestation of Groupthink?

With the wage-price freeze of late 1971 and the subsequent limitation placed on price increases in 1972, fundamental analysis, always difficult, became vastly more so. Caught up in the increasing uncertainty of the times, professionals looked to the "certainty" or visibility of the earnings growth of the high-tier stocks. The large growth stocks were the best-performing companies during this period. Under the difficult conditions of 1972 it was easy for many analysts to associate with the widely held opinions of the time, favoring one-decision stocks and avoiding all other companies, regardless of price. These views were extensively held, reinforcing the decision maker's and his firm's own thinking. The decisions were empirically backed by series of selected statistics. Some professionals also displayed a degree of intolerance and perhaps disdain toward criticism and the critics themselves.

Let us examine the major premises of one-decision thinking to see how well they tie in with fundamental investment analysis, since almost all professional investment organizations ascribe their investment decisions to this discipline. The central thesis of one-decision theory was that large companies with highly visible earnings outlooks and well above average rates of growth could be purchased at high P/E multiples relative to the rest of the market; these P/Es valued each dollar of earnings as much as ten times more than other companies of comparable size and financial strength. Many of the major institutions shared the idea that this course of action was prudent and did not involve excessive risk taking.

In their excellent textbook, *Security Analysis,* on which a good part of the industry (including this author) has cut its investment teeth, Graham and Dodd warn against precisely this kind of reasoning. In discussing how in the late 1920s investors abandoned time-tested standards for evaluating common stocks, they write:

> The only quantitative factor that remained was the specific rate of growth, either historical or projected. But while *this concept might lead the investor to the "best" companies, it could not possibly protect him against paying too much for their shares* [italics mine]. On the contrary, the acceptance of the growth stock principle as the only guide to investment made the payment of excessive prices its inevitable consequence.
>
> The stock market of 1928–29 was highly discriminating, in accordance with its single touchstone of value. Nearly all companies that had failed to expand their profits during the current period of good business were held to have mediocre prospects at best, and thus they sold at low multiples of earnings.[26]

In discussing the difficulties of buying companies with the best prospects, Benjamin Graham noted: "The chief obstacle to success lies in the stubborn fact that if the favorable prospects of a firm are clearly apparent, they are almost always reflected already—and often overdiscounted—in the current price of the stock. Buying such an issue is like betting on a topheavy favorite in a horse race. The chances may be on your side, but the odds are really against you."[27]

The institutional investors who identified the "best" company as the "best" purchase at any price were making the same serious mistake that has been made throughout the history of financial markets. That so many professionals would do this at the same time, with so little realization of the inherent risks, can be attributed to the process of groupthink.

The error was compounded because visibility has all too often proved ephemeral. Graham and Dodd note that if a company was assured of a high rate of growth indefinitely while less attractive companies were likely headed for bankruptcy, the analyst's only real course of action would be to buy the former and sell the latter. But, they say, "The truth of our corporate venture is quite otherwise. Extremely few companies have been able to show a high rate of uninterrupted growth for long periods of time. Remarkably few, also, of the large companies suffer ultimate extinction. For most their history is one of vicissitudes, of ups and downs, of changes in their relative standing."[28]

Graham and Dodd were astute clinicians. Their findings were confirmed by extensive empirical evidence almost three decades later. You may recall the discussion in Chapter 2 of Oxford Professor I. M. D. Little's article, "Higgledly Piggledy Growth." While working with English companies, he discovered that the pattern of previous earnings per share and their changes were useless in predicting future earnings results. A number of American studies have also reached much the same conclusion. Earnings changes seem to follow a random walk. If earnings cannot be predicted with any high degree of accuracy, paying high multiples for current prospects may be extremely dangerous if not foolhardy. Chapter 7 was strewn with the charred wreckage of "high visibility" companies that failed, confirming Little's findings. We further saw how consistently the "best" companies as a group provided the worst subsequent performance as a result of continually overpaying for immediate visibility.

There are many reasons why companies show outstanding earnings and sales growth for periods of years and then slow down. Sometimes it is simply accounting gimmickry (which we shall look at more closely in Chapter 10). Or, a company may have a short-term competitive advantage, which the market, enraptured by the high profit margins and earnings, interprets as a long-term trend. The showroom-warehouse concept of Levitz is just such a case. At its height of popularity the company sold at a P/E ratio of over 100 times earnings before being dashed to smithereens by competition and management problems. Only a little more than two years later, this highly popular institutional favorite had declined over 97% at its low point and was trading at a P/E under seven times lower earnings.

The more successful a company becomes, the more diffi-cult it is to continue the record; competition, governmental controls, and increasing market saturation all play a role in slowing growth. Too, a management team skilled at running a rapidly growing $50 or $100 million corporation may prove totally inadequate at the $300 to $500 million sales level. Products and markets seemingly invulnerable to competition are suddenly inundated by it. Untouchable patents are circumvented by new discoveries. Costs cannot be controlled adequately or selling prices cannot be raised, and profit margins are squeezed. Markets that appeared open for years of brisk growth rapidly become saturated. Political or economic events occur, such as the oil embargo or a sharp recession totally beyond the control of even the most astute management, and temporarily wreak havoc in the marketplace. These, then, are some of the factors behind the empirical findings that future earnings cannot be predicted with any degree of accuracy.

History constantly reminds us there is no absolute "visibility" of prospects in an uncertain world. Suppose, for example, we take the case of the investor who in 1913 decided to invest a large amount of money. The world had been at relative peace for almost a hundred years, with minimum inflation. Being conservative, the investor chose only bonds and, to be fully secure, he picked only government securities. To be extra sure, he went one step further and diversified by buying the obligations of the six strongest powers on earth. If he had put them in a safety deposit box unacessible to him for 10 years, upon opening the box a decade later he would have found the bonds of Russia, Austria-Hungary, and Germany to be valueless, and those of England and France to have only a small fraction of their former worth because of inflation. Only the bonds of the United States would still possess the greater part of their value. His investments had been decimated; yet at the time he made them, the "visibility" for his investments was unquestionably superb.

Such factors argue decisively against the top-tier strategy of buying "visibility," adopted by the institutions in 1972 and the first half of 1973. Disregarding the serious capital-raising problem of the bottom tier for the moment, the strategy was extremely dangerous from a financial viewpoint, as was confirmed dramatically within months.

The danger of overemphasizing current visibility was brought home time and again to the proponents of one-decision stocks. Whenever the certainty of "visibility" was questioned, there was a rush to liquidate, which often ended in near panic. At the height of the two-tier mania, it reminded one investment advisor of "an Agatha Christie novel where there is a new dead body every time you turn around. God help any company that experiences so much as a single flat quarter. When current earnings are lowered by only $.10 or $.20 below the original estimate of $3.50 (3 to 6%) and the stock promptly drops from 55 to 28 (50%). That's really sad."[29] In Chapter 9 we shall see the constant recurrence of this syndrome.

The top-tier advocates focused solely on "visibility," almost always measured by immediate earnings. In a dynamic and rapidly changing world, such visibility is most often impossible. Yet many institutional investors, apparently under the influence of groupthink, rode "into this Valley of Death," paying five- or tenfold more for one-decision companies than for other large companies with poorer "visibility."

The shared rationalizations on a colossal scale, which allowed these institutional investors to believe that their excessively risky course was actually prudent, defied historical and recent market experience, fundamental analysis, and the statistical findings of respected academics. So specious did the reasoning appear to be that even if the "visibility" of earnings had been correct, in many cases the stocks would have still been overpriced. Using basic security analysis and reasonable assumptions, in October 1973, *Fortune* valued Avon at between $33.14 and $45.20 a share at a time when the stock was trading at $110 (down from the year's high of $140). In 1974 it traded at under $20. The formula used by *Fortune* appears at the end of this chapter.

Fortune's analysis could have been applied to many of the other upper-tier stocks with very similar results. The exercise clearly shows that for Avon to be worth a price of $110 at that time, unwarranted optimistic assumptions had to be made about the company's growth rate.

Using the same analysis, a "mundane" company like

Goodyear would have been worth its low P/E ratio only if the 8.2% growth rate in the 1967–1972 period were to decline sharply in the future. Overly pessimistic assumptions were required to justify the price of a lower-tier stock.[30] Many of these latter stocks were valued almost on a "going out of business" basis. One wondered where the growth for 50 or so favorites would come from if most of United States industry, as judged by its stock valuation, was likely to become extinct.

The people who embarked on this disastrous upper-tier course were highly qualified professional investors, probably in many cases not terribly different from successful upper-echelon corporate executives or government policymakers. Not only was the decision maker reinforced by the manifestly strong opinions of other members of his organization and by other investment groups but the groups interlocked with members of a number of investment organizations serving on the policy committee of a hospital, a college, or a religious or a union organization. The interlocking structure, so much a part of the modern investment scene, served to more firmly embed the consensus.

Some of the comments made at the time are illustrative, I believe, of the groupthink phenomenon. The head of Trust investments for Bankers Trust said in mid-1973, "It bothers me that everybody is doing the same thing." But he found "solace" in the quality of his research, and was not really surprised that the research effort led the banks "to so many of the same stocks."[31]

A senior trust officer of a major New York bank clearly shows the confusion between "best company" and "best value." In discussing a popular high P/E group in March 1974, when most of the previous favorites selected by the same standards had already toppled sharply, he said:

> There's been, of course, some question about price. This [the oil service companies] is a group that has been rather heavily exploited in the market, and I have no way of getting around the fact that some of these stocks are high priced. It's just that, as I said earlier, I think in the long run the market recognizes growing sales and earnings, and *questions of price*

earnings multiples tend to be quite contemporary.* They're short run problems. We don't throw caution to the wind and buy extravagant multiples all the time, but we do try to buy the best stocks we can find in the industry groups we favor even if the multiples are a bit high.[32]

The term "best," used by so many large professional investors, filters out the inherent riskiness of the situation. The stocks of "best" companies can be both terribly overpriced and subject to drastic downward reappraisal if "visibility" deteriorates. The repeated use of the term "best" by experts, investment committees, and hundreds of organizations inoculates the groups against serious analysis of the risks. According to Janis this is a major symptom of groupthink: "They [groups] develop a set of shared beliefs that rationalize their complacency about the soundness of their policy decisions. . . . [These widely accepted rationalizations] contribute to the members' unresponsiveness to impressive information that otherwise would incline them to rethink the pros and cons of alternative courses of action."[33] The groupthink hypothesis seems to be particularly appropriate in the investment situation, where we repeatedly see large numbers of investment firms converge with only limited serious opposition to the same widely accepted rationalizations.

In the two-tier syndrome the "best" companies in terms of past record and present outlook become the best companies to buy, with limited emphasis on price even though this course had always been fraught with danger. The whole category of "not best" (that is, the second tier), which meant the very large majority of strong, moderately expanding, and often essential companies of American industry, were avoided. With institutions increasingly becoming more dominant, narrowing "best" to only 60 or 70 companies and ignoring the rest made it difficult if not impossible for a large part of American industry to raise equity capital, the primary function of securities markets.

---

*Italics mine. A marvelous rationalization to avoid seriously considering risks! The trust officer realizes the group is very highly priced. By stating that valuation is a "contemporary" problem, he ducks the question of paying too much and thus justifies paying often exorbitant prices.

The idea of the one-decision stocks as "best" was not substantiated statistically, historically, or theoretically and was shortly abandoned in chaos by many of its most outspoken advocates. Its rise and rapid fall must be attributed largely to the process of groupthink. On this point Janis writes that to the outsider "one of the most incomprehensible characteristics of a cohesive group . . . is the tenacity with which the members adhere to erroneous assumptions despite the mounting evidence to challenge them."[34] When the assumptions were finally abandoned, near panic often ensued. Groupthink on the part of many major institutional investors led in this case to major investment errors for the tens of millions of investors who had entrusted the institutions with their funds, and for a while it threatened to have the most serious consequences on the economy itself.

Although professionals under the influence of groupthink believed their analysis justifying the purchase of "best" stocks reached far into the future, when the news turned negative, market and client pressures very often made them focus on immediate events. Any lack of visibility in one of the "best" companies, even a disappointing quarter, could cause a stampede of selling. It appears that most professionals, like most other investors seem unaware of the importance of immediate events in the shaping of their own and market opinions. At the height of the energy crisis in late 1973, 25% of Kidder Peabody's "top 50" were energy related. In November 1975, although none of the nation's energy problems had yet been solved, not one energy stock was left in the group as investor attention shifted.

"Best" seems at times to be like a game of musical chairs. Between December 1973 and November 1975, fully 44% of the Kidder Peabody's "top 50" changed. This would be quite acceptable if the new companies were even better than the ones replaced. Most often, however, it is the "visibility of the moment" that is bid up. Many of the old favorites were sold at distress prices when their visibility turned out to be less than was thought at the time.

It would be encouraging to note that the two-tier market was a brief instance of institutional groupthink which was unlikely to recur. Unfortunately, the increasing concentration of investment funds in large institutions, the tremendous similarity of the informational flow from experts, and the reinforcement of opinion, both within the group and from myriads of similar groups, make this hope appear excessively optimistic.

In this chapter we have examined some of the effects of groupthink applied to stock selection and concentration. Next let us look at risks such actions overlooked and at the panic that often ensued when institutions lost faith in their previously commonly held beliefs.

Fortune formula

Fortune used the following standard valuation formula for assessing the present value of a common stock:

$$p = \frac{D}{1+k} + D\frac{(1+g)}{(1+k)^2} + D\frac{(1+g)^2}{(1+k)^3} + \cdots + D\frac{(1+g)^{n-1}}{(1+k)^n}$$

The p is defined as the present worth of the stock. It is found by discounting the future stream of dividends. D is the dividend received each year (presumably growing with earnings); g is the dividend growth rate; k is the discount rate which includes a premium for risk; and n is the number of years for which it is possible to make estimates. The risk premium must be added to the current long-term interest rate. It will vary, depending on how assured the investor believes the company's prospects to be.

At the time of the analysis, the interest rate on highly rated long-term bonds was about 8%. Avon had a 17.2% compound earnings growth rate in the ten years ending in 1972. For the 1967–1972 period the earnings growth rate had slowed to 13.6%. *Fortune* assumed n to be 20 years. Beyond 20 years, g was considered constant because the company is mature. Therefore the formula used for each year after 20 was

$$p = \frac{D}{\text{discount rate} - g}$$

Fortune postulated growth rates of 14%, 12%, 10%, and 8% for four consecutive five-year time spans. Beyond 20 years, a 5% growth rate was used and the company was considered mature. These estimates were considered realistic to slightly optimistic at the time. In the computation, the dividend stream increased from $1.60 in the first year to $11.27 in the twentieth. By applying a 14% discount rate, which included a not inordinate 6% risk premium over what could be obtained on high-quality bonds, a present value of $33.14 was arrived at for the stock.

Reducing the discount rate to 12%, which was only 4% above long-term bonds and seemingly too little in the light of the problems of visibility discussed, the present value of the stock became $45.20. Using a 9% discount rate, which was only a 1% premium for risk and far too aggressive, a price of $88.21 was arrived at, still below the market price. To arrive at the then-current price of $110, the following assumptions had to be made: Growth at 14% over the next ten years (above the previous five-year rate), 12% for the next five years, followed by another five years at 10%, followed by 6% indefinitely, and discounted at only 9.5%. No "prudent man" would hang his hat on those assumptions.

9

Panic

The Liquidity Trap

The large sums of institutional money flowing into the select group of favorites in 1972 and early 1973 made it a foregone conclusion that these stocks would appreciate—for a time. The phenomenon was similar in principle to the operations of the Enterprise Fund and the Mates Fund in the late 1960s. The enthusiastic buying of Fred Carr or Fred Mates and their legions of admirers would push the prices of the small, relatively thinly traded companies they selected, sky high. But when the music stopped, disaster followed. The institutional accumulation of top-tier stocks was the same game played on a larger scale.

In 1972 Morgan Guaranty alone accounted for 14% of the daily trading in Walt Disney, 12% in Philip Morris, and 5% in American Home Products. Morgan was, of course, the largest institution, but it had only 7% of all bank trust accounts and 11% of bank-administered pension plans.[1] Many other large banks, mutual funds, insurance companies, and investment advisory firms purchased exactly the same narrow group of stocks. The syndrome was fostered by both group-think and the pressure applied by enthusiastic clients. Among mutual funds, only some of the better performers, the ones that usually bought the "nifty fifty," were receiving any new investor money. Overall there was a pattern of steady redemptions by disenchanted investors.

An old Street story relates how a man began to buy a thinly traded stock. He bought 500 shares at $6.00 and the price rose to $7.00. His purchase of an additional 500 shares sent it to $8.00. He continued to buy and watched happily as the price moved steadily to $12. Satisfied with doubling his money, he instructed his broker to sell. "To whom?" asked the broker.

To a large extent this was the problem faced by the major institutional investors who had concentrated on the same stocks. If many changed their minds at the same time, as was likely if discouraging news came along, there simply was no way they could eliminate their holdings without drastically driving down the price. Lord Keynes saw the liquidity problem clearly in the mid-1930s when institutional investing was still in its infancy: "The fact that each individual investor flatters himself that his commitment is 'liquid' [though this cannot be true for all investors collectively] calms his nerves and makes him more willing to run a risk."[2] Keynes was writing in an era when 10,000 shares was considered a big trade. With large institutions often holding a million shares or more of a particular favorite and with the tremendous concentration of the same favorites among institutions, the risks, if anything went wrong, were much greater. James Needham of the New York Stock Exchange was clearly alarmed by this danger. In mid-1973 he warned:

> Although an institution may take weeks or even months to accumulate a substantial position in a particular stock, it often happens that at the slightest whiff of bad news—disappointing earnings or what have you—the portfolio manager will rush for the exits, with the idea of liquidating that position almost immediately without any serious impact on the price of the stock. Obviously, that is not a reasonable expectation. Yet institutional investors often express surprise when such actions trigger a sharp decline in the market price of the stock.[3]

That many institutional money managers "calmed their nerves" in this manner and disregarded the actual risks may be attributed to a significant extent to the process of groupthink.

Previous Warnings Ignored

Adequate warning of the danger of overconcentration had been provided years prior to 1972–1973. Bad news in heavily held institutional issues had often triggered large sell-offs. SEC Commissioner Hugh F. Owens recalled that in 1966 over 500,000 shares of Motorola, a glamour stock of the time, traded in a single day. Trading opened at the high for the day, and then disappointing news on earnings was received. The stock closed 19⁵/₈ points (16%) lower. Mutual funds bought 1,500 shares, one-quarter of 1% of the day's volume, but sold nearly 250,000 shares. Included in their sales were block trades of 25,000, 32,000, and 137,000 shares.

Often in bad markets, relatively little of a stock can be disposed of, as this harrowing experience of a 1970 fund manager illustrates. "We tried to get out of a fair sized, over-the-counter stock at $15. We got off 1,000 shares at $13 and then they found out who was doing the selling. Before we knew it, the stock was $5. As soon as the traders smelled a big sell order, you were dead,"[4] But this example was in the over-the-counter market, where volume even for larger issues was normally much thinner. What about favorites on the New York Stock Exchange? In fact, even near the crest of the 1971–1972 market the problem was very severe.

In July 1972, Handleman Company, an institutional favorite, reported disappointing earnings in one quarter. By 10 A.M. there was a flood of institutional sell orders. Because of the paucity of buy orders, the stock did not trade that day (Friday) nor on the following Monday morning. The stock finally opened in the afternoon at 10¹/₈, down 51%. Some 837,900 shares traded that day, 19% of all stock outstanding. Numerous institutional pets dropped precipitously in the latter part of 1971 and early 1972 in the face of a very strong market. The corpses included William Wrigley, STP, Holiday Inns, Genesco, Liggett and Myers, Max Factor, and Wang Laboratories. The news most often launching the selling was disappointing earnings in companies that were supposed to have "high visibility." In every case, as one trader noted, there was "an incredible—and I mean incredible—vacuum of buying."[5] When trading finally resumed, it was at a substantial discount from the former price.

The pattern repeated itself with regularity in 1972. Bausch & Lomb dropped over 20 points in mid-March 1972 after disappointing earnings news. H&R Block, an institutional favorite, dropped 75% over some months when earnings for the year were 16% below expectations. Management hadn't lied; their forecast had simply proved inaccurate. But in the rarefied atmosphere of a 60 P/E multiple where it traded, such mistakes were fatal. Levitz Furniture, among the top ten institutional choices for appreciation in both 1972 and 1973, fell on huge volume from 47 to 33 in half an hour because of disappointing news. Never paying a dividend, it had had a P/E ratio of 110 at the top and a market value of $885 million dollars.

July 1972 was a particularly bad month for former institutional favorites, as Table 21 indicates.

The tremendous concentration had already proved extremely dangerous in the bull markets of 1971 and 1972, but the danger signs were all ignored and the convergence into the top 50 became more acute. With such concentration there was no escape. Like World War I fighter pilots, whose planes were crippled in battle, they could either leap from them without parachutes or go down in flames. Under the influence of the groupthink-compliance syndrome, money managers had voluntarily placed themselves in as dangerous an investment cockpit.

In spite of the litter of previous one-decision stocks strewn along the road, the underlying assumptions were not questioned. Instead, clearer and clearer "visibility" was demanded by the top-tier cult, and the concentration narrowed further. When a disappointment occurred, the immediate reaction of many was to sell, and just the suggestion of other professionals selling could trigger a chain reaction. One trader that summer (1972) recalled he had received an order to sell 150,000 shares of stock, "so I made my customary two or three calls to institutions I knew had been buyers. Wouldn't you know, on the first call I made the guy shot back 'if you've got 150,000 to sell, you can add 110,000 more.'" Often in the scramble to sell no limits were placed, the seller would sell "at market,"* which results in devastating price

---

*At whatever price he could get.

TABLE 21

Company	On this day . . .	The stock closed at . . .	Down this many points from the previous close . . .	On volume of . . .	And at its low was off from the previous close by . . . (%)
Max Factor & Co.	July 10	31¼	− 7	9,100	18.61%
Wang Laboratories, Inc.	July 10	48½	−11	66,700	18.49
Family Dollar Stores, Inc.	July 11	22	− 5	53,700	19.44
Genesco, Inc.	July 11	15½	− 5⅝	459,700	29.02
Curtiss-Wright Corp.	July 12	36⅛	− 9⅞	232,300	21.46
Handleman Co.	July 17	12½	− 9⅛	837,900	51.47
McDonald's Corp.	July 17	52⅜	− 5½	78,300	13.62
Liggett & Myers Corp.	July 19	46⅜	− 6⅛	44,700	15.47
Westinghouse Electric Corp.	July 20	45	− 3⅛	113,700	7.02
New Process Co.	July 26	21	− 8⅜	413,900	30.23
Grumman Corp.	July 27	13⅞	− 3⅝	130,900	28.57
Holiday Inns, Inc.	July 27	42½	− 7½	478,300	20.00

Source: *Institutional Investor*, September 1972. The table carried the descriptive line, "A midsummer nightmare."

drops if there are few buyers. Stock prices were trampled underfoot on bad news. One professional said, "The only thing faster than the herd selling on bad news is the Egyptian Army in retreat." Even this comparison may be outdated.

The tremendous concentration of funds in the hands of powerful institutions—$80 billion in pension funds in 1974 held by ten banks alone—and the striking similarity of their thinking was like a fuse approaching a gigantic powder keg. The ensuing explosion would blow the one-decision stocks to smithereens.

What happened was inevitable. Through 1973 and 1974, accelerating inflation, discouraging economic news, the oil embargo, increasingly more restrictive monetary policy, and soaring interest rates resulted in the stock market breaking badly. Between the end of 1972 and September 30, 1974, the S&P 500 dropped 46%. By comparison, the Kidder Peabody Index of the 50 highest multiple stocks on the New York Stock Exchange declined from a median multiple of 54.6 to 16, some 70%. If both indexes had been adjusted for dividends, the disparity would have been worse. But even these disturbing figures were only a part of the story because many of the former favorites no longer included in the "top 50" had declined substantially more. The 1973–1974 collapse of one-decision stocks and the ensuing widespread panic were of a magnitude not seen since the Great Crash.

A salesman with one of Wall Street's prime research houses said at the time, "just about everyone in the ranks of professional investment has gotten involved in the fever and done something to depress the market." The battering that individual one-decision stocks took was terrifying. Avon, one of the ultimate "vestal virgins," reached a high in early 1973 of $140. In the disillusionment of 1974 it traded as low as 18⅞, a decline of 87% in 20 months. Polaroid, another "religion" stock, was 149½ at the height of its visibility. It dropped 91% to its 1974 low of 14⅛. It seems very safe to say that institutions owned well over 50% of both issues at the end of 1972. The "visibility," so assured in both companies, had dissipated as both theory and statistical findings predicted it might.

So dramatically had professional opinion changed on Avon that its yield, under 1% in the past, had gone up to 8% at its low because of the price drop. At the bottom, judging by its higher yield, Avon was considered more ordinary than most electric utilities, tire companies, and other perennial dwellers in the darkness of the bottom tier. Its P/E multiple had fallen from a high of 60 in 1973 to under 10, and in spite of its vaunted "visibility," earnings declined 17% in 1974. The descent to darkness was stormy, and large amounts of stock were dumped on the market as investors desperately tried to escape.

Polaroid was meted out the same fate. As Charles Elia, the widely read market columnist for *The Wall Street Journal,* put it, "Polaroid was a prime one-decision stock at the height of the institutional fascination with glamour stocks last year. . . . Polaroid is still a "one-decision" stock except that the decision seems to have become sell."[6] A disappointing second quarter resulted in the stock's declining 11 3/8 points (32% to 24 1/4), and being most active trader on the New York Stock Exchange on July 2.

One after another the "high flyers" were abandoned, often in circumstances of near panic. To the outsider unaffected by events, the spectacle of such faulty decision making and the ensuing disaster had the appearance of bedlam.

The Market Collapse Viewed Within Groupthink

An important manifestation of groupthink is the ignoring or discounting of serious and obvious risks. In their shared rationalizations of buying the "best" companies, many institutional investors overlooked the following danger signals:

1. Overconcentration in the same stocks. This was extremely dangerous because the large holdings of numerous institutions usually cannot be sold without depressing the price. •
2. The transitory quality of "visibility" of outlook given the dynamic nature of economic change.
3. Paying too much for the "best" companies. Market history is filled with such examples. Even if the growth

objectives were met, a reappraisal of the P/E might reduce the price drastically.

Only in the latter part of 1973 and in 1974 when the market began to fall rapidly did a critical reappraisal of the dangers of current policy begin among many professionals. The process was stimulated by the Bentsen committee, and by warnings from other congressional and business sources about the negative effects of overconcentration. The fact that the top-tier stocks began to decline far more rapidly than the market undoubtedly fueled the critical assessment process.

Psychological experiments have indicated that the more central a belief is, the more resistant it is to change. However, when strongly held beliefs are finally changed, the new course is often radically different from the old. Some psychologists have called this the "shock effect" phenomenon. When a person who has had forceful central beliefs becomes strongly disillusioned, he will often embrace the opposite viewpoint with as great or greater conviction. Atheists become powerful believers, and powerful believers become atheists, alcoholics become formidable teetotalers, and lovers have nothing but hate for their former partners. In the stock market, professionals with brutal logic now saw clearly the flaws in companies and strategies they had previously favored, and perhaps assessed them overcritically.

Experimental work on economic behavior at the Survey Research Center of the University of Michigan had indicated that when expectations change, they do so simultaneously, radically, and in the same direction. George Katona, professor of both economics and psychology at the University and viewed by many as the leading authority on the psychological influences on economic decisions, directed this program for over a quarter of a century. He and his colleagues studied the changes in expectations of both consumers and businessmen. In his most recent work, *Psychological Economics,* Katona writes:

The systematic factor that brings about a fairly uniform change at about the same time among very many people may be readily identified. It is the acquisition of information. Because the same information, or very similar information, reaches millions of people at the same time and is apprehended by them in a similar manner, changes in attitudes resemble contagious diseases rather than movements in opposite directions which cancel out.[7]

In the course of his extensive research, Katona was surprised at the similarity in new thinking once a change had occurred: "The uniformity of opinion among the majority of people [after opinion change] . . . is an unexpected finding."[8]

Katona identifies the paramount importance of new information in changing opinion. In the environment of the stock market a torrent of such information and expert opinion is released, and it most often follows the trend of current price movements. Graham and Dodd observed long ago that it seemed an "inevitable rule of the market that the prevalent theory of common stock values has developed in rather close conjunction with the change in level of prices."[9]

As we observed in the history chapters, the irrationality of crowds operates both on the way up and on the way down. The same is true of groupthink.

When prices decline, people look for reasons. And reasons are invariably found. The more severe the decline, the more open to new thinking the professional becomes. We have seen how people under stress have an increased desire to affiliate. In the marketplace, as Avon continued to fall from $140 to $100, then $60, then $30, analysts and money managers whose careers were on the line became almost frantic to find out what other top analysts and money managers knew. Most were negative. Were they right? The market certainly supported their view.

Like a battlefield, the incoming reports are confused and contradictory, but one sees clearly that values are steadily retreating. Rumors and opinions, always abundant, seem to reach a peak at such times. Leading analysts previously totally committed to Avon, McDonald's, Disney, Polaroid, and dozens of other favorites now begin to see problems as the prices sink lower. Each analyst and money manager is influenced by the course of the market and by respected colleagues both inside and outside the firm.

With numerous influential authorities changing opinion markedly, all within a short period of time, and with the falling market confirming the correctness of such changes, it is hardly surprising that the fulcrum of group opinion often shifts dramatically. Each change is reinforced by thousands of others shifting in a similar direction.

Because careers are often at stake, such decisions are anything but academic. Professionals are under increasing stress and anxiety as important decisions for which they are responsible begin to disintegrate. In laboratory experiments, high-anxiety subjects, regardless of their original opinion, changed their opinion more often than do people in a low-anxiety state.[10] Experiments have also demonstrated that the greater the fear aroused in a person, the more likely he is to take action.[11] These psychological influences help to explain why opinion can change so dramatically when underlying fundamentals have changed so little. As previous decisions prove disastrously wrong in the market, institutional investors are far more open to fresh viewpoints and approaches even if they clash drastically with their former convictions. Avon will no longer grow at 15% or better. It seems to be a mature company; perhaps 8% is realistic. Rather than looking like an outstanding success, Polaroid's SX-70 camera, into which so much research and money was poured, looks like a massive failure similar to Ford's Edsel. In such an anxiety-producing environment, perceptual processes that had screened out many of the dangers now focus sharply on them. The Street is awash with bad news. A new interpretation of events emerges, widely held and dramatically different from its predecessor.

Many forces converge to make the new consensus. Institutional research firms are asked if they still believe in the "one-decision stocks" when so many others are expressing their doubts. Disgruntled clients become increasingly vociferous in demanding that money managers explain their mistakes. The pressures of groupthink and compliance are never so strong as under tremendous anxiety. Not only is it dangerous career-wise to stand alone at such times, but it is also psychologically very difficult to do so. Under these conditions, perceptions do very often change. The professional becomes hypervigilant to negative information and often begins to overemphasize it. The analyst and the money manager see major flaws in previous favorites, as do most authorities both within and outside the firm. Mutually reinforced under conditions of stress, they arrive at a new interpretation of events, most often directly in line with current market action.

Thousands of investment firms interlinked in thought and action are realigning their interpretations of events at the same time. The new course of action widely emerging is dramatically contrary to the old. One-decision stocks are sold instead of purchased. Rather than blaming the original investment decision, the failure most often is attributed to "different conditions," "changed times," high interest rates, poor advice, or the sharp stock market break. The professionals involved almost never blame the failure on groupthink or the "herd instinct."

That a dramatic change in thinking occurred is evidenced by the ensuing tableau. Before Senator Bentsen's committee in late July 1973, we saw numerous leading advocates of the upper tier justify the purchase of such stocks because of their visibility in an increasingly inflationary environment. Samuel Callaway of Morgan Guaranty Trust made one of the strongest defenses of this policy. Yet, mighty Morgan, the strongest influence on the two-tier market, shifted course 180 degrees not too long afterward.

In 1973 it added 1,742,483 shares of American Home Products; 766,166 shares of Philip Morris; 1,797,051 shares of Kresge's; and 1,131,250 shares of McDonald's. Through 1975, Morgan was a heavy seller of these and many other growth stocks.*

In an interview with *Business Week* in September 1975, Samuel Callaway of Morgan gave the reasoning for the change

---

*Among its heaviest sales for the fifteen months ending March 31, 1976 were 2.2 million shares of American Home Products, 2.5 million shares of Philip Morris, 2.2 million shares of Xerox, and 2.1 million shares of McDonald's.

of course: "It is our judgment that over the next two or three years other stocks will be more attractive . . . inflation affects growth stocks in a way recession doesn't. . . . The kind of inflation we've seen in the recent past has changed our judgment in the sense that it's difficult to hold on to these stocks through thick and thin."[12] To the Bentsen committee in July 1973 Callaway had said, "It became apparent that many companies could not produce earnings increases at a rate greater than continuing inflation. The stocks of these companies naturally suffered, and this served to accentuate the preference for companies more favorably situated [the top tier]."[13]

If the reader is somewhat confused by this logic, so am I. Inflation was the reason the top tier was bought, and now it's the reason they are sold. Both reasons were the prevailing expert opinion of the time. Even first-rate money managers can succumb to the influence of groupthink, and if many do, it can have a disastrous effect on both investors and the economy.

Morgan's thinking, along with that of most other major institutions, had absolutely reversed itself. By the spring and summer of 1974 many institutions began to sell one-decision stocks with abandon.

With the new polarization of opinion, the decimation of the former favorites was horrendous. Table 22 gives the 1971–1973 high, the 1974 low, and the percentage change of some institutional favorites. Each of these companies (with the exception of Tandy and Westinghouse) were on the Kidder Peabody top-50 list at some time in 1973 or 1974.

When a position of excessive risk taking fared badly, a stance of excessive conservatism is often adopted.* In a sharply falling market, survival for not a few professionals consists of selling at any price. The extent of the panic in

---

*Social psychologists have performed a number of experiments to demonstrate how the level of risk-taking increases in a group from what is acceptable to the members, when tested beforehand. This process is termed the "risky shift." It would be interesting to devise an experiment to show the excessive conservative position a group can adopt when a risky course of action fails. This appears to be the repeated pattern of groups in the market.

TABLE 22

Company	Prices 1971–1973 High	Prices 1974 Low	Prices 1975 High	% Decline 1971–1973 High to 1974 Low	% Appreciation 1974 Low to 1975 High	P/E Ratios 1971–1973 High	P/E Ratios 1974 Low	P/E Ratios 1975 High
Alcon	42⁷/₈	12¹/₈	26¹/₈	−71.7	116.5	52	12	24
Auto. Data Proc.	99³/₄	20³/₄	65	−79.2	213.3	105	13	33
Avon	140	18⁵/₈	51¹/₄	−86.7	175.2	60	9	24
Clorox	53	5¹/₂	11³/₄	−89.6	113.6	43	6	12
Colonial Penn	70	12⁵/₈	41³/₈	−82.0	227.7	44	6	17
Curtiss-Wright	59¹/₄	5	11¹/₂	−91.6	130.0	106	4	7
Damon	70³/₈	6	16³/₄	−91.5	179.2	63	5	62
Data Gen.	49	10¹/₂	39	−78.6	271.4	59	9	26
Disney	119¹/₈	16⁵/₈	55³/₈	−86.0	233.1	74	10	27
Dr. Pepper	30	6¹/₂	15¹/₈	−78.3	132.7	59	13	27
Jack Eckard	43¹/₂	10	27³/₄	−77.0	177.5	56	8	23
Electronic Data	85³/₄	10¹/₂	22¹/₈	−87.8	110.7	96	8	18
MGIC	97³/₈	6¹/₈	19¹/₂	−93.8	218.3	51	—	—
Marriott	38¹/₈	6¹/₈	16⁵/₈	−83.9	171.4	56	8	24
Masco	32³/₄	9¹/₂	27³/₄	−71.0	192.1	46	9	23
McDonald's	77³/₈	21¹/₄	60¹/₂	−72.5	184.7	82	13	29
Nat'l. Semiconductor	36¹/₄	6¹/₄	48⁵/₈	−83.0	674.0	27	5	35
Polaroid	149¹/₂	14¹/₈	43¹/₂	−90.6	208.0	115	16	31
Ponderosa	86¹/₄	3⁵/₈	11³/₄	−95.8	224.1	40	7	48
Rite-Aid	56³/₄	2¹/₂	11³/₄	−95.6	370.0	71	4	12
Rubbermaid	50³/₄	9³/₄	20¹/₂	−80.8	110.3	39	12	10
Simplicity	58⁷/₈	6¹/₄	16⁵/₈	−89.4	166.0	52	10	19
Sony	18¹/₄	4	10⁷/₈	−78.1	171.8	45	9	35
Tandy	49	9³/₄	50³/₈	−80.1	416.7	35	6	13
Tropicana	60³/₈	6¹/₂	26	−89.2	300.0	65	8	18
Wal-mart	17¹/₂	3³/₄	15³/₄	−78.6	320.0	50	8	32
Westinghouse	54⁷/₈	8	20	−85.4	150.0	24	26	10
Average				−84.0	+220.7	59.8	9.6	23.6
S&P 500 (without div.)	120.24	63.54	95.19	−47.2	+ 49.8			

All companies adjusted for stock splits.

the list of institutional favorites becomes more apparent when we observe the sharp recovery, often of 200 to 300% or even 400%, in a matter of months from the bottom of late December.

Any unfavorable news touched off massive waves of selling on the part of professional investors. Combustion Engineering, for example, dropped 24¾ points (38%) in one day* as a result of an unsubstantiated story appearing in *The Wall Street Journal* that the company had underestimated its costs in bidding for a number of nuclear power contracts. The stock was the most active trader on the New York Stock Exchange, turning over 337,800 shares. Research Cottrell† and Damon Corp., other prime one-decision stocks, each fell a shattering 60% in a day of large volume because of disappointing earnings news.

The Nature of Panic

Enrico Quarantelli writes in *The Nature and Conditions of Panic* that the most important condition for the emergence and continuation of panic is a feeling of entrapment with an impending threat.[14] Whether the person is independent or part of a group, the feeling of being trapped predominates. Psychological experiments have also duplicated conditions of near panic. In one experiment, corks were placed in a bottle attached to strings. The neck of the bottle was so narrow that only one cork could be passed through at a time. The bottle was slowly filled with water and the subjects were told they would have to get their cork out before the bottle filled or they would receive an electric shock. As the bottle filled with water slowly, there was adequate time to do this if each subject went in order. This, of course, did not happen. A wild melee ensued, similar to panic at a theater fire, and very few got their corks out in time. The situation of many institutional sellers trying to sell large blocks of stock in a bad market with only a narrow market exit is

---

*May 8, 1974.
†63% institutionally owned at the time.

similar, but considerably worse, for even if order could be established, only a few would escape because of the often overwhelming size of total holdings.

Quarantelli, although discussing physical panic, accurately describes many of the conditions observed in the securities market. People see the threat as immediate, and believe that their survival is dependent on taking instant action. In panic there is a total collapse of the constraints to flee. In the overwhelming desire to save oneself, self-control is overcome by fear and actions become highly self-centered.

In the two-tier market, when a new consensus occurred there was a sense of entrapment in the narrow tier of favorites, a realization of the danger, and a desire to flee. Even with the knowledge that their actions could trigger a stampede, numbers of professionals rushed for the exit at the same time, only to be trampled by the mob.

As the 1974 market continued its grinding, annihilating path, evidence corroborating groupthink was produced with abundant regularity. Expert opinion turned negative on companies whose names were long uttered in only hushed and reverent tones—IBM, Coca-Cola, Xerox, Polaroid, Avon, and Eastman Kodak.

In fact, in the space of only a few days in early December 1974, near the market lows, *The Wall Street Journal*'s widely read "Heard On the Street" column featured the negative views of well-known research analysts about the prospects of Coca-Cola, Eastman Kodak, Disney, Hewlett-Packard, Perkin-Elmer, Thomas & Betts, and other top-tier stocks. In each case the stocks had been previously recommended by the same analyst at substantially higher prices.

The unanimity of the new prevailing opinion is sometimes overwhelming. In the final quarter of 1974, Westinghouse Electric declined to as low as $8 from a high of $26 earlier in the year. So prevalent was the negative thinking in that quarter that there was not one purchaser of the stock among 128 banks surveyed, although 14 sold 524,165 shares. Mutual funds and other institutional investors were also heavy sellers. By Spring the stock had doubled.

In the next year many of these same banks accumulated the stock heavily at substantially higher prices.

The Institutional Role in the Break

It would be nonsense to attribute all the events that contributed to the 1974 decline to institutional investors. Financial markets were swept by greater uncertainty than at any time in the post-war period. Tight money, record interest rates, fears of a liquidity crisis, the unfathomable ramifications of the energy crisis, prospective shortages of many raw materials, and uncontrollable inflation, all contributed to the prevailing mood of fear.

It would be equal nonsense to say that the major institutions as a group did not accentuate the decline through their actions. Technimetrics, a financial research concern, monitored the results of the portfolios of 261 United States banks, insurance companies, investment advisors, and mutual funds, as well as 47 European counterparts.[15] In the fall of 1974 when the market was approaching its exact bottom, the cash positions of these institutions climbed to 19% from 13.5% in 1973 (an inordinately high figure in itself). Rather than aggressively purchasing stocks at the best relative values seen in decades, these professional investors were selling securities.

Financial theory would lead us to expect exactly the opposite course from rational professionals observing these astounding values. Yet to increase cash reserves, most institutions sold and some did so fairly heavily. Mutual funds entered October with a record 13.5% of their $32 billion of assets in cash. The 100 leading growth funds proved to be even more wrong. Their cash positions, raised through selling securities, increased to 23.9% on September 30 from 18% on March 30. The heavy liquidation of stocks was a destabilizing force in a highly illiquid and frightened market.

The market's liquidity, its ability to absorb sales or purchases, had decreased drastically in 1974. With the reduced liquidity, institutional selling served to further, and perhaps dramatically, accentuate the general market decline. A 5 to 7% shift in institutional holdings between stocks and cash at the time was a shift of between $17 and $23.5 billion.

Amivest, a financial services firm, attempted to measure the extent of the illiquidity by tracing the dollar value of stock trades required to raise or lower the price of a stock 1% on a monthly basis over a number of years. Between the end of 1972 and December 1974 it estimated that the liquidity of the Dow Jones Industrial Averages had dropped over 70%. This meant that in 1974 it took only about a third as many dollars as it took in late 1972 to change the price of these stocks a fixed amount. Decreasing liquidity magnifies the size of the price movements caused by large sales of stock. Amivest found that whereas it took $4 million to change the price of Burroughs stock 1% in December 1973, by December 1974 only $1.3 million was required. With Xerox it was $4.2 million versus $2.3 million; with Sears Roebuck, $3.8 million versus $974,000. On the American Stock Exchange, liquidity had fallen far more drastically—84% during the same time span.[16]

Liquidity thus decreased sharply just when institutional selling pressures were at their worst. Large blocks were thrown on the market in response to bad news, precisely when the market was least able to digest them. The institutional action then appears to accentuate declines and destabilize markets.*

In the 1970 break, institutions were also heavy sellers at the bottom. Donald Regan, chairman of Merrill Lynch, said afterward, "Institutional buyers alleged to be stabilizers of the market, and pretty cool customers making emotionless decisions, were just as susceptible to panic, if not more so as anyone else. They sold on the way down, and waited until after the upturn before they started buying again."[17] In June 1970, as the market was reaching its low, the mutual fund cash position was at 11.4% and hit a record 11.8%

---

*The *Institutional Investor* "Study Report" of 1971 investigated the effects of institutional investors on markets in 1968–1969. In the time period studied, the Dow Jones fluctuated within a fairly narrow 150-point range. The report concluded that professional portfolios were not a destabilizing influence on markets. It would be most interesting to see what would be concluded from a study of the institutional actions taken with their favorites in 1973 and 1974.

the following month. By March 1971, as the market rallied
sharply, the ratio declined to 6.2%.[18] Near the interim top
in June 1971, the funds' cash declined to 4.9%, the lowest
since 1965.[19] The floor traders, also supposedly terribly astute,
have a 30-year record of being most negative near bottoms
and most positive near tops.[20]

Some of the financial press began to call the institutions
the "new odd-lotters." The odd-lotters in Wall Street lore
have almost always been wrong in the market. Surprisingly,
in both 1970 and 1974, it was the much disparaged odd-lotters
and the rest of the public who stopped the market decline
from going even lower. The "irrational" public were large
buyers at the bottom while the "rational" institutions liquidated heavily.

Possible Economic Implications of Institutional Investing

From a high of 124.6 in 1972, the S&P declined 50%
to a low of 62.28 in early October 1974. But the real losses
were far more severe. The Value Line Composite Index
declined 74% between late 1968 and late 1974. Between
year-end 1972 and 1974 it was down 57%. Market losses
in real terms were staggering. Over $500 billion in dollar
values was lost between the end of 1972 and the 1974 low.
This was more than ten times the amount of all mutual
fund assets at the time. In 20 stocks, $84 billion was lost
in the first nine months of 1974, as Table 23 shows.[21]

Barry Bosworth, in an economic paper for the Brookings
Institution, concluded that the stock market decline had a
direct effect on consumption. His figures suggest that the
1973–74 decline which cost $500 billion in paper losses,
resulted in between $15 and $25 billion less in consumer
spending, and may have cut business outlays by an additional
$15 billion. Bosworth's computer calculations indicated that
approximately 25% of the sharp economic decline in real
output in the first quarter of 1975, adjusted for inflation,
may have resulted from the stock market drop.[22]

Francis Modigliani of MIT, a former president of the

TABLE 23

Stock	Price Sept. 30, 1974 Close	9 Months % Change	Sept. 30 Mkt. Value ($ billions)	9-Month Value Drop ($ billions)
IBM	159	−35.6%	$23.4	$−12.9
Eastman Kodak	65³/₄	−43.3	10.6	− 8.1
Exxon	58³/₄	−37.6	13.2	− 7.9
Gen. Elec.	31¹/₄	−50.4	5.7	− 5.9
AT&T	41	−18.2	22.8	− 5.1
Xerox	64³/₄	−47.3	5.1	− 4.6
Sears, Roebuck	51⁵/₈	−35.7	8.1	− 4.5
Coca-Cola	51¹/₄	−59.5	3.1	− 4.5
Minn. Mining	49	−37.2	5.6	− 3.3
Gen. Motors	35⁵/₈	−22.8	10.2	− 3.0
Citicorp	22⁷/₈	−50	2.8	− 2.8
Phillips Petr.	34	−50.4	2.6	− 2.6
Avon Prod.	19¹/₄	−69.8	1.1	− 2.6
Shell Oil	30⁷/₈	−54.5	2.1	− 2.5
Brit. Petr.	6³/₈	−50	2.5	− 2.5
DuPont	108	−32.1	5.2	− 2.4
Merck	50¹/₄	−37.8	3.7	− 2.3
Texaco	21¹/₄	−27.6	5.8	− 2.2
Std. Oil (Cal.)	22	−37.1	3.7	− 2.2
Johns. & Johns.	75¹/₂	−33	4.3	− 2.1

Source: *The Wall Street Journal*, October 2, 1974. Reprinted with permission of *The Wall Street Journal.* © Dow Jones & Company, Inc., 1974. All Rights Reserved.

American Economic Association, estimates that for every $10 billion drop in stock prices, consumers cut their spending about $600 million (6%). Bosworth estimates this at 3 to 5%. Modigliani calculates that the 1973–1974 break alone reduced consumption by $25 billion. Both James Tobin of Yale and Irwin Friend of Wharton support this thesis, though their figures are somewhat different. Thomas Juster of the Survey Research Center at the University of Michigan also thinks there is a ripple effect. People not directly owning stocks but participating in pension funds who watch a sharp drop in stock prices realize they will not receive as much upon retirement and so cut back their spending.[23]

While such work is not universally accepted in economics, it is certainly worth examining. For if, as the evidence appears to indicate, institutions as a group magnify the swings in stock prices, the result is both destabilizing and harmful to the economy. The rapid growth projected for large institutional holdings of investments, along with the concentration pattern that will often occur if the groupthink-compliance hypothesis is correct, would suggest further wide market swings in the future.

The Effect of Increasing Institutionalization of the Market

As we have seen, it was the noninstitutional investor who came in at the bottom and purchased securities while institutions were selling in both 1970 and 1974. From the standpoint of the groupthink-compliance hypothesis, this would make sense. The individual does not have the performance pressures that frequently make professionals comply, and he is possibly less subject to the pressures that lead professionals to groupthink. George Katona's work at the Survey Research Center appears to substantiate this. He writes:

> One might expect that business leaders would not be easily swayed by others from their decisions made on the basis of solid knowledge, while the less wise mass of consumers could readily be shifted from one position to another and thus have an unsettling effect on the economy. In fact, our studies revealed practically the opposite to be true. . . .[24]

By entering the market in large numbers in December 1974, the public stopped the decline from becoming even worse. Tony Zulica, the head floor trader for Bache, a large brokerage firm, attributed the first two months of the upturn almost entirely to individual investors buying. Bear Stearns, another firm with a large retail business, reported a tremendous surge in public buying in January 1975, the first full month of the rally. The public picked up stocks at "wholesale" prices as numerous institutions continued to sell. Many were happy to unload, and others even sold short to these "naive" buyers. But as the market continued to rise, much of the stock was repurchased by institutions at far higher prices.

The individual investor has a very important role to play

in the marketplace. Assuredly he is unsophisticated and often wrong, but all the same he may not be so subject to the dangers of groupthink or compliance. Thus he may both invest in a far broader range of stocks and help to narrow price swings.

As individual investors have increasingly left the market in recent years, some evidence suggests price fluctuations have become more volatile. A study by *Financial World* indicates that throughout the 1960s, there were 11 up-or-down market moves of 10% or more. By late 1975, 13 such moves had already taken place since 1970. Another statistical work done by the Lenthold economic group of Piper Jaffrey and Hopwood, a Minneapolis-based brokerage firm, indicated that in the 27 months ending mid-April 1974, there were 61 days of high volatility (defined as the market's moving 2% or more). There were only 57 such days in the 24 years from 1949 to 1972. According to the study, in the 1897–1972 time span only 3% of the trading days each year on average were volatile. This increased to 6% (14 days) in 1973 and 16% (41 days) in 1974, about the same percentage as 1929. The study suggested that the larger institutional blocks destroyed the cushioning effect of specialists.[25]

The demise of the small investor is unfortunately well documented and comes at a time when he is most sorely needed. His exit from the market has actually been welcomed in some quarters where he was believed to be a nuisance. Institutions, it was contended, could get along well without him.

In a survey conducted in late 1975, the New York Exchange found the number of shareholders had declined over 18% in the five-year period ending June 1975. This was the first such decline in 23 years. The survey showed that combined shareholders of both common stocks and mutual funds fell from 30.8 to 25.2 million. Prior to this time, share owners had risen almost steadily from 6.5 million in 1952. Younger people appeared particularly disenchanted with stocks. The age of the average holder was 53 in 1975, compared with 48 in 1970. Thus, a case can be made that the demise of the individual investor is due to both more

210

volatile markets and large sudden drops in the value of their holdings, both of which can be ascribed to increasing institutional concentration.

The number of investment clubs* has also declined sharply. The National Association of Investment Clubs projected that its membership in late 1975 had declined 48% from the peak in the spring of 1970, when there were an estimated 50,000 groups in existence.[26] Although their assets were relatively small, themselves, such clubs were instrumental in getting many people interested in the market. Their steady demise is a further sign of decreasing individual participation.

As large institutional holdings have increased, both major brokerage firms and money managers have followed fewer and fewer companies. A survey made of 800 large financial institutions and 200 brokerage firms indicated that the typical bank trust department, money management company, and broker in early 1975 followed about 200 companies, down from 230 a year earlier. The decrease in coverage is probably due to institutions' seeking investment opportunities in progressively larger companies as the funds under their management grow. To cover large numbers of smaller companies, research costs would have to be expanded considerably, which is not feasible in the current operating squeeze that both brokers and institutions are experiencing. In addition, large-money managers would be in the difficult position of having to decide how to apportion shares in good smaller companies to extensive lists of clients. A report by a brokerage firm on one of the thousands of smaller companies often meets with little interest and proves uneconomical.

Institutional concentration in a relatively narrow group of large companies is enormous, and is expected to continue to grow at a rapid rate as a result of both large flows of new money and their continued preference for this type of investment. In 1969 an SEC study indicated that the biggest individual holdings in the stock portfolios of each of the 50 largest bank trust departments represented 10.5% of the

*Individuals banded together to invest a pool of money to which they contribute.

portfolio. A recent survey by Computer Direction Advisors, Inc., of the holdings of 159 banks indicated the largest single holding to be 13% of the portfolio, a 24% increase in concentration.[27]

Institutional flows of funds are immense. Pension funds alone have been estimated to rise from $130 billion at the end of 1973 to over $200 billion by the end of the decade. Just how fast will institutional investment grow overall? Robert Soldofsky in his carefully researched book, *Institutional Holdings of Common Stock 1900–2000,* published in 1971, was courageous enough to make some projections. Forecasting ahead a decade or more is extremely hazardous because the forecaster has no way of anticipating a vast number of future political, economic, and sociological events that could badly upset his projections. After carefully stating his assumptions, including gross national product (GNP), growth, inflation, and the continuation of past P/E multiple and dividend relationships, Soldofsky forecasted that institutional holdings would expand at a 12.3% rate from 1968 to 1980, and at 10.3% between 1980 and the year 2000. Institutions would own approximately 36.3% of total stock in 1980 and 55.2% in the year 2000.[28] New York Stock Exchange figures, which included more classes of professional investors than did Soldofsky's* figures, indicated institutions held 45% of big-board-listed equities at the end of 1972. Using this much larger base, the growth rate should, of course, be lower, but increasing institutional domination appears inevitable. Within a decade, institutions with a turnover rate approximately three times that of the public may account for over 80% of total trading, as against 70% at the present time.

The problem of the increasing concentration of assets and the size of large investors is thus extremely grave. With a narrowing of the research effort because of the need for large capitalizations and the constantly decreasing importance of the individual investor, a serious and continuing problem

---

*His figures do not include investment advisory money, bank trust departments (over 10% of stock held in 1973), hedge funds, and other smaller institutions.

in raising essential equity capital may exist for most public companies. If unattended, this problem could affect future levels of employment and production. In the last two market breaks, the individual investor played a major role in stopping the declines. With his decreasing presence, institutions under groupthink-compliance pressures may very well make future market swings even wider, with increasingly negative consequences for the economy. The market landscape could become as barren and pitted with craters as the surface of the moon, as each new institutional concept that fails leaves its own giant hole. The concentration of assets in the hands of very large and like-minded institutions is a problem that simply cannot long be ignored.

Have Things Changed?

The disaster of 1973 and 1974 put many of the previously favored one-decision stocks into the trash can of financial history. It was totally in accord with the groupthink-compliance hypothesis that most of the major institutions abandoned the concept within months of one another. Some stopped buying these stocks in late 1973, and by mid-1974, the top-tier buying had almost ground to a halt. Through 1974 and into 1975 these stocks were being liquidated by institutions with abandon. When the buying stopped, the top tier disintegrated.

The large institutions began to buy the lower tier. Westinghouse, which as we recall was taboo near its lows of 8 in the fourth quarter of 1974, was among the largest First National City purchases nine months later, at prices more than 50% higher. The bank acquired 273,980 shares. Throughout 1975 a dramatic change occurred in institutional portfolios. The once despised "great unwashed," as one financial reporter alluded to them, were now being acquired. Union Carbide, General Electric, General Motors, ATT, the steels, and the electric utilities were all purchased as the former favorites were sold.

Have things, then, really changed? Many professionals think not. In the words of a well-known money manager,

John Westergaard of Questrion Research, in April 1974, "I think the herd instinct and the tendency toward dominance of conventional wisdom is still there, and therefore the flow of money is going to tend to continue to be concentrated."[29]

At the present time, most institutional investors have not made major attempts to analyze the flaws in their methodology which have led them repeatedly to failure and sometimes to disaster. Perhaps this is not surprising, for the groupthink-compliance hypothesis is certainly new, and in any case neither fundamental theory nor EMH has ever come to grips with the importance of psychological influences on the decision maker. If behavioral influences are indeed as important to investment decision making as they appear, it is essential that they be far better understood by practitioners and theorists alike. The increasing size and importance of institutional investment on the economy make this process of reappraisal and recognition all the more urgent.

If the groupthink-compliance theory has validity, then it is probable that many will again march out after new concepts, bands blaring and drums beating, following another sure course with the same almost inevitable consequences.

In Chapters 5 through 9 we have developed the groupthink-compliance hypothesis as a major explanation of professional behavior in the marketplace. In the subsequent chapters we shall compare it with the efficient market hypothesis to see which of these two more adequately interprets the evidence we have viewed to date.

Part IV
Can an Investor Beat the Market?

10

Market Information: the Forest and the Trees

The efficient market hypothesis has been likened to a new religion, which in many ways is a particularly fitting analogy. This powerful new creed has swept through the academic institutions of this country in the past decade and a half, gaining thousands upon thousands of converts. Today it influences SEC and other governmental thinking as well as numerous professional research and money management organizations. On the theory that the markets cannot be outperformed, market index funds have been organized and portfolios assembled which attempt only to duplicate general market results. Management fees are reduced substantially because no judgment is exercised once stocks are selected, which should parallel market performance.

The new religion comes at a time when there is little to oppose it. The old gods of fundamental and technical analysis are dying. An increasingly larger percentage of the market populace view them indifferently or with outright cynicism or contempt. None of the ancient rituals seems to work, no matter how rigorously they are applied or how extensive the training, or how broad the experience or how intelligent the practitioner.

Into this vacuum the seductive idea of EMH has appeared, offering a very plausible explanation of the professional's failure, absolving investors of blame (for it preaches it is not in their power to change things), bringing order and structure where there had previously been bewilderment and chaos. Although there are serious questions about the foundations upon which the new theology is built, there is nothing better, nothing to give a more rational explanation of how the financial world exists. And so the converts continue to flock to the new gospel.

As with every new idea, many are still unaware of it, others find that it conflicts with their old beliefs, and some stand aside pondering and wishing to ask questions. Most do not question, recognizing that questions by those who have not yet seen the light are at best tolerated, if not treated with amusement or ridicule, by zealots of a new faith.

How the new church views the old may be judged from some of the following statements.

Lorie and Hamilton, in discussing the implications of the efficient market hypothesis, write: "The most general implication of the efficient market hypothesis is that most security analysis is logically incomplete and valueless."[1]

Hagin and Mader acknowledging that the new religion hasn't permeated everywhere, write: "Today, many investors, as well as some Wall Street professionals, are reluctant to disregard their 'childhood' beliefs in the light of the overwhelming body of evidence gleaned from scientific investment research." A little later they clearly fly the "no-quarter flag" in analyzing the implications of EMH: "The efficient . . . market theory questions the value of the investment management profession. An industry based on the value of investment advice is braced against the weight of research evidence concluding that much advice is useless."[2]

These conclusions are tightly tied into a massive amount of academic research evidence that has been produced. Hagin and Mader continue: "The essential point, however, for anyone truly interested in understanding the securities markets, is that the quality of the evidence adduced by the academic community is the highest attainable. On the other hand, high-quality support for 'professionals' is almost entirely nonexistent."[3]

The academic case against fundamental analysis is not that it is no good but rather the contrary—it is too good!

In order for markets to be efficient, thousands of analysts, money managers, and other sophisticated investors search out and analyze all available information, constantly keeping prices in line with value.

EMH thus creates something of a paradox, for if the professionals are important to the operation of the efficient market, if they do help to keep price synonymous with value, they must also, according to EMH, be dismal failures in the primary goal of their profession—helping their clients outperform the market. Those professionals who somehow survived the tidal waves of the 1969–1970 and 1973–1974 markets now find themselves relegated to an ambiguous limbo.* Moreover, the millions of people who enjoyed the high excitement of trying to "beat the market" now know it cannot be done. The only remaining way left to invest is stable but dull. One cannot help thinking of Mark Twain's jocular description of heaven as a place where a person, as his reward, would have to sit with his fellows appearing pious and singing hymns throughout eternity, denied all the earthly frivolity that gave life its sparkle.

Let us now put EMH under the microscope, for if it is correct, an entirely new and revolutionary approach to the stock market is called for. This discussion will lay the groundwork for the investment strategy outlined in the final chapter of this book.

The Necessary Assumptions of EMH

The idea that stock-market participants have immediate access to new information, and react rationally to it, fits in snugly with the behavior of buyers or sellers in the perfectly competitive markets of microeconomic theory. As one academic noted: "You can see why the idea [of perfectly knowledgeable investors in the stock market] is intriguing. Where else can the economist find the ideal of the perfect market? Here is a place to take a stand if there is such

*The Labor Department estimated 50,000 jobs were lost in the securities industry between 1969 and 1975, three-quarters of these in New York.

a place."[4] Is the stock market really a perfectly competitive market? Or is the idea of a completely knowledgeable and rational securities market an exciting yet unachievable ideal, like "the best of all possible worlds" of Voltaire's Dr. Pangloss? Is it an idea that unfortunately exists only in the minds of those who wish it so?

To begin, let us examine the seemingly simple statement that enough buyers and sellers are aware of the meaning of all public information to keep prices in line with value. A number of important and enormously complex premises are subsumed in this statement. If any one of them can be shown to be inaccurate, the hypothesis in its present form will be severely weakened.

The first key premise is that all past information, no matter how large the company, how difficult the accounting, how extensive the public information, or how complex the operating picture, is known and understood by a large enough percentage of market participants (henceforth collectively referred to as Supersleuth) to keep prices constantly in line with value.

Similarly, all current information is correctly dealt with by Supersleuth no matter how vague, muddled, or difficult. For example, if the chairman of Bethlehem Steel says in answer to a reporter's query that the second quarter "doesn't look too great" and walks away without saying anything more, and the company makes no further comment, Supersleuth can immediately quantify this statement and arrive at the proper new value for the stock.

The first premise thus assumes Supersleuth not only has complete knowledge but can correctly interpret all this information, both past and current.

The second premise assumes that the sophisticated investors in the marketplace (Supersleuth) are rational in the classic economic sense of excluding all behavioral influences but one, the maximization of gain or the minimization of loss. Given new information, then, decision making is as routine, automatic, and mechanical as the changing of a traffic light.

Thus, EMH involves very explicit assumptions about both behavioral and interpretive capabilities of major market participants.

Interpretive Capabilities—The Story of Supersleuth

Can sophisticated investors really assimilate tens of thousands of disparate facts? Can all these data, past and present,
be exactly shaped, properly indexed, and infallibly interpreted
in making a decision? For this processing is essential in order
to be able to arrive at the absolute value of a security at
any given time. And can it be done, not only by one person
but also by a great many people, our seemingly omniscient
group known as Supersleuth? This would be a difficult enough
case to argue under conditions of certainty; under conditions
of uncertainty it becomes all the more complicated. To
examine the problem, let's look at the kinds of information
available and required to evaluate Union Carbide, one of
the 30 largest corporations in the country.

From the 1974 annual report and a prospectus issued
in connection with a debenture offering in January 1975,
we find that the company operates nearly 500 plants, factories,
laboratories, mines, and mills around the world. It has
subsidiaries and affiliated companies operating in nearly 30
countries, with foreign business accounting for approximately
one-third of both sales and earnings. In 1974 it employed
110,000 people and had sales of $5.3 billion. Sales are grouped
into three major product areas: chemicals and plastics; gases
and related products, metal and carbons; and consumer and
related products. Although dividing the product line into
three major groups makes the analysis appear more manage-
able, it is still extremely complicated. In chemical operations
alone, for instance, the company manufactures three build-
ing-block chemicals: ethylene, propylene, and benzene. These
building blocks then provide 800 derivatives, which fall into
the general categories of glycols, acids, alcohols, amines,
ketones, ethers, and silicones.

There are normally a number of manufacturing steps
between the production of the original chemical and the
final end-product, and many of the chemicals go into a wide
variety of end-uses. Ethylene is one of the basic raw materials
for antifreeze, polyester fiber (which can be used in products
ranging from apparel to tire cord), plastics (serving a wide
range of markets), adhesives, products for the construction

industry, packaging, and agricultural chemicals, to give only a partial list.

Varying amounts of information are normally available, not only about the product lines but about each market served. It is not hard to see that the company is involved directly and indirectly in thousands of separate markets, both domestic and foreign. The company notes in its statements that each market it serves is highly competitive.

Our group of sophisticated investors, Supersleuth, must understand at any moment the exact competitive position of a company putting out thousands of products, many of which go through numerous intermediate manufacturing stages. In addition, the effect of the thousands of competing goods in these markets must be correctly appraised.

It must be remembered that Supersleuth is at best working with very limited information to do this remarkable job. It might hear, as an example, that the price of ethylene has dropped 1¢ a pound. How important is this information? Supersleuth may know the company's capacity to produce it and the operating rate, but even so, it is not given the actual profit-or-loss figures. Any attempt to estimate such a number is extremely arbitrary and, as often as not, is far off the mark. Whether there will be further price cuts depends on the current markets for the scores of derivatives of ethylene, often intermediate products themselves. Thus, Supersleuth has to know the competitive situation in each of these markets. The uncertainty repeats itself for each of the thousands of other products that the company sells all around the world.

While companies may go so far as to give actual breakdowns by major product groups in sales and pretax profits (as Carbide does), they do not normally do this for individual product lines. No company releases all the information needed to analyze a market, such as unit volume, profitability, sales, inventories, pricing, and market share. Management will normally give partial information on a market, often much of it qualitative. It may state, as has been my experience, that production is up "nicely" or is "not bad" for a product and refuse to say more, telling the analyst that it is his job to fathom the explicit meaning. Whether "nicely" is 5%, or 25%, or even 50% is left to the analyst's judgment. While information can be scoured from records of customers, competitors, and trade sources, again much of it will be qualitative and difficult to analyze.

Thus, if EMH theorists are correct, our Supersleuth is truly an amazing creature. With the speed of light it can translate obscure information about a product—like an "O.K." or a "so-so," or other partial, incomplete, and at times inaccurate data—into accurate, quantifiable terms. When one realizes the immense amount of time and data it takes to accurately gauge the operating situation in one large market involving dozens of competitors and scores of substitute products worldwide, with the constant introduction of new products or the discontinuance of old ones, one can only stand in awe of the way Supersleuth can do it so effortlessly for hundreds or even thousands of products. Management, too, must be overwhelmed by Supersleuth. Product managers spend many years studying a market, have excellent staff support from teams of trained experts, are in constant touch with suppliers and customers, and yet are very often wrong in assessing a single market. Yet Supersleuth has the analytical capabilities to fully understand the current situation, not in one market, but in hundreds or even thousands!

Let us go on. Supersleuth can also correctly assess Carbide's capital spending plans for new plant and equipment relative to the plans of hundreds of other chemicals companies. Early in 1975 Carbide indicated its intention to spend $800 million in 1975, $1 billion in 1976, and an additional billion in 1977. To know just how good Carbide's spending plans are, they must be broken down between products and countries and then compared with other United States chemicals companies such as Dow, DuPont, Hercules, Grace, Celanese, and many others as well as with those of another dozen or so foreign giants. Such a step alone probably requires thousands of additional man-hours to get the necessary information. Considering many billions of further calculations are required once it is obtained, this is not a bad trick by itself.

In addition, Supersleuth is an excellent industrial psychologist and can correctly evaluate a company's management. With equal unerring judgment it can properly interpret the meaning of all important management changes. Then there is labor relations. Supersleuth understands perfectly the cost to a company of a new labor settlement, even if there are numerous unions and the settlement runs to perhaps 200 pages with many complex clauses on pensions, overtime, inflation adjustments, and scores of other provisions.

We are only scratching the surface of Supersleuth's problem-solving capabilities. It also considers the complex areas of accounting, lawsuits, antitrust actions, finances, research and development, and literally dozens of others. But apparently Supersleuth can handle them all. Not only does it digest the many billions of bits of information of the past but the information is always updated. The vast stream of raw new fact, much of it apparently contradictory, flowing piecemeal from thousands of different sources is flawlessly built into the new assessment.

We have not as yet touched upon one of Supersleuth's most important capabilities, that of determining whether the corporate information given is totally objective. Groupthink-compliance pressures may work within the corporation, which can result in misleading information being presented to professional investors both unintentionally and at times deliberately. Often a "party line" determines what executives will disclose to outsiders and how they will explain various corporate developments. Executives are human and would like to regard themselves as first-rate managers. Acquiring or sustaining the reputation of an excellent management team will aid both egos and the price/earnings ratio of the stock. It is a very natural inclination to believe a new product or plant expansion program will be highly profitable or a new acquisition is exactly tailored to company requirements. Similarly, there is a strong tendency to underplay negative events. Such information may be difficult to ferret out and may be heavily edited and sugar coated, making it hard to gauge the true extent of adverse developments. Thus, we find that a substantial portion of information received from management is qualitative and can be immensely difficult to interpret as well. Apparently Supersleuth can also do this with total infallibility.

Thus, even if only a fraction of Supersleuth's alleged capabilities are real, we are indeed guilty of wasting the greatest natural resource ever discovered on the securities markets. Supersleuth could certainly supplant the CIA and all other intelligence agencies with ease, put the space program years ahead, straighten out the post office, and have time left over to solve New York City's financial crisis.

I have been somewhat tongue-in-cheek in my approach, but the problem is very real, and one that not enough academics or perhaps even fundamentalists take cognizance of.

As we have seen, the amount of information available can be staggering and difficult to quantify. There is still a large, albeit diminishing, number of institutional research firms staffed by intelligent, experienced analysts who attempt to make meaningful earnings forecasts based on their extensive knowledge of a company. Many of these houses strive to improve the quality of their inputs. Ph.D.s with technical backgrounds are hired to study industries such as mining, electronics, or computers and MDs to research drug stocks. Extensive use is made of trade sources, and management consultants are utilized where appropriate. Nevertheless, the potential incoming material is so extensive that an analyst could devote a lifetime to the study of a company and still have major gaps in his knowledge.

And suppose that he knows more "facts" per se, will he necessarily be able to interpret them correctly? In practical terms, it is uneconomical for an analyst to spend more than a fraction of his time on any one company. His responsibilities are extensive; at the very least he must cover dozens of companies in one industry and devote time to other duties, such as customer contact and report writing.

Even if the analyst is fully aware of the "facts" of a company, he must make many assumptions about economic conditions, interest rates, taxes, government policies, growth rates of numerous markets, raw material costs, and the success of various plant-expansion programs. Any one of these assumptions can turn out wrong and destroy the earnings projection. We can now see how difficult interpretation of information actually is. Perhaps this is why analysts so often have projected the continuance of current trends to arrive at earnings forecasts. Earnings forecasts depend on so many rapidly changing underlying assumptions that their accuracy can always be questioned. Some observers go so far as to say that the complexity of the situation is such that these predictions are of no value at all.

Top management has infinitely more information on which to base a decision than has any research analyst or Supersleuth. It also has hundreds of full-time managers and their staffs, who constantly report new developments. Yet, management is often wrong. Union Carbide made overly optimistic earnings forecasts in early 1975 about their expectations for that year, and later had to revise them downward. The error was not due to chance happenings. Management had simply underestimated the magnitude of the recession, not at all surprising with the extremely complex 1975 business picture. There were some investors who believed management's original expectations were too high. Among professionals, these investors were very much a minority, and yet they proved correct.

Although large numbers of sophisticated investors are often in agreement on the course of the market and the value of individual stocks, the difficulties of the interpretational problems by themselves (to say nothing of the group-think-compliance pressures) may result in their being far off base very often.*

The arena of the professional investor is not much different from that in which economists perform. Economic forecasting and fundamental stock market analysis are both based on a tremendous number of complex variables and hundreds of underlying assumptions, a good many of which

*This is not to say that Supersleuth may not often realistically appraise value, but given the complexity of the operating environment, the generalization that it will always be done correctly cannot be made.

are held in common. Economists are often wrong because of the immensity of the task. We need only go back to October of 1974 when most leading economic authorities were preoccupied with inflation and stopping the boom at a time when the economy was already moving rapidly into a severe recession and production was beginning to free fall. For some reason, economists have chosen to devote considerable time and effort to the study of the forecasting results in the stock market while largely ignoring their own forecasting records and errors: perhaps that's just human nature.

Suppose we are feeling mischievous and impose the logic of EMH upon economists themselves. We would then assume that a sophisticated group of economists known as Supersleuth II* would be able to absolutely gauge the economy at a moment of time just as the more primitive Supersleuth I can gauge the market. Strangely enough at any given time there seems to be a good deal of doubt within this group about the actual conditions of the economy, and there are often errors such as the one we just witnessed.

And here we have the problem—by the logic of EMH, Supersleuth II can never be wrong on the basis of existing facts just as Supersleuth I cannot be wrong about the stock market. Like Supersleuth I, it can take hundreds, and perhaps thousands of underlying assumptions, and choose the correct ones in reaching its decision. If it is wrong it is only because new developments have occurred. I rather doubt any economist would claim that an important consensus of his colleagues has any such record of infallibility. Yet this is precisely what is claimed for Supersleuth I.

Raw data do not equal knowledge, although in an increasingly computerized society the two are often thought of as the same. There is a great deal of difference between simply amassing facts and correctly understanding their significance, something seemingly overlooked by the EMH theorists.

A substantial gap also exists between the availability and the utilization of data. An article in *The New York Times*

---

*Since by definition economists are the most rational of rational creatures, we would assume this group to be an advanced model of Supersleuth I.

delineates this point clearly. A test was devised by Dr. Harold
C. Neu of the Columbia University School of Medicine to
find out how conversant doctors were with the antibiotics
they were prescribing. Antibiotics, the single most commonly
prescribed class of drugs, cause serious and sometimes fatal
reactions among patients when incorrectly administered. The
test, admittedly stiff, was a 50-question multiple-choice type
given to 4,513 doctors. The average score was only 67.2%.
Only 17.2% of private practitioners scored 80% or better,
as Figure 6 indicates. Hundreds of facts on drug reactions
would have to be known if all questions were to be answered
properly. Such information, however, was readily available
and easy to interpret. Even so, we see in practice that a
wide sample of professionals did not have the prerequisite
information on which to properly make the correct decisions.

EMH assumes not hundreds but thousands, and perhaps
millions, of facts far more difficult to obtain and correctly
interpret. Many thousands of investors are expected to score
far higher in an exponentially more complex undertaking.
This line of reasoning, never subjected to testing, must be
seriously questioned.

One defense of the EMH theorist against the foregoing

Figure 6. Breakdown by percent of doctors who scored 80% or
better on a test of their knowledge of antibiotics.

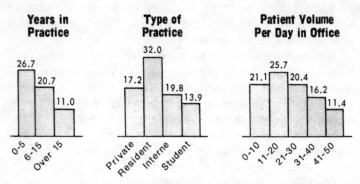

SOURCE: *The New York Times,* January 28, 1976. ©1975/1976 by The New
York Times Company. Reproduced by permission.

discussion might be that the analysis of raw data by itself is too complicated to serve as a major base for decision making. Instead, he would say, recent earnings statements and the current trends of earnings, which management often indicates, accurately reflect the many millions of facts that may well defy interpretation by themselves. Thus, according to our mythical EMH theorist, it is through the systematization of accounting that the meaning of information is provided to investors. Let us, then, look at accounting more closely.

Accounting—Order Out of Chaos?

Most investors, including a considerable number of professionals, are relatively innocent when it comes to accounting. This should come as no surprise. Accounting has always been considered a painstakingly accurate profession, almost a science, and we tend to be in awe of the perfectionism of its practitioners. Even in a brief glance at a balance sheet, an income statement, or a statement of source and application of funds, we see a highly organized format in which figures are stated, often to the last penny. If a company reports earnings of exactly $6,444,256.26 in 1975 on sales of $97,-256,345.75, it appears to be an unassailable measurement, as absolute as 5,280 feet in a mile or 2,000 pounds in a short ton. The sad fact is that accounting measurements are nowhere near so absolute as they seem. Under varying accounting assumptions, all of which are quite legitimate, the $6,444,256.26 might become considerably more, considerably less, or even in some cases an actual loss.

Why is this so? Accounting statements are prepared under broad guidelines set up by the accounting profession and usually called "generally accepted accounting principles," which is condensed to the acronym "GAAP." Under GAAP procedures the accountant has a wide range of options in treating various income-statement and balance-sheet items. The rationale for allowing these options was to give management a significant amount of flexibility in choosing the procedure best suited to a company's unique requirements, while still reporting fairly to shareholders. In theory, this is an excellent and a progressive idea. In practice, it has fostered misleading reporting by companies, resulting in lawsuits having been filed by investors against all of the major accounting firms and a lowered public confidence in company reporting. To quote *Fortune* magazine on the subject:

> The basic problem is not dishonesty on the part of corporations or their auditors, but the amorphous nature of accounting itself. The wide range of accounting options permits companies enormous leeway, with various paths to take in consolidating earnings of subsidiaries, depreciating assets, evaluating inventory, and accounting for various drilling costs. Thus, identical earnings figures for two similar companies with identical sales do not necessarily represent equal performance by management.[5]

In looking at earnings, the main problem faced by the investor is the allocation of costs and revenues under GAAP procedures. Since future earnings are considered to be the major consideration in securities evaluation, their accurate determination is of crucial importance. As analysts are acutely aware, the measurement of a company's actual earnings is often a most difficult, at times seemingly impossible, undertaking. Giving only a partial list, each item containing complex nuances of its own, the accounting discretion in the treatment of any of the following can have an important effect on reported earnings: revenues, depreciation, inventory valuation, pension liability, investment tax credit, taxes and tax refunds, nonrecurring items, capital gains and losses, contingent liabilities, evaluation of investments, the method of determining various reserves, foreign currency gains and losses, prepaid expenses, and deferred charges.

In an excellent book entitled *Unaccountable Accounting*, Professor Abraham Briloff of City College, who is both a CPA and Ph.D., takes the accounting profession to task for the wide leeway it has allowed in reporting information to investors.[6] The resulting distortion has led many highly sophisticated professionals to purchase what they believed to be companies with rapidly growing earnings, only to find in the end that the growth was a figment of the accountant's imagination.

It is often very much to management's advantage to report earnings results as favorably as possible. For one thing, a rising level of earnings often entitles management to higher salaries. For another, if stock prices increase with earnings, management may also benefit from the stock options granted to them at lower prices. It also allows capital to be raised through new stock issues at better terms, makes possible the acquisition of other companies on more favorable terms, and makes it more difficult for the company to be swallowed up by an "unfriendly" predator.

For the reasons just discussed, the "game plan" is usually designed to show a pattern of steadily rising earnings. The great majority of companies report their results fairly, but if there is a choice of options, a strong predilection exists for accepting the option that will show the most favorable results. In difficult periods, the inclination to take advantage of options that will minimize the unfavorable results is even stronger.[7]

There are two types of game plans, offensive and defensive. The offensive game plans are designed to make a company's earnings record as favorable as possible. Some very tough players participate in this competition, as we have already seen in Chapter 4. They program earnings by adopting accounting treatments very definitely bordering on the unacceptable, even with the liberal standards in effect. The loosest treatments are necessary to show the growth record they desire. The auditor may grimace, but if the option or options chosen by management are at all plausible, he had better use them, or his successor will.

Defensive game plans may be used by companies to present a better picture to avoid the numerous unfriendly predators, the "financial Jaws," constantly swimming around searching for a delectable new morsel. These predators love to swallow up cheap, asset-rich, financially conservative companies, change their accounting options, and begin to come out with higher earnings and a higher price for their stock.

At this point the reader may ask just how important are these options overall to a company's reported earnings. One source estimates the swing from using the most conservative accounting practices to the most liberal from 30 to 50%.[8] In my experience, the change has been even more in the cases of computer leasing, franchise, and land development companies. A good number of companies in these industries achieved high P/E ratios on reported earnings, fabricated by using ultraliberal accounting techniques. If more conservative accounting procedures had been adopted, many would have had no earnings at all. In fact, large losses were often recorded after the adoption of more conservative standards.

As a simple example, let us assume that two companies operating in the same industry in reality have equal revenues and expenses. Revenues are accounted for in the same manner, but widely different options in accounting for their expenses are used. Modonic's earnings are then double those of Jersey Scrap (Table 24).

TABLE 24

	Modonics	**Jersey Scrap**
Sales	$20,000,000	$20,000,000
Net Profit	$ 2,000,000	$ 1,000,000
Shares Outstanding	1,000,000	1,000,000
Earnings per Share	$2.00	$1.00
P/E Ratio	10–15–20	10–15–20
Price	20–30–40	10–15–20

An unqualified acceptance of the earnings report might put Modonics at double the price of Jersey Scrap. Modonics also looks considerably better by some important ratios used in security analysis. It is earning 10% after tax on its sales compared with Jersey Scrap's 5% and, assuming both had a net worth of $10 million, a 20% return on net worth versus 10% for Jersey Scrap. Thus, without a careful scrutiny of the "quality" of these earnings, Modonics might even trade at a higher P/E multiple than Jersey Scrap. We could then have a situation where Jersey Scrap, although actually earning the same amount as Modonics, trades at only a small fraction of the latter's market price. The complexity of the measurement grows more difficult, of course, when companies in different industries are compared.

Imaginative Accounting in Action

In his book, Professor Briloff goes on to give some classic examples of creative accounting in action. He makes a detailed analysis of various companies and industries that were major institutional favorites in recent years, such as Leasco Data Processing in the computer leasing industry; Performance Systems; in the franchising industry; Memorex and Telex in the computer peripheral industry; Great Southwest Corporation in the land development industry; U.S. Home, and Kaufman and Broad in the home-building industries; and an old favorite, National Student Marketing. The evidence makes it quite clear that the accounting employed in each case was ingeniously, if not nefariously, complex—so complex, in fact, that none but the most sophisticated investors might be able to follow it. To quote Briloff:

> If financial statements were "understandable," could Penn Central have disposed of its commercial paper to some of the most astute and prestigious banks, insurance companies, and other professional investors? Could there have been the psychedelic conglomerate craze of the 1960s? Would the land developers and leasing companies . . . have gotten away with it as long and as well as they did?[9]

Briloff's work illustrates that even highly sophisticated investors were again and again taken in by exciting "concept" companies whose only real asset was exceptionally creative accounting. Institutional holdings of many of these stocks were extremely large for considerable periods of time. When these stocks finally plummeted in price, it was not only the small unsophisticated investor who was burned badly, but just as often the well trained professional.

To be fair, it must be said that even with the complex accounting procedures described, a highly trained investor could often ferret out enough information, either from the text or the footnotes of the financial statements, to deduce that all was not well. He certainly would not be able to discern how sick the situations actually were, but by recognizing the basic lack of conservatism in the methods used, he could at least avoid the stock. But, in practice, very few professionals actually did.* The accounting was either ignored or misunderstood by large segments of the professional market population.

Although information was available for a substantial period through careful analysis of financial statements,† it was not until the quality of these companies' earnings was widely questioned publicly that their stocks dropped sharply. More recent examples of the same phenomena were Memorex and National Liberty Insurance, both of which had extensive deferred charges for long periods. With mounting public awareness and criticism of their accounting, these securities plummeted in price.

The myriad of accounting options available to the corporation is a labyrinth through which even the most skilled practitioner may stumble for weeks, months, or sometimes years. Corporation financial officers also have ways of allocating revenues between divisions, the basis of which the analyst may not know. A good division can be made to look better, or an exciting new product, much in the investor's eye, may become even more alluring through such allocations. Earnings growth can be smoothed to gain favorable investor attention.[10] A case in point is a large cosmetics manufacturer's use of timing when introducing a major new perfume. The introduction was made in the *first quarter* of 1972 rather than in the fourth quarter of 1971 because the final quarter's profitability was already sufficient to impress investors, while the next year's could use the boost.

Clearly, it is extremely difficult to determine the quality of earnings accurately. The sophisticated investor has some

---

*Professor Briloff wrote a number of articles based on such information, warning investors of the accounting pitfalls of specific companies.

†It is possible the false sense of security implicit in groupthink made many professionals not seriously consider the accounting dangers of favorites.

knowledge of the reporting standards used, but this knowledge is often, at best, only partially complete. While GAAP standards have been tightened in the past several years (possibly following a rash of lawsuits by disenchanted investors against each of the "big eight" accounting firms), they still leave managements a considerable earnings latitude.

As Arnold L. Thomas, a professor of accounting at McMaster, recently wrote, "To generalize, whenever accountants try to match costs with revenues *there will be no way to verify or refute the results.** Instead, any of a wide variety of possible calculations will be just as good (or bad) as any other. These are sweeping conclusions, and they violate most of what we have been trained to believe about accounting."[11]

Earnings, as we have already seen, are normally considered to be the prime consideration in determining the price of a stock. Even among professionals the basic complexity of the problem just described allows a good deal of room for significantly different interpretations as to what a company's true earnings actually are. Comparing many companies of different sizes, some of which have many divisions and international operations, simply multiplies the interpretational problems manyfold.

The reader may now see the complexity involved in determining what the real earnings of a company are at any time. Many professionals either cannot or do not have the time or interest to analyze the accounting in detail. For those who do, and they are a small minority, it is still impossible to absolutely quantify earnings. But enough clues can probably be found to at least avoid being taken in by a numbers game, and in most cases, with diligent effort, to make a reasonable assessment of how conservative (or nonconservative) management reporting actually is.

The Interpretive Problem in Perspective

I have tried to show that the analysis both of basic information and of a company's earnings are terribly involved

*Italics mine.

questions which require immense interpretative skills. Because of the vast amount of raw data, the large number of premises that can be made about operating and economic conditions, and the wide latitude of difficult accounting options employed, even Supersleuth's conclusions may at times be widely off the mark. High P/E multiples were paid at one time by a great many professional investors for computer leasing, computer peripherals, franchising, land development stock, and conglomerate stocks, when at least some knowledge was available that accounting was loose and had been for a long period.

To say that even if no one individual may have all the information, it is still impounded in the market, simply begs the question. The decisions of market participants determine price. Decisions are made by thousands of investors, and if enough are wrong because of the difficulties outlined, the market is wrong! Price can, and often does, diverge significantly from value.

EMH theorists might disagree with such statements. We saw in Chapter 2 the results of a number of their experiments designed to prove that the market responds rapidly to new information. These tests were considered to have provided strong support for the thesis of the rationality of investors and the efficiency of markets.* The strength of such assertions should be questioned. Even if there is full understanding of the effects of a stock split or a secondary offering, it should be rudimentary to most professionals and a large number of other investors. It is certainly not on a par with the difficulties outlined in this chapter. To use these findings as proof of market efficiency is equivalent to saying that because many millions of chess players understand how to properly move the pieces on a chess board, they all play the game with equal ability. Millions of chess players, then, play as well as Masters, Grandmasters, or Bobby Fischer himself.† Obviously, this statement is untrue. Unfortunately

---

*I expressed some doubts in Chapter 2 about several of the findings.
†Here the author may be displaying faulty interpretive capabilities in still recognizing Fischer as the world's best.

the enormity of the interpretive problem has not been examined by market researchers to date.

Before bidding adieu to our overworked Supersleuth group, we can now sympathize with the task it has been allotted to perform by the efficient market hypothesis. Like the Polish cavalrymen who charged the German tanks in the first days of World War II, they have been assigned a mission not humanly possible to fulfill. The complexities of the interpretational problems leave ample room for Supersleuth to be wrong fairly often. And if it can be wrong except on the rarest of rare occasions, then EMH fails, for it categorically states this cannot happen.

The difficulties both of interpreting information and of understanding accounting should not lead us at this point to throw up our hands in despair. It is precisely because of these problems, as we shall see presently, that there may be hope for outperforming the market.

The Foundations of EMH—Bedrock or Quicksand?

Suppose for a moment that the informational and interpretational problems we discussed in the last chapter were whisked away. We would now find an even larger barrier for the efficient market hypothesis to hurdle.

The Problem of Investor Behavior

The second premise of EMH states that enough professionals and other sophisticated investors will react to the same facts in exactly the same rational manner so that prices will always stay in line with basic value. Investors, we are told, react like human computers: feed them measurable data, and out comes the only possible answer.

Do investors really act with total rationality in making their investment decisions? The evidence we have viewed to date indicates that they assuredly do not.

In our study of speculative bubbles, both historical and recent, we saw gigantic changes in prices with only minor changes in underlying conditions. During tulipmania in Holland, tulips were traded for the equivalent of $8,300 one day and almost nothing three months later. Many stocks in March 1975 traded for 200, 300, or even 400% more than they did in December 1974. Often much of the gain took place in weeks. The moves resulted from violent shifts in investor psychology.

Man's capriciousness unfortunately makes him a most unreliable automaton. In *A Random Walk Down Wall Street,* Burton Malkiel relates how the market responded to the announcement by GE in 1955 that its researchers had developed a synthetic diamond. The scientists stated at the time that the man-made diamonds were not suitable for jewelry and were too costly to profitably manufacture for industrial purposes. Nevertheless, the market value of GE stock rose $400 million within 24 hours. This was approximately twice the value of total annual worldwide diamond sales and six times the value of sales to industrial markets.[1] Unquestionably, a thorough study of market reactions to new information would uncover hundreds of similar situations all quite contradictory to EMH theory.*

The attack on the assumption of rational behavior also comes from another source—economic researchers who have made studies of the decision-making characteristics of consumers and businessmen. George Katona, whom we met in an earlier chapter, writes that although consumer and business behavior at times appears to be "purposive" and "intelligent," a great deal of evidence has also turned up which shows it often is not. Particularly pertinent for us are the studies made of the decision making of businessmen in deciding to build new facilities, because such decisions are both important to the corporation's future and because the criteria are quite similar to those involved in investment decisions. Katona found that many such decisions were automatic or "rule-of-thumb" rather than made after careful deliberate investigation. The absolutely rational behavior so central to EMH precludes such mechanical decision making.[2]

With the accelerating advance of the behavioral sciences in this century, it is no longer accepted that man is always completely rational. In *Managerial Psychology,* Harold Leavitt writes: "Man is an irrational animal if by irrational he does not do what we always think best for him. But though

---

*Simply because prices react to new information does not mean that the response is necessarily appropriate. If price levels are far removed from basic value beforehand, they may still be so after the new information is received.

irrational, there is an internal logic to his behavior."[3] The behavior of investment professionals viewed in Chapters 5 through 9 may at times have been wildly irrational with regard to security values. But for the individuals it was entirely logical in terms of career and group relationships.

A Pact With Mephistopheles

It would be unfair to say that EMH theorists are entirely unaware of the simplicity and vulnerability of their assumptions. The assumption of economic rationality is one that has perplexed economic theorists for a long time. This premise was derived in the golden age of rationalism in the eighteenth and first part of the nineteenth centuries.

In the eighteenth century the attitude toward the role of the individual in society began to change. Rather than needing a rigid code to hold him in check in the interests of an organized and rational state, as was the prevailing thinking of the seventeenth century, man was now believed to be far more able to shape his life according to the principles set forth by his own reason. In so doing, it was assumed he would arrive at decisions that would be in the best interests of the state (Adam Smith's famous invisible hand). The acceptance of this philosophy led to the reversal of the far-reaching economic restrictions of the preceding century. Now the individual was to be granted as much freedom as possible so that he could exert his rationality for the benefit of all.

Since that time, the concept of the absolutely rational man has been primarily discarded in philosophy. With the revolutionary advances of the behavioral sciences, it is commonly accepted that although at times man may act rationally, very often he does not. Market and economic history strongly support the findings of the behavioral scientists.

Why, then, do many economists persist in utilizing an outmoded concept of human behavior as the cornerstone of their theory?

To partially answer this question, we quote briefly from Stonier and Hague's excellent textbook on economic theory:

> Rationality in the theory of the firm implies that the individual producers aim at earning the greatest possible money profits. Now no economist believes that all businessmen do, in fact, always maximize profits, nor does he necessarily believe that they should do so. But, if no such assumption were made it would be difficult to produce any definite explanation of the way firms fix output and prices at all.[4]

Thus the authors acknowledge that the concept of economic rationality so central to EMH is not realistic; still they defend its usefulness, adding: "But to introduce a more realistic assumption would make economic theory very difficult, quite apart from the fact that no one really knows what the correct assumption would be."[5]

Economic theory is thus caught on the horns of a major dilemma: Should it espouse realistic assumptions, and if so, what would they be? Or should the assumptions, although acknowledged to be unrealistic, allow extensive analysis, however flawed in terms of practical value?

Most economists have chosen the latter approach. By accepting the concept of rationality, they have proceeded to make an intensive analysis of economic data, such as supply, demand, income, capital, and interest rates, and have constructed cohesive and far-reaching theory through the integration of many such variables. The decision making, which to a significant extent shapes each of these variables, remains largely unexamined, since it is always assumed that the decision maker will behave in the predictable fashion of an automaton. Some economists have called this the reification of economic data.

The same kind of thinking has been brought to bear by economists in stock market analysis. Investor decision-making processes are believed to be entirely a function of external circumstances. The decision-making process has thus become, for economists, a kind of Pandora's box which, once opened, might quickly swallow up the existing theory.

Have economists paid perhaps too high a price for developing integrated economic theory? Like Dr. Faust have they given up far too much as their part of the bargain?

Economists recognize these problems and note that their

models may have limited or no applicability to the real world. The trouble, in the words of Sherman Maisel, a past president of the American Finance Association, is that "We warn that our assumptions and techniques are limited. We point out that other variables may be significant. We recognize the danger of partial analysis, but we still act as if the difficulties do not exist. We persist in rendering advice or drawing strong implications from our limited analysis."[6] EMH is a classic example of a theory that draws far-reaching conclusions from at best a most limited and partial analysis.

As we have seen, EMH makes a very important psychological assumption about investor behavior. An interesting question at this point might be, how scientific is the assumption of rationality—this far-reaching psychological law proposed now it seems only by economists? We might indeed ask how well such assumptions tie into a scientific approach. Robert Plutchuk, in his book on scientific method, states: "The observation of natural occurring events is the starting point of all science."[7] This principle has been accepted by scientists for many hundreds of years. In the fifteenth century, Sir Francis Bacon related the following engaging tale to illustrate the importance of observation to establish evidence, rather than reliance on the writings of previous authorities, or merely speculating:

> In the year of our Lord 1432, there arose a grievous quarrel among the brethren over the number of teeth in the mouth of a horse. For 13 days the disputation raged without ceasing. All the ancient books and chronicles were fetched out, and wonderful and ponderous erudition, such as was never before heard of in this region, was made manifest. At the beginning of the 14th day, a youthful friar of goodly bearing asked his learned superiors for permission to add a word, and straightway, to the wonderment of the disputants, whose deep wisdom he sore vexed, he beseeched them to unbend in a manner coarse and unheard-of, and to look in the open mouth of a horse and find answer to their questionings. At this, their dignity being grievously hurt, they waxed exceedingly wrath; and, joining in a mighty uproar, they flew upon him and smote him hip and thigh, and cast him out forthwith. For, said they,

surely Satan hath tempted this bold neophyte to declare unholy and unheard-of-ways of finding truth contrary to all the teachings of the fathers. After many days more of grievous strife the dove of peace sat on the assembly, and they as one man, declaring the problem to be an everlasting mystery because of a grievous dearth of historical and theological evidence thereof, so ordered the same writ down.[8]

The generally agreed upon starting point of scientific method is very thorough observation. General laws come only after careful study and classification of the phenomena under observation. This critical stage in the development of theory cannot be avoided. Surprisingly enough, no observational evidence has ever been presented by EMH theorists that market participants behave according to their assumptions. The crucial observation stage has seemingly been bypassed. Furthermore, EMH both overlooks and is contradicted by extensive psychological findings as well as market history. The evidence previously presented that large samples of professionals perform worse than the market and the evidence that the low P/E stocks consistently outperform high P/Es also directly contradict its basic premise.

Viewed in the context of proper scientific procedures, EMH seems almost to have been put together back to front. Its starting point is a correlation discovered between the performance of money run by financial institutions, primarily mutual funds, and the market averages. From the correlation, the hypothesis then works backward to the assumption that it is rational investors who always keep prices in line with value.

Writers on scientific methodology warn that though findings appear to support a hypothesis, the correlation could just be chance. The correlation may even be statistically significant, as are the EMH findings that professionals do not outperform the market. But this is not evidence of a cause-and-effect relationship; it does not prove the hypothesis that all investors are rational and have equal interpretive capabilities. There may be another hypothesis (for example, that of groupthink-compliance) which also explains the same results and is far more realistic when carefully scrutinized.

Thus, correlation does not indicate causation.

A humorous example that illustrates this point clearly was the clever correlation recognized some years ago between the length of the hemlines of women's dresses and the level of the Dow Jones Industrial Average. A hypothesis could be offered that the length of the hemline dictated the course of the Dow Jones Industrial Average. (See Figure 7.)

Figure 7. The hemline indicator.

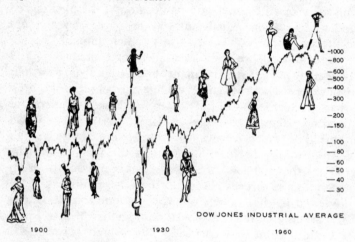

SOURCE: Ralph A. Rotnem, dec. Smith Barney, Harris Upham & Co, Inc., successors to Harris, Upham & Co. Inc.

Though hemlines in the 1920s were rising and stock prices followed, both fell sharply in the early 1930s (fortunately, before this writer could be affected by either). In the first years of the 1960s, both hemlines and stocks worked higher. With hot pants came the market surge of the early 1970s. The hypothesis seems repeatedly vindicated, but I doubt that even the most strident woman libber would back this line of reasoning.

We can see how dangerous it is to simply reason backward to a theory because a correlation is proven between market performance and expert results. Almost an infinite number of explanations can be derived to explain this phenomenon.

Perhaps professional investors have transmitters hidden in the boardrooms of the companies they invest in and so get precise information to accurately gauge prices; perhaps they all secretly go to the same clairvoyant to get their information; perhaps the correlation is best explained by the groupthink-compliance hypothesis. The only way of knowing is to test the assumptions, something these theorists have never tried to do.

To be scientifically acceptable, a hypothesis should not only be tested against findings, as EMH has been, but it should also be grounded in previous findings, as EMH is not. A scientific hypothesis must never be spuriously constructed but instead should be based on what is already accepted as fact. Isaac Newton's famous dictum, *"Hypothesis non fingo"* (not formed or shaped) put it succinctly hundreds of years ago. There is no evidence yet produced that would support the EMH case that people are always rational, but there is substantial evidence to the contrary. The groupthink-compliance hypothesis, on the other hand, is strongly supported by existing psychological evidence, and it also explains the findings of inferior professional results and the constant overvaluation of high-visibility and undervaluation of low-visibility stocks, phenomena that are dismissed out of hand by the very definition of EMH. Thus, if several theories appear to explain the facts on the market behavior of professionals, as do EMH and the groupthink-compliance hypothesis, the more substantially documented one that "fits the facts" better is the scientifically acceptable one. After examining all the evidence, the assumptions of EMH seem most suspect. It may well be in the words of Thomas Huxley, "A beautiful theory killed by nasty, ugly little facts."

Is There Another Defense of EMH?

Perhaps, in spite of the foregoing discussion, one can simply ignore the need for realistic assumptions. Some EMH theorists have taken this position: to quote one highly regarded source, "Fortunately, it is now generally understood that the value of a model lies in its predictive or explanatory power and that the model cannot be judged by reference to the realism of its underlying assumptions. This point has been expressed with great clarity and persuasiveness by Milton Friedman:[9] 'The relevant question to ask about the assumptions of a theory is not whether they are descriptively realistic, for they never are, but whether they are sufficiently good approximations for the purpose in hand. And the question can be answered only by seeing whether the theory works, which means whether it yields sufficiently accurate predictions.' "[10]

EMH theorists have used Friedman's passage to justify their hypothesis because the model indeed seems to explain why professionals do not do better than the market. Defending assumptions that are acknowledged to be unrealistic because the resultant model seemingly explains other observations leaves EMH theorists skating on dangerously thin ice. Friedman himself warned in the essay previously quoted: "Observed facts are necessarily finite in number, possible hypotheses infinite. If there is one hypothesis that is consistent with the available evidence there is an infinite number that are."[11] It is crucial, then, to choose the hypothesis that best fits the facts. This can be done only by thorough observation.

The efficient market hypothesis appears to be totally unrealistic. It is not merely simplified to eliminate irrelevancies but is directly contradictory to repeated observations. Under these conditions, we cannot accept the contention of these EMH theorists that the "predictive" and "explanatory" powers of the model justify its divergence from observed fact. To illustrate the flaw in such reasoning, let's take two important historical examples—the Ptolemaic system and the Phlogiston theory.

The Ptolemaic System. This school of astronomy held that the earth was the center of the universe, a dictum accepted as scientific fact for over 14 centuries. The system stated that all planets and stars traveled around the earth, which is stationary. The moon was closest, Mercury, Venus, and the sun extended out in that order, followed by Mars, Jupiter, and Saturn, and what were known as the fixed stars. The sun and the moon moved in extended circles around the earth. The planets traveled in a circular path, called an "epicycle," about a point, and this point traveled in an eccentric circle about the sun.

With time, as irregularities were observed through more accurate observation, the model became increasingly complex in order to incorporate the newly discovered information. The planets and stars moved around each other and around the earth in a combination of circles, epicycles, and eccentrics (large deferent circles around whose centers the epicycles simultaneously revolved). The result of this hodge-podge was a mind-boggling whirl.

The Ptolemaic system meets the two major criteria of a useful hypothesis in the narrow sense these EMH theorists proposed. It is "predictive" in correctly forecasting where various celestial bodies will be at future points in time, and it is "explanatory" because it gives us a system of planetary motion. The only trouble, unfortunately, is that it's totally wrong.

The Phlogiston System. This theory, developed by George Ernst Stahl about 1700, was an early attempt to explain the major facts observed in combustion. Combustible materials such as coal or wood were held to be rich in a substance called "phlogiston" (from the Greek word "to set fire"). In the combustion process, phlogiston escaped to the air, giving off heat and light. The remaining residue, having lost its phlogiston, was reduced in weight. Later contributors broadened phlogiston theory to cover the rusting of metals. In the latter process, phlogiston was thought to escape at a much slower rate than in combustion. The hypothesis thus explained the two widely independent processes of combustion and rusting.

Additional explanations were found as time passed. The hypothesis was also able to accurately predict certain chemical results, which were subsequently verified through experiments.

Again, we have an appealingly simple, yet comprehensive, hypothesis meeting the requirements that a model be both "predictive" and "explanatory." But, because the assumptions are wholly false, they explain the phenomenon in a completely incorrect manner.

While there is certainly reason to question whether assumptions need be all-inclusive, covering large amounts of minor and irrelevant information, the major axioms of any theory must accurately describe the phenomena from which the deductions are made. This requirement is basic to the proper scientific approach. Otherwise, using the narrow criteria of usefulness of a hypothesis, we can accept the world as motionless or believe that phlogiston explains combustion.

Evidence must be accumulated, if at all possible, to prove that the major assumptions hold, and hold better than any potential challengers. In the marketplace, a better application of the scientific method should attempt to carefully observe, categorize, and analyze the complex interrelationships that result in investor decision making and only then should a hypothesis be formulated. Science must begin, as we have seen, with observing the world as it really is, not as one wishes it to be. Mathematical and statistical methods cannot substitute for scientific observation. If the mathematical or statistical analysis is built on major assumptions that are incorrect, neither the complexity of the model nor the many man-hours that went into its construction will make is useful in the real world. The important disciplines of mathematics and statistical analysis in theory building can be of value only in conjunction with properly formulated assumptions based on scientific observation.

There is a tendency by some to think that the production of a great deal of statistical material is by itself enough to prove a case. Peter Drucker in *Management* makes clear that it is not. He writes,

> Scientific is not—as many management scientists naively seem to think—synonymous with quantification. If it were true, astrology would be the queen of the sciences. It is not even the application of the scientific method, after all; astrologers observe phenomena, derive the generalizations of a hypothesis therefrom, and then test the hypothesis by further organized observation. Yet, astrology is superstition rather than science

because of its childish assumption that there is a real zodiac, that the signs in it really exist, and that their fancied resemblance to such earthly creatures as a fish or a lion defines their character and properties (whereas all of them are nothing but the mnemonic devices of the navigators of antiquity).

In other words, "scientific" presupposes a rational definition of the universe of the science (that is, of the phenomena which it considers to be real and meaningful) as well as the formulation of basic assumptions or postulates which are appropriate, consistent and comprehensive . . . if it is not done, or done wrongly, the scientific method cannot be applied.[12]

The history of science teaches us that, given capable, intelligent people, large errors normally do not occur in the development of a case, but rather in the assumptions upon which the work is based. People want to continue practicing what they have been trained to do, in the manner in which they have been trained to do it. Change undermines their basic approach. Is it not also possible that EMH and other such economic axioms also allow people to proceed in the manner they know best? After all, they are trained far more thoroughly in statistical method than in psychology. There may well be too much eagerness to push on with the building of the structure more and more grandly, and too little interest in ensuring a solid foundation.

If I have been somewhat harsh on EMH, it is simply because I cannot accept the manner in which its case has been built. Although I do not believe the hypothesis, I certainly respect the arduous experimental efforts made by the many researchers in this area. They have brought the major winds of change to Wall Street, where they were long overdue. Investors who are really interested in how the market works must genuinely appreciate the findings of the university researchers. Much of the work was necessarily tedious, dull, and time consuming but absolutely essential for building the foundation of a new investment structure.

Without the thorough measurement of both technical and fundamental performance records, Wall Street would continue in the old, unsuccessful—often disastrous—ways, with no impetus toward change. As it is, the academic findings

250   *Can an Investor Beat the Market?*

are still largely ignored by professionals. But with the increased exposure given to these results in undergraduate and graduate finance courses, and the interest expressed in them by governmental bodies, legislators, the press, and practitioners, the boundaries of this ignorance are gradually receding. It is of little consequence that the first hypothesis based on the empirical findings appears not to be correct that the evidence itself is paramount.

This work can easily be extended to test the groupthink-compliance hypothesis for which a great deal of further research is required. As Janis and other sources indicate, the process of groupthink may permeate business, industry, the professions, and even the highest levels of government decision making. To establish empirical evidence that substantiates or rejects the hypothesis would be a major undertaking, but it would be an invaluable contribution to the social sciences. It could lead to revolutionary changes in the formulation of financial, economic, managerial, and organizational theory.

Because the securities markets often reflect in a few years, or less often, major attitude changes not seen elsewhere in a decade or sometimes a generation, it is a fascinating laboratory to study the nature of opinion change. It provides the interested researcher with a vast treasure house of the most detailed information of investment decisions, of expert opinions, of price movements, and of underlying fundamental and economic data from which to work. This information can be categorized and analyzed systematically, going back sometimes 50 years or more, by utilizing the numerous financial periodicals available. Large samples of expert opinion, such as those presented in Chapter 7, could be procured to corroborate or disprove the groupthink-compliance hypothesis in the securities market. In no other area of government, professional activity, or business can successful or poor decision making be so accurately measured.

It is the EMH researchers, with their excellent knowledge of financial statistical techniques, who could play a major role in such an undertaking. If substantial empirical findings corroborated the existence of the groupthink-compliance hypothesis, which current evidence certainly points to, the ramifications could extend far beyond the stock market. Within the financial world such findings would be invaluable as a framework to properly assess the current institutional role and to accurately gauge the value of current investment theory.

Where Do We Go from Here?

A good portion of this book has been devoted to what I believe are the real reasons why professionals do not do better. The fact that most do not does not mean that it is impossible. A number of students of EMH have themselves pointed out that there is little or no recorded evidence of how sophisticated individual investors, whether professional or amateur, have performed over a period of time. My own repeated observation is that this type of investor most often does well and is knowledgeable and independent enough to fight off the destructive addiction of the groupthink-compliance process. Sometimes his rewards have been spectacular. In the final chapter of this book, we shall synthesize the psychological and financial findings that may allow an investor to put a successful investment program into practice.

12

A Contemporary Investment Strategy

To this point the reader may be ready to believe that no one can beat the market. Even if EMH is not a realistic description of how the market operates, behavioral and interpretational problems prevent most professionals from outdoing the averages. Some measurements indicate that many professionals have done consistently worse. Many books have been written on the subject of the market, telling investors how easy it is to make a killing in stocks. The formulas offered are alluringly simple, but no real evidence is given to support their effectiveness. The popular reception of some of these authors indicates that there is still room in this world for the old-time patent medicine salesman. While I cannot concoct a magic formula that will grow hair on bald heads and double the readers' net worth in a month, I can formulate a strategy which, if rigorously applied, will give the investor a good chance of success. My formula contains no magic, no "open, Sesame"; rather, its ingredients comprise the important aspects of both the psychological and the statistical findings we have viewed to date.

Psychological Variables in the Investment Formula

To be of value to the investor, a practical stock market approach must factor into the formula the behavioral and interpretational obstacles we have discussed. This is not done by either EMH or current fundamental investment theory.

To convert our previous discussion into a simple algebraic formula, EMH states that most sophisticated investors always properly determine the value of a security (V) by the price (D) they assign to it. At any time, $D = V$.

We have seen how value can appear to change with kaleidoscopic rapidity. A slight tilt of the investor's views and an entirely different pattern is formed, with a new and often drastically altered price structure. Both the investor's current psychological reaction to the individual security and to the market, and his interpretation of information, affect value. The price of a security (D) is a function (f) of actual value (V), the interpretation of information (I), and the investor's current psychological state (P). The formula is thus expressed as

$$D = f(VIP)$$

The two complex interacting variables I and P can very often be the dominant influence on price. Value is extremely elusive, as we have often seen. Incorrect interpretation of information and emotional factors can carry price far away from actual worth. The IP variables are most often influenced in the direction of current market movement.

Overlooking the important influence of these variables very often leads to below-average market results. As currently practiced, too much fundamental analysis concentrates on exactness, particularly in the building of near-term earnings estimates. The tremendous difficulties of interpretation in a complex, rapidly changing environment are not fully considered. We have seen that under such conditions, it is difficult if not impossible to make such precise estimates consistently. Yet a major portion of current institutional research tends to exaggerate the importance of this one factor of stock evaluation while downgrading all others.

There are limits to forecasting ability beyond which even the most astute investor cannot go. Because these limits are not recognized by many, powerful behavioral reactions are initiated when such estimates prove inaccurate. The interpretational and psychological reactions normally work in the same direction at a given time and tend to magnify any change in actual value. Thus, if actual value changes by only 5 or 10%, the *IP* change can be many times this amount. An excellent example of how rapidly the *IP* variables can change is provided by the price movements of popular favorites, shown in Table 22. From a price/earnings multiple that averaged 59.8 for the 27 stocks in this sample at their 1971–1973 highs, the average multiple declined 84% to the 1974 low. Was this a proper reflection of new conditions? Hardly, for within a matter of months the average multiple of the group had more than doubled, with little change in underlying fundamental prospects. The 1975 high P/E ratio of the group was 23.6, 146% above the 1974 low of 9.6. It would appear that most practitioners and researchers do not take account of these major attitude changes, which culminate in mammoth price movements with only minor changes in basic facts.

The *P* of the equation is devilishly tricky, and can often have a substantial and at times overwhelming influence on *I*. In periods of ebullience or panic, *P* dominates both *I* and *V*. In more normal times, *V* and *I* can be more important than *P*. We have seen the constant recurrence of this theme throughout this book. *V*, although appearing almost invisible for long periods of time, is eventually the determining factor on stock prices. Value (*V*) can never be measured precisely and is constantly changing with conditions, but it exists in the stock market as surely as it exists in any other economic aspect of our lives. If there were no such thing as real value, a peanut butter sandwich might cost as much as a house in the country, which in anything but wildly abnormal circumstances is not the case. Because of the rapidity of price change, value often appears ephemeral and evasive. Still, like gravity, its tug normally restores prices to levels of real worth.

To understand why fundamental analysis as it is usually practiced may not adequately cope with the problems outlined, let us look more closely at how a practitioner of this art determines the value of a particular security. Both EMH researchers and fundamental theoreticians agree that the future course of earnings and dividends growth is eventually the most important determinant of stock prices. One of the most rigorous methods of security analysis used to determine true value is the intrinsic value theory. According to this theory, a security is worth the discounted present value of the future stream of dividends.

In order to arrive at this future stream of dividends, the competent analyst makes an exhaustive study of the company. He carefully assesses its history and performance record, measuring competitiveness, growth, and profitability of the business. He makes a thorough analysis of the company's position in its major markets and the probable rate of their expansion. He considers the quality of its management, the location and condition of plants, its expansion plans, and the adequacy of its financial resources. He tries to appraise the soundness of the accounting and, by applying various ratios, determines its financial strength. The analyst also uses a large number of other ratios to assess the profitability of the basic business. Two of the most commonly used are the pre-tax margins (income before taxes as a percentage of sales) and the return on equity (the net profit as a percentage of net worth).*

The analyst then makes his earnings estimates for the future, usually starting with a sales forecast. Using his knowledge of the company and its position in the industry, he projects the profitability of these sales. This will be reflected in the pre-tax margin. He then calculates the estimated tax rate, the earnings, and the earnings per share. Based on his estimates of the probable financial strength of the company and his knowledge of the past pattern of dividend payments, he estimates the percentage of earnings that will be paid out as dividends, called the "payout ratio."

Professor J. Peter Williamson states that this theory, or one closely akin to it, is the heart of the fundamental or value approach. Williamson presents a formula that discounts

*The higher these ratios are and the more consistent their record from year to year, the more highly regarded the company usually is. These ratios can vary from about 10% or less for the average company to 15 or 20% more for the supergrowth companies.

the future stream of earnings and dividends to arrive at the present worth of a stock.[1] The formula, developed by Nicholas Molodovsky, the late editor of the *Financial Analysts Journal,* is written as follows:

$$V = \frac{e_1 \times M}{1 + R} + \frac{e_2 \times M}{(1 + R)^2} + \frac{e_3 \times M}{(1 + R)^3} + \cdots +$$

and so on,* where

V = present value of stock
e_1 = earnings per share in first year
e_2 = earnings per share in second year
e_3 = earnings per share in third year
M = dividend payout ratio
R = rate of return the investor demands on his investment (the discount rate)

To illustrate, let us assume a company earns $5.00 per share and will increase its earnings at a 12% rate in the first several years, the payout ratio is 50%, and the discount rate selected is 10%. The first three years of the equation would then read

$$V = \frac{5.00 \times 0.5}{1 + 0.10} + \frac{5.60 \times 0.5}{(1 + 0.10)^2} + \frac{6.27 \times 0.5}{(1 + 0.10)^3}$$

$$= 2.27 + 2.31 + 2.36$$

The present value of the first three years is $6.94. To get the present worth of the stock, one would discount this stream over the company's entire expected life.

The method is extremely logical; the flaw is that people often are not. There is a dangerous false precision in this approach, for it appears that we can accurately calibrate value to two or three decimal places. What is overlooked is that in arriving at an earnings estimate, hundreds of implicit assumptions are made far into the future, as we discussed

---

*The exposition is actually more complex, for it is assumed that earnings will grow at one rate for a specified period of years and at another rate beyond that period. For our purposes, the full mathematical exposition is unnecessary.

in detail in Chapter 10. The assumptions are heavily colored by the current state of psychology for both the individual stock and the market. Thus, the *IP* variables will differ drastically with changed circumstances and will affect both future earnings estimates (e) and the expected rate of return (R), if not perhaps the dividend payout ratio (M) itself.

Professor Williamson demonstrated this point by using his formula to determine a value for IBM. Initially, he forecast earnings increases at a 16% rate for 10 years and 2% thereafter. Using a 40% dividend payout ratio and a 7% discount rate, he got a value of $172.90, about half of the then-current market price (in 1968). Extending the 16% growth rate for 20 years, the value became $432.66, well above the market. Changing the discount rate to 10%, the value became $205.73, again well under the market. Raising the discount rate to 16% and changing the growth rate to 18% for 30 years, with residual growth of 4% thereafter, the value became $151.21.

Williamson clearly shows how much intrinsic value can swing with the changes of these variables. We sometimes tend to think investment decisions are as clear-cut as business school problems. No matter how complicated the question, there is usually an optimal answer found by working in a straight line from fixed assumptions. The investment decision, however, requires a large number of assumptions about the economy, the stock market, the industry, rates of growth, competition, profit margins, earnings, dividends, and rate of return, each of which allows a wide range of possibilities. Because forecasting is so imprecise and is dependent on numerous rapidly changing underlying variables, the analyst has wide latitude in his choices. In the end nothing prevents changes in the underlying *IP* factors that influence these assumptions significantly.

In determining a value by intrinsic formulas, the investor may be heavily influenced by subjective factors that creep into the assumptions without his being aware of them. He can thus very often mislead himself into believing that his decision is reached on the basis of "the facts," when in reality his choice of assumptions has predetermined what the facts will be. In Professor Williamson's examples, only moderate changes in assumptions for IBM changed the price as much as 186%. The analyst who is optimistic need only extend the number of years IBM will grow at the projected rate, or raise the rate a percentage point or two, lower the discount rate, or increase the payout ratio, and *voilà*! IBM is undervalued. If the prevailing psychology is negative, the process is reversed. An intricate valuation formula is therefore no fortress against subjectivity, for the basic assumptions underlying the most essential calculations are often determined by it.

Because neither professionals nor academics usually place much emphasis on the *I* and *P* variables, I believe there is a far greater opportunity to outperform the market than is generally acknowledged. To understand this more clearly, we must look carefully at what occurs when a "factual" estimate proves incorrect.

Visibility Revisited

What we saw in the groupthink-compliance chapters was that too high a price was consistently paid for current visibility (or the presently forseeable future stream of earnings) in both the concept stocks such as Levitz, Teleprompter, and Damon, and in the large growth stocks. Many professionals believed that forecasts based on current trends could be made with assurance extending well into the future. The cancer of modern investment practice is its absolute obsession with current quarterly and annual earnings, and the downgrading of most other important fundamental evaluation standards. There seems to be an almost mystical belief that if the estimates turn out to be correct, everything else will fall into place. Such security analysis, as numerous critics have argued, may well be incomplete. In the first place, no allowance is made for the information being already fully discounted or overdiscounted by investors. If the stock is at a high P/E multiple, even if earnings forecasts are met, it is very vulnerable because investors' preferences change drastically and P/E multiples can tumble sharply. We also know that earnings forecasts are highly precarious no matter how skilled the practitioner. Visibility is often illusionary. As we have seen in a number of studies, earnings appear to follow a random walk. Disappointing earnings in companies believed to have high visibility often trigger large sell-offs.

We have seen how, in choosing a popular favorite, the projected time span of earnings growth was lengthened many years to justify the price, while if bad news came in, even for a single quarter, the frame of reference usually shifted to the immediate. The inclination of many amateur and professional investors to overemphasize the importance of current prospects in choosing their securities is self-defeating. Of course, one may point to many growth stocks that have done far better than the market averages over the years. The performance of Automatic Data Processing, Burroughs, IBM, Johnson and Johnson, and other such firms seems to justify the soundness of the growth school approach. The problem is that the companies selected are the survivors, not the losers. The original lists were longer and many of the former favorites fell by the wayside.

The brings us back to the evidence presented in the latter part of Chapter 9 which shows that the companies with the best visibility consistently did far worse than the companies that investors considered to have the poorest prospects.

These findings clearly demonstrate that investors have consistently paid too much for companies that appear to have the best prospects at the moment, and with equal consistency react too negatively to companies considered to have the poorest prospects. In the formula $D = f(VIP)$, the IP variables in the favorite companies are repeatedly too high, and are too low in the companies in disfavor. We have also viewed the rapidity with which the self-correction process begins to take effect, usually within a year.

Choosing the favorite stocks leads to consistently inferior results, but this is precisely the game played by a large number of professionals and the public alike. The findings discussed above are impressive evidence that markets are not nearly so efficient as EMH theorists claim. Because people, including professionals, will regularly repeat the same errors, there

is some chance for the investor to outperform the market
if he is aware of these patterns.

A Proposed Investment Strategy

The evidence shows that the odds are heavily stacked
against the investor who purchases stock currently in vogue.
On the other hand, the odds in playing the unpopular low
P/E stocks seem much more on the investor's side.* Like
the song "The World.Turned Upside Down," which the
British regimental bands played when they marched out to
surrender to the Continental Army at Yorktown, the extensive
empirical findings suggest a major realignment of thinking.
The "best" companies frequently seem to make the worst
investments, and the "worst" companies, the best.

Our strategy must be one of avoiding high-multiple growth
and concept stocks. Some coups will be made with them,
but the odds are very much against the individual. Likewise,
we should be very careful about accepting exciting new issues
with little substance. Here, again, the odds appear to strongly
disfavor the investor because such issues can be sold only
in rising markets when speculative fever is increasing. The
conservative investor would do well to avoid them.

The best chance for success definitely appears to be in
selecting large companies currently out of market favor. Far
greater safety exists in choosing major companies, since
relatively few have gone out of business but many have had
substantial price turnarounds. With the constantly shifting
conditions of a dynamic economy, a profitability decline that
appears entirely irreversible can show a substantial reversal
within a short space of time. This self-correction process
goes on with enough regularity so that even though some
companies may fail, enough do unexpectedly well to result
in the bottom P/E multiple group outperforming the other
groups. The companies with the lowest P/Es in the market

---

*I hate to do it, but I must borrow the economist's phrase *et ceterus paribus*
(all else being equal), for the fascinating thing about markets is that if
enough people were to practice this method, it would no longer provide
better results.

have consistently done better than other P/E groups in every study I have been able to locate. How, then, do we choose the "best" large companies in the low P/E ratio group? Again there is no instant answer, for the process can involve the whole field of securities analysis.

The Concept of Earnings Power

The important concept of earnings power is often used in securities analysis. The earnings power of a company is determined by analyzing a company thoroughly, looking at its past record for a number of years, and then making a forecast of the future earnings, usually from projected sales and pre-tax profit margins.* The past earnings record for larger companies usually provides some foundation on which to base future projections. We look at the past, not to predict the following year exactly, but to determine the company's viability and profitability over time.

Stocks quite often trade at extremely low P/E multiples because it is anticipated that their future earnings will decline sharply from levels of the recent past. For example, Mohasco in late 1974 traded as low as 8½, which was four times its 1973 earnings of $2.21. But earnings were expected to decline to under $1.00 for the 1974 year. Based on an estimate of $0.95, the multiple was almost nine times earnings. Mohasco's record looked like this in the 1968–1974 period:

1968	1969	1970	1971	1972	1973	1974
1.96	1.91	1.57	2.07	2.32	2.21	0.93

An average of the period, including the depressed 1974 year, would come to $1.85. The P/E on this average is only 4.3. A number of problems arise when using patterns of earnings from the recent past as a base for determining earnings power. In the case of a rapidly growing company, an average of results in the recent past is usually too conservative. Because

---

*In *The Intelligent Investor*, Graham recommends analyzing the records for the past seven or ten years and then forecasting sales and earnings seven years ahead.

of their high P/E ratios, however, such companies are always eliminated from our approach and this is of no consequence. The second and more important problem is that there may be a permanent decline in the companies' earnings power, justifying the lower market evaluation. While the decline in earnings power is sometimes enduring, in more cases it is not. Large companies have amazing staying power. Favorable events that an investor did not anticipate often enter the competitive picture, causing a resurgence of earnings. It is the constant tendency of the market to overdiscount negative news and then pay handsomely in a reappraisal when this original assessment proved too gloomy. Thus, if a company has a sharp fall-off from a fairly stable level of past earnings, and the market places a low valuation on the depressed earnings, it quite often represents an interesting investment opportunity.

Earnings may drop so sharply that the P/E multiple is still high, even though price has declined significantly. An analysis of such situations is necessary to determine whether the downturn is temporary or permanent. It is unlikely you will get much instructive advice from your financial advisor. The evaluation of companies with earnings declines or losses is complex, and it is probable that most expert thought will conform to the current market opinion and paint an overly negative portrait of the company's prospects. Some experts at the time may even be recommending the sale of such stocks. The investor must use his own judgment of a company's prospects, remembering that most often the market is too pessimistic on this score.

In the case of Mohasco, for example, the company is the nation's largest independent producer of carpets and furniture, solidly entrenched in its major markets. Its finances at the time were reasonably conservative, with its current assets 2.6 times its current liabilities and its long-term debt only 38% of the capital structure at the end of 1974.*

Another measure of a company's worth resides in its

*The capital structure is the book value of the common stock, preferred stock, and bonds of the company. Usually, for an industrial company, debt and preferred stock above 45% of the total are considered high, and when they are above 50% a warning light is flashed.

book value per share (the tangible assets minus the liabilities divided by the number of shares of the company outstanding). Usually, the book value is a conservative figure because the replacement cost of assets, with steadily rising inflation, may be two or three times as high. Book value for most major industrial corporations is normally below market value. However, in a very depressed market the book value can be above the market value, sometimes substantially.

Mohasco in December 1974 had a book value of $24.35 a share, almost triple its market value. The stock had dropped sharply from its high of 48⅝ in 1972. In 1974 it was hit with a serious cost/price squeeze. Costs of synthetic fibers for carpets, and raw materials for furniture, rose rapidly, but the company could not raise its selling prices as quickly because of slackening demand and contracted future shipments at fixed prices. The company also changed its methods of inventory accounting to LIFO from FIFO.* The combination of these two factors reduced Mohasco's 1974 net to 93¢/share. The market took too dim a view of the company's prospects. By early 1976 it was trading at $23, up over 170% from its 1974 low and about triple the increase in the S&P 500 for the same period. As it turned out, Mohasco earned $1.87 in 1975, fairly close to its average of $1.84 for the 1969–1974 period.

Values such as Mohasco can often be discovered by utilizing such earnings-power analysis. Two problems arise to complicate successful application of this approach. The first is that the investor must have a comfortable working knowledge of both accounting and fundamental analysis. The second, and to me more important, caveat is that too many subjective

*The last-in–first-out (LIFO) method of inventory accounting as contrasted to the first-in–first-out (FIFO) method. Under LIFO, the most recent cost of labor and materials in the units of a product sold is charged against the sale. Under FIFO, the oldest cost of labor and materials of the units in inventory still on hand is charged against the sale. The difference can sometimes be substantial because, in periods of rapidly rising prices, the new unit cost may be significantly higher than that for the units produced some years earlier. A switch from FIFO to LIFO in an inflationary environment thus can sharply raise the cost of goods sold and thereby sharply decreasing profitability significantly, which is what occurred with Mohasco.

factors can filter into these earnings forecasts, causing them to swing widely with varying circumstances. If unclouded by emotional biases, fundamental analysis can be an extremely effective tool, but it can often be misapplied. For the truly conservative investor, unless he more fully understands the nuances of such analysis, it may prove disappointing.

The strategy that would appear the safest, from the results of the tests we have examined, is to buy very large companies at low P/Es relative to the market. One might attempt to buy the lowest P/Es of the Dow Jones Industrial Average or of companies in the S&P 500.

Our investment strategy hinges on the assumption that the economy that we are dealing with is not materially different from the one of the immediate past, nor has the existing political or sociological framework changed significantly. That being the case then major companies such as those represented by the S&P 500 will continue to be expanding and profitable on the whole, and expectations will continue to change far more drastically than actual events.

It is true that mechanical guidelines, such as the P/E rule of thumb, will occasionally prove inadequate, but the mechanical failures will be far fewer than the behavioral errors involved in fundamental analysis. To take a number of specific examples of the application of these rules, you may recall that the auto and tire companies traded at extremely depressed prices in late 1973 and through 1974 as a result of investor beliefs that the energy crisis would drastically change our transportation patterns. Even at that time, such views appeared too alarmist. While it was true auto sales and average car usage declined for some months, the time period was certainly not long enough to determine that a major long-term change in driving habits was occurring. Yet, the stocks in these industries dropped very sharply, apparently anticipating the very worst possibilities. When by 1975 and early 1976 it became evident these fears were greatly exaggerated, auto and tire stocks appreciated far faster than the averages.*

---

*Using the low P/E approach, the big three auto producers could have been bought in 1973, but not in the following year. In 1974, sharply declining

The investor willing to buy the low P/E giants at a discount from the market often benefits from both improved earnings following depressed levels and a higher multiple on these earnings. In 1974 the earnings of Goodyear, the country's largest tire and rubber fabricator, dropped from $2.22 a share the previous year to $2.04. At its low, the stock traded at 11³/₄, or at 5.3 times these depressed earning (the average of five years, 1970–1974, had been $2.29). This was one of the lower multiples in the Dow Jones Industrial Average at the time. In 1975 it earned $2.24, and its P/E multiple at year's end had risen to almost ten times these higher earnings; by then, the market was already anticipating further earnings increases in 1976. By the end of 1975, Goodyear's price had increased 100% from its low versus 48% for the Dow Jones Industrial Average.

When the market loses faith in a former favorite, it will often drive it to extremely low price levels as a result of both interpretational and psychological overreactions. A good illustration is Honeywell, the second largest computer manufacturer after IBM (although a very distant second, with under 10% of the market). A number of its divisions have always appealed to investors, and even before it doubled the size of its computer operations in 1970 by acquiring the loss-ridden GE division, the company commanded a high P/E multiple. By 1972, when it appeared that the computer division was beginning to show a major increase in profitability, the stock traded as high as $170 or 41.7 times that year's earnings. But then Murphy's Law came into effect—anything bad that could happen did happen. For a variety of reasons, including strikes, tight money, the introduction of a new line of computers, and the sharp recession, earnings proved disappointing in both computer and noncomputer operations from the latter part of 1972 to 1974. In 1974, earnings

---

earnings resulted in their having P/Es equal to or above the P/E of the S&P 500. If we had bought the market bellwether GM in the high 40s in 1973 (when it was trading at a P/E of about 5, well under that of the S&P 500) we would have unhappily watched its price decline to as low as 28⁷/₈ in 1974. But by adhering to our rule and continuing to hold the stock (see footnote on page 269), we would have been well rewarded. By the spring of 1976 it rose to as high as $74.00.

dropped to $3.74 from $4.79 the previous year. Because Honeywell was an institutional favorite, the collapse of the stock was more dramatic than the general market drop. Honeywell declined from its 1972 high of $170 to 17½ by late 1974. Rumors swept the Street: The company was headed for bankruptcy*; Honeywell would be forced to dispose of its computer business. Traditionally yielding about 1%, Honeywell at its low provided a return of over 8%. Its P/E multiple on depressed 1974 earnings had declined to under 5. Little tangible evidence existed for this dour market appraisal. In the subsequent market recovery although there was only moderate improvement in the company's operations and outlook, Honeywell rose as high as 58 in early 1976, some 231% above its low and significantly more than the popular averages.

All three cases are good examples of the exceptional value possible with the low P/E multiple approach. Since many professionals would have advised investors to avoid these stocks, we now face the important question of how best to utilize expert advice.

Using Expert Advice

If psychological influences play an important and often incorrect role in professional conclusions, the investor cannot place his major emphasis on the expert's opinions. This is not to say that the expert's knowledge of a company or an industry may not be thorough and in some cases outstanding. But we have found that the expert, like everyone else, can be swayed by the current emotion of the marketplace. In periods of either ebullience or deep gloom, his projections can often by influenced in the direction of current market movements, thus tending to be too extreme. In using expert knowledge, the investor must substitute his own judgmental factor. The expert might have been quite right in saying

---

*The emptiness of the bankruptcy rumor is indicated by the fact that an issue at that time of a subsidiary company's debentures was given an A rating (above average) by a major corporate bond-rating service.

that the immediate outlook for Honeywell and Goodyear was not encouraging. The investor must determine whether the earnings power of these companies is permanently destroyed. The broker or the broker's research department should be of some help in providing him with details of the company's financial position and its competitive muscle within its industry.* The odds are very much in favor of the investor who buys these large low P/Es at a significant discount from the P/E of the average sizable company in the marketplace. The investor who chooses "reverse" tactics in this manner will probably be right far more often than wrong.

The careful investor should also begin to record the results of the professionals who give him advice. All the advice of the advisor should be measured and then a relationship established with the advisor who has the best record over a long period of time. This precludes advice from professionals who simply happen to have several winners in a boiling stock market. Remembering Galbraith's dictum, "genius is a rising stock market," the more speculative the investment in such an atmosphere, the more brilliant the advisor appears. The investor should try to weigh all recommendations made to him by each advisor for at least a five-year period covering both rising and falling markets.

It is also important to realize that some stocks are far more volatile than others. They will perform better in an up-market and worse in a down-market.† Thus, if an advisor with a number of highly volatile stocks beats the S&P 500 significantly in a rising market, this record is not impressive by itself. Too often in the past when the market turned down, the client eventually lost not only his profits but also a good part of his original investment. To judge success, at least a full market cycle (both rising and falling markets) is required.

*But again, the interpretation can suffer from either positive or negative psychological bias.
†See the discussion on beta in Chapter 2. A number of investment services measure beta. The *Value Line Survey*, for example, provides the beta measurement on over 1,400 widely held companies.

The individual who wishes to undertake this approach would do best to find an advisor with a basic investment philosophy attuned to his own. But here again the advisor's performance must be carefully evaluated.

Other Components of a Successful Strategy

As has been stated previously, the less experienced the investor, the larger the companies he should invest in. Not only do large corporations have less chance of failing entirely, but an improvement in their results is noticed by the market more quickly than for medium-size or smaller companies. There is also another advantage. A major corporation with a long record is usually subject to relatively less accounting gimmickry. This provides some protection for an investor not sophisticated in this field.

Accounting is a complex and often baffling discipline, to most people. The investor should use expert advice, where available, to determine how conservative the accounting of a company really is. One of my own rules of thumb for small and medium-size companies is to carefully scrutinize the number of footnotes to the financial statements. If there are too many, or they appear to be unfathomable, an amber light should be flashed. While this method is somewhat primitive, in view of the evidence it is better that the unsophisticated investor depend on such intuitive reactions and stay clear of medium-size or small companies with complex accounting.

Diversification—An Essential Ingredient

The proposed approach recognizes that our information on a company can never be complete. It acknowledges that it is almost impossible to continually know more about a company than many other investors. Even if we do know more in one case, it is likely we shall know less in the next, so that on average we shall know about the same as most other astute investors. Our approach is not to know more, but to react less emotionally to both positive and negative information. We are striving for a balanced assessment in an environment that continually goes to extremes. Even so, we must recognize the method is not foolproof. Any single company selected in the manner outlined may turn out to be a failure.

Interpretational and psychological problems are too complex for an investor to choose stocks with absolute confidence. Too many things can go wrong. It is thus essential to diversify extensively so that bad choices should be offset by a predominance of good ones. A portfolio should ideally consist of 15 to 20 stocks in a minimum of ten or more industries. The stocks listed in Table 25 were selected according to the principles outlined in previous sections. Most of the companies are very large. Ten were ranked by *Fortune* among the 100 largest industrial corporations in the country and four more were in the top 500. INA, not included in the industrial rankings, is a giant in the insurance industry. Only one company, Dennison Manufacturing, is not listed in the top 500 industrials. All have sales of over $150 million. The portfolio is also a widely diversified one among 15 different industries.

The investor who adopts the policy of buying a portfolio of well-diversified, large-company, low P/E stocks must restructure it periodically as the P/Es of particular companies rise to the market P/E or above.* Such stocks might be sold annually and replaced by other large low P/E issues, making sure that the principle of wide industry diversification is not discarded. This approach is designed for the investor who wishes to always remain fully invested and does not wish to attempt to outguess the market.

Market timing, the attempt to forecast market movements in order to buy or sell stocks more advantageously, is appealing to many investors. If successfully implemented, it can greatly enhance investment results, but it is difficult to practice and introduces a much higher element of risk. If the investor misjudges the direction of the market, he will do worse than

---

*If the multiple has increased as a result of a decline in earnings as in the General Motors example, this procedure should not be followed.

TABLE 25

Company	1974 Sales ($ millions)	1974 Earnings ($ millions)	1974 $ EPS*	Fortune 500 Rank	12/7/74 P/E (Latest 12-month earnings at the time)
Alcoa	2,727	173	5.14	65	5
Bendix	2,481	76	4.65	77	4
Beth St.	5,381	342	7.85	21	4
Control Data	1,085	35	1.22	187	5
Dennison Mfg.	245	11	3.63	555	3
Exxon	42,061	3,142	14.04	1	4
Firestone	3,676	154.0	2.71	40	5
Goodyear	5,256	158	2.18	23	4
INA†	1,466	80	2.10	—	6
Johns-Manville	1,106	72	3.88	181	5
Jim Walter	1,293	63	3.65	155	6
Mohasco	552	6	.93	315	4
Monsanto	3,498	323	9.25	43	4
Phelps Dodge	1,026	113	5.47	195	4
RCA	4,594	113	1.45	31	5
Reynolds Metals	1,993	111	6.23	95	5
TRW	2,486	101	3.05	76	2
Union Carbide	5,320	907	8.69	22	4
U.S. Steel	9,186	635	11.72	12	5
Westinghouse	6,466	28	.31	19	6

*EPS, earnings per share.
†Premiums written.

simply buying and holding stocks. I have known some outstanding money managers who were exceptionally competent in their selection of stocks but who, nevertheless, often misjudged the direction of the market. A more conservative investor should avoid market-timing plans, changing the composition of his portfolio only as the P/Es of individual holdings increase relative to the market.

The Cold-Turkey Road to Success

Because the major barriers are psychological, the best chance an investor has is to stand apart from popular thinking. He must be able to forgo the thrill of being in unison with the market, in agreement with expert opinion and with the exciting, seemingly surefire ideas currently in vogue. He must give up the thrill of playing an absorbing game in good company. This is no small sacrifice. To own the "right" stocks in a rising market is a heady experience. There is a wonderful blend of monetary gain and ego satisfaction in being right in a popular manner.

Informed opinion often stands behind the current course of the market, and so to stand apart means to disagree with most expert advice. As a people, Americans have become increasingly dependent on experts. The investor who wishes to succeed must steel himself to assume the posture of a financial loner. Undoubtedly the stocks he doesn't buy will perform better in the short run than will the unpopular ones that he chooses. If he buys stocks in a bad market, people will consider his actions rash. When he discusses his preferences, people may raise their eyebrows at his seeming simplemindedness, for everyone can see that the obvious course is *exactly* the opposite. Not much excitement can be gleaned from the strategy being outlined. Not only does the lone wolf have to buck the opinions of most other investors, including experts, but he must also be constantly able to reassure himself that the course adopted is sound despite the seemingly endless evidence to the contrary.

Man is a social animal. To succeed, the investor has to be able to withstand the tremendous pressures leading to conformity. He will have no positive reinforcement in the course he adopts, but will instead face a continuing flow of negative feedback from the market, from experts, and from groups of people he respects. For the professional, the pressures described in Chapters 7 and 8 make the problem far more acute. The reader may feel a little like the patient whose doctor has just recommended that he give up sex to preserve his health. Some of us might just prefer to die happy.

Another Alternative

The independent procedure, if it is to be used at all, must be applied rigorously. This is difficult, but if properly carried out, the rewards appear far better than average over time.

Some readers may question their ability to exhibit such psychological independence and may also conclude that their financial knowledge is not sufficient to allow them to attempt it. If so, there is still another quite acceptable way for them to participate in the stock market, that is, through no-load mutual funds with broad, widely diversified portfolios.* Buying these funds avoids the commission charges of the normal mutual fund. Since we have seen that there is no evidence of superior performance by the front-end-load funds,† such a course is both reasonably safe and should, with a widely diversified fund, provide results not too dissimilar from the market's.‡

A broad portfolio of stocks can also be acquired through the purchase of a closed-end investment company. These companies usually trade at a discount from asset value. The

*If any random walkers remain at this point, I acknowledge I am steering very close to your beliefs on this issue.
†This was one of the findings of the exhaustive Friend, Blume, and Crockett report referred to in Chapter 2.
‡Information on no-load mutuals can be obtained by writing to the No-Load Mutual Fund Association, 475 Park Avenue South, New York, N.Y. 10016. The telephone number is (212) 532-8811.

TABLE 26

Fund	Asset Size, $ millions	Average Discount 5 Years, to 1975, %
Adams Express	$180.9	8.2%
General American Investors	96.7	14.4
Lehman Corporation	412.3	16.6
Niagara Share Corporation	18.8	4.8
Tri-Continental Corporation	567.8	16.4
U.S. & Foreign Securities	102.1	16.4

Source: Wiesenberger & Co. Inc., *Investment Companies Survey*, 1976.

average discount for the past five years is given in Table 26.

The discounts are given on a weekly basis in *The Wall Street Journal, The New York Times, Barron's,* and other publications. If the discount is larger than normal, the closed-end funds may provide interesting buying opportunities. However, since the funds are listed on stock exchanges, buyers must take into consideration the commission charges that must be paid in both buying and selling.

A Final Word

As I have noted earlier, the stock selection methodology I propose is primarily mechanical, and purposefully so, for it best checks our emotions. These emotional reactions are overwhelmingly the most important source of stock market errors. Professionals utilizing far more sophisticated methods than I suggest here have most often failed because the methods themselves were not adequately structured to eliminate emotional biases. Because we tend to constantly overreact to events, a mechanical formula designed to moderate such overreactions will work, provided the recent past is not too different from what is to come. The future for any single company or industry may certainly be different, but for the economy and overall industry, radical change is unlikely. Years of sweeping changes will occur, and the formula will not function, but such years are very rare. The odds appear very much with the investor who uses the method proposed.

Investing is a truly fascinating game, one in which we should all act totally rational, but often do not. Each of us has an instinct for gambling, an excitement induced by risk and a desire to be successful in the approved manner. Human nature is the major deterrent to our carrying out a successful investment program, even though many of us are extremely well trained and have planned our strategies in detail.

I am often reminded of the famous German "swinging door" plan that von Schlieffen prepared in the 1890s for use against France in the event the two nations ever warred again. It was terribly intricate and had many thousands of details on virtually every aspect of assembly, movement, timing, and supply of millions of men, down to the most minute item. The plan was thoroughly rehearsed for years prior to 1914, and nothing was overlooked in the attempt to ensure its proper functioning. And yet, when the war with France did break out in 1914, the plan was abandoned after the initial stages. According to the plan, it was crucial that the strength of the German armies be concentrated on the right. This wing would encircle the French in a wide arc reaching to the North Sea. In von Schlieffen's words, "the last man on the right will brush his arm against the sea." Von Schlieffen feared the tendency to abandon the plan in the heat of action, and among his last words was the warning not to weaken the right. But the right was weakened, exactly as von Schlieffen feared, and the armies of this wing drifted inward toward Paris, allowing the French to sharply counterattack at the Marne. This deviation from the plan caused the stalemate of trench warfare over the next four years. Even the absolutely efficient German general staff could not adhere to the plan it considered essential to win the war.

Thus, for the investor, a great challenge is posed. The plan for success is relatively easy to design. Its implementation, however, depends on a very independent and determined nature. To those of you who, like me, have the gaming spirit in your blood and find the challenge fascinating, good luck.

References _____

Chapter 1
The Riddle of Professional Investing
1. *Money Market Directory* (New York: Money Market Directories, Inc., 1973).
2. Peter F. Drucker, "American Business's New Owners," *The Wall Street Journal*, May 27, 1976.
3. David B. Bostian, Jr., "The De-Institutionalization of the Stock Market in American Society," *Financial Analysts Journal*, Nov.–Dec. 1973.
4. "The Top Ten Stocks," *Institutional Investor*, Jan. 1972.
5. Charles J. Elia, "Heard on the Street," *The Wall Street Journal*, Feb. 11, 1975.
6. Frank Russell and Company, Tacoma, Washington, 1976.
7. John Quirt, "Benjamin Graham, the Grandfather of Investment Value, Is Still Concerned," *Institutional Investor*, April 1974.
8. President's Message in the 1966 Annual Report of the Ford Foundation.
9. *SEC Statistical Bulletin*, April 23, 1974.
10. *Public Transactions Study, 1974*, New York Stock Exchange.
11. "Look Who's Talking," *Fortune*, Aug. 1967.
12. "Ford Foundation to Halve Staff Over Next Three Years," *The New York Times*, March 31, 1975.
13. "Fiduciary Giants," *The Wall Street Journal*, Jan. 7, 1975.
14. *Forbes*, July 1, 1975.
15. Ibid.
16. A. F. Ehrbar, "Index Funds—An Idea Whose Time Has Come," *Fortune*, June 1976.

17. Benjamin Graham, David Dodd, and Sidney Cottle, *Security Analysis,* 4th ed. (New York: McGraw-Hill, 1962), p. 740.

18. Irwin Friend, Marshall Blume, and Jean Crockett, *Mutual Funds and Other Institutional Investors: A New Perspective,* a Twentieth Century Fund Study (New York: McGraw-Hill, 1970).

Chapter 2
The Academic Onslaught

1. Paul H. Cootner (ed.), *The Random Character of Stock Market Prices* (Cambridge, Mass.: MIT Press, 1964), pp. 17–78. (A translation by A. James Boness from Louis Bachelier, *Théorie de la Speculation,* Gauthier-Villars, Paris, 1900.)

2. Harry V. Roberts, "Stock Market Patterns and Financial Analysis: Methodological Suggestions," *Journal of Finance,* March 1959.

3. M. F. M. Osborne, "Brownian Motion in the Stock Market," *Operations Research,* March–April 1959.

4. Fisher Black, "Implications of the Random Walk Hypothesis for Portfolio Management," *Financial Analysts Journal,* March–April 1971.

5. John Magee, *The General Semantics of Wall Street,* 6th ed. (Springfield, Mass.: John Magee, 1967), p. 242.

6. John Brooks, *Seven Fat Years* (New York: Harper & Row, 1958), p. 158.

7. Samuel Nelson, *The ABC of Stock Speculation* (Wells, Vt.: Fraser Publishing Co., 1964, reproduction).

8. Mansfield Charting Service (New York City).

9. John L. Springer, *If They're So Smart How Come You're Not Rich?* (Chicago: Henry Regnery, 1971), pp. 56–57.

10. Eugene F. Fama, "The Behavior of Stock Market Prices," *Journal of Business,* January 1965).

11. ———, "Efficient Capital Markets: A Review of Theory and Empirical Work," *Journal of Finance,* May 1970.

12. ———, "The Behavior of Stock Market Prices," op. cit.

13. Fisher Black, op. cit.

14. Burton G. Malkiel, *A Random Walk Down Wall Street* (New

York: W. W. Norton, 1973), p. 126.

15. Ibid., p. 127.

16. Fisher Black, op. cit.

17. Eugene F. Fama, "Efficient Capital Markets," op. cit.

18. J. G. Cragg and Burton G. Malkiel, "The Consensus and Accuracy of Some Predictions of the Growth of Corporate Earnings," *Journal of Finance,* March 1968.

19. I. M. D. Little, "Higgledly Piggledly Growth," *Bulletin of the Oxford University Institute of Economics and Statistics,* November 1962.

20. I. M. D. Little and A. C. Rayner, *Higgledly Piggledly Growth Again* (Oxford: Basil Blackwell, 1966).

21. Richard A. Brealey, *An Introduction to Risk and Return from Common Stocks* (Cambridge, Mass.: MIT Press, 1968).

22. James H. Lorie and Mary T. Hamilton, *The Stock Market: Theories and Evidence* (Homewood, Ill.: Dow Jones-Irwin, Inc., 1973), pp. 71ff.

23. Robert Hagin and Chris Mader, *The New Science of Investing* (Homewood, Ill.: Dow Jones-Irwin, Inc., 1973), p. 88.

24. Irwin Friend, Marshall Blume, and Jean Crockett, *Mutual Funds and Other Institutional Investors: A New Perspective,* a Twentieth Century Fund Study (New York: McGraw-Hill, 1970), pp. 56, 60–63.

25. Eugene F. Fama, "Efficient Capital Markets," op. cit.

26. Ibid., and James H. Lorie and Mary T. Hamilton, op. cit., pp. 83–87.

27. Roy Ball and Phillip Brown, "An Empirical Evaluation of Accounting Income Numbers," *Journal of Accounting Research,* Fall 1968.

28. Myron S. Scholes, "The Market for Securities: Substitution Versus Price Pressure and the Effects of Information on Share Prices," *Journal of Business,* April 1972.

29. J. Peter Williamson, *Investments—New Analytic Techniques* (New York: Praeger Publishers, Inc., 1974), p. 184.

30. Eugene F. Fama, "Efficient Capital Markets," op. cit.

31. James H. Lorie and Victor Niederhoffer, "Predictive and Statistical Properties of Insider Trading," *Journal of Law and Economics,* Vol. 11 (1968).

32. A. F. Ehrbar, "Index Funds—An Idea Whose Time Has Come," *Fortune,* June 1976.

Chapter 3
Bubbles, Bubbles, Bubbles

1. Gustave Le Bon, *The Crowd* (New York: Viking Press, 1960), pp. 23, 27, 30.
2. Ibid., pp. 41, 62, 66.
3. Charles Mackay, *Extraordinary Popular Delusions and the Madness of Crowds* (New York: The Noonday Press, 1974), p. 55. Originally published in London in 1841 by Richard Bentley.
4. Ibid., pp. xix–xx.
5. Frederick Lewis Allen, *Only Yesterday* (New York: Harper & Row, 1931), p. 280.
6. Calvin Coolidge in a speech to the Society of American Newspaper Editors, Jan. 17, 1925.
7. John Kenneth Galbraith, *The Great Crash* (Boston: Houghton Mifflin Co., 1961), p. 9.

The following publications have also been used in preparing this chapter:

Angly, Edward, *Oh Yeah.* New York: Viking Press, 1931.
Brooks, John, *Once in Gloconda.* New York: Harper & Row, Colophon Books, 1970.
Chandler, Lester V., *Benjamin Strong: Central Banker.* Washington, D.C.: Brookings Institution, 1954.
Clough, Shepard B., *European Economic History: The Economic Development of Western Civilization,* 2nd ed. New York: McGraw-Hill, 1968.
Cowing, Cedrick B., *Populists, Plungers, and Progressives.* Princeton, N.J.: Princeton University Press, 1965.
Cowles, Virginia, *South Sea, the Great Swindle.* London: Crowley Feature, 1960.
Durant, Will and Ariel, *The Age of Voltaire.* New York: Simon & Schuster, 1965.
Lynd, Robert S. and Helen M., *Middletown: A Study of American Culture.* New York: Harcourt, Brace, 1929.

Melville, Lewis, *The South Sea Bubble*. London: Burt Franklin, 1968.

The New York Times, 1927–1932.

Posthumus, N. W., "The Tulip Mania in Holland in the Years 1636 and 1637," in *The Sixteenth and Seventeenth Centuries*. Warren C. Scoville, J. Claybouch, and T. La Force, eds. Lexington, Mass.: D. C. Heath and Company, 1969.

Rogers, Donald I., *The Day the Market Crashed*. New Rochelle, N.Y.: Arlington House, 1971.

Sakolski, A. M., *The Great American Land Bubble*. New York: Harper & Row, 1932.

Sobel, Robert, *The Great Bull Market*. New York: W. W. Norton, 1968.

———, *The Money Manias*. New York: Weybright and Talley, Inc., 1973.

Thomas, Dana L., *The Plungers and the Peacocks*. New York: G. P. Putnam & Sons, 1967.

Winkleman, Barnie F., *Ten Years of Wall Street*. New York: John C. Winslow, 1932.

Zumthor, Paul, *Daily Life in Rembrandt's Holland*. New York: The Macmillan Co., 1963.

Chapter 4
The Tulips of the Sixties

1. "The Great Corporate Talent Hunt," *Forbes,* Sept. 15, 1961.
2. "The Money Men," *Forbes,* Jan. 15, 1969. An interview with William Berkley.
3. Israel Shenker, "Galbraith: "29 Repeats Itself Today," *The New York Times,* May 3, 1970.

The following publications have also been used in preparing this chapter:

Adler, Bill, *The Wall Street Reader*. New York: World Publishing Co., 1972.

Baruch, Hurd, *Wall Street Security and Risk*. New York: Penguin Books, 1972.

Brooks, John, *Seven Fat Years*. New York: Harper & Row, 1958.

The Editors of Fortune Magazine, *The Conglomerate Commotion.* New York: Viking Press, 1970.

Kaplan, Gilbert, and Chris Welles, *The Money Managers.* New York: Random House, 1969.

Regan, Donald T., *A View from the Street.* New York: New American Library, 1972.

Shulman, Martin, *Anyone Can Make a Million.* New York: McGraw-Hill, 1966.

Smith, Adam, *The Money Game.* New York: Dell Publishing Co., 1969.

———, *Supermoney.* New York: Popular Library, 1973.

Tobias, Andrew, *The Funny Money Game.* Chicago: Playboy Press, 1971.

Chapter 5
A Poisonous Competitive Environment

1. Irving L. Janis, *Victims of Groupthink* (Boston: Houghton Mifflin Co., 1972), p. 3.
2. Ibid.
3. Ibid., p. 9.
4. Ibid., pp. 11, 13.
5. Ibid., p. 197.
6. John Quirt, "Confessions of an Underperformer," *Institutional Investor,* July 1973.
7. "The Splitting Sweepstakes," *Institutional Investor,* Dec. 1974.
8. Edward Malca, *Proceedings,* hearings by the Bentsen Committee, Subcommittee on Financial Markets, U.S. Senate Committee on Finance, 93rd Congress, 2nd Session, on S2787 and S2842 (Washington: D.C.: U.S. Government Printing Office).
9. "Are the Institutions Wrecking Wall Street?" *Business Week,* June 2, 1973.
10. Roger G. Kennedy, "The Uses and Abuses of Performance Measurement," *Institutional Investor,* Nov. 1973.
11. Nancy Belliveau, "Are Pension Administrators Monitoring Their Managers to Death?" *Institutional Investor,* Jan. 1974.
12. Ibid.

13. Ibid.
14. Nancy Belliveau, "Why Pension Funds Are Firing Their Money Managers," *Institutional Investor,* Feb. 1974.
15. Ibid.
16. Nancy Belliveau, "Are Pension Administrators Monitoring Their Managers to Death?" op. cit.
17. Ibid.
18. John Quirt, op. cit.
19. ———, "Benjamin Graham, the Grandfather of Investment Value, Is Still Concerned," *Institutional Investor,* April 1974.
20. John Maynard Keynes, *The General Theory of Employment, Interest and Money* (New York: Harcourt Brace Jovanovich, Inc., 1969), p. 156.
21. Ibid., p. 158.
22. *Wall Street Transcript,* Sept. 23, 1974.
23. Christopher Elias, *Fleecing the Lambs* (New York: Fawcett World Library, A Crest Book, 1971), p. 104.
24. Burton Malkiel, *A Random Walk Down Wall Street* (New York: W. W. Norton, 1973), pp. 145–148.
25. Fred Bleakley, "End of an Era," *Institutional Investor,* Feb. 1972.
26. Dana L. Thomas, "Analysts Insecurity," *Barron's,* May 27, 1974.
27. Dan Dorfman, "Why Can't Research Directors Hold Their Jobs?" *Institutional Investor,* Oct. 1973.
28. Reba White, "Are the Days of Superspecialization Numbered?" *Institutional Investor,* Oct. 1974.
29. "1974: The Year Stock Picks Didn't Matter So Much," *Institutional Investor,* Oct. 1974.

Chapter 6
A Flourishing Environment for Groupthink

1. S. E. Asch, *Social Psychology* (Englewood Cliffs, N.J.: Prentice-Hall, 1952), p. 197.
2. M. Sherif and C. W. Sherif, *Social Psychology* (New York: Harper & Row, 1969), pp. 208–209.
3. William Samuels, *Contemporary Social Psychology* (Englewood Cliffs, N.J.: Prentice-Hall, 1973), p. 10.

4. David C. McClelland, *The Achieving Society* (New York: Van Nostrand Reinhold Company, 1961).

5. ———, "The Urge to Achieve," in *Behavioral Concepts in Management*, 2nd ed., David Hampton, ed. (Encino, Calif.: Dickenson Publishing Co., Inc., 1972), p. 81.

6. Harold Leavitt, *Managerial Psychology* (Chicago: University of Chicago Press, 1972), p. 109.

7. S. Milgram, "Some Conditions of Obedience and Disobedience to Authority," *Human Relations*, Vol. 18 (1965), pp. 57–75.

8. Harold Leavitt, op. cit., p. 288.

9. C. A. Kiesler and S. B. Kiesler, *Conformity* (Reading, Mass.: Addison-Wesley, 1969), p. 66.

10. David J. Lawless, *Effective Management: A Social Psychology Approach* (Englewood Cliffs, N.J.: Prentice-Hall, 1972), p. 260.

11. William H. Whyte, Jr., *The Organization Man* (New York: Simon & Schuster, 1956), p. 245.

12. J. L. Freedman, J. M. Carlsmith, and D. O. Sears, *Social Psychology* (Englewood Cliffs, N.J.: Prentice-Hall, 1970), p. 122.

13. Ibid., p. 221.

14. Irving L. Janis, *Victims of Groupthink* (Boston: Houghton Mifflin Co., 1972), p. 119.

15. Ibid., p. 120.

16. H. A. Simon, "Theories of Decision Making in Economics and Behavioral Science," *The American Economic Review*, June 1959.

17. M. Alexis and Charles Wilson, *Organizational Decision Making* (Englewood Cliffs, N.J.: Prentice-Hall, 1967), pp. 68–69.

Chapter 7
The Ascendancy of Groupthink

1. "What's in the Cards for 1972?" *Institutional Investor*, Jan. 1972.

2. *Vickers' Favorite 50*, Dec. 31, 1971 (New York: Vickers Assoc. Inc.).

3. Peter Landau, "Where Do We Go from Here?" *Institutional Investor*, Oct. 1970.

4. Ibid.
5. Francis Nicholson, "Price Ratios in Relation to Investment Results," *Financial Analysts Journal*, Jan.–Feb. 1968.
6. William Breen, "Low Price-Earnings Ratios," *Financial Analysts Journal*, July-Aug. 1968.
7. Francis Nicholson, "Price-Earnings Ratios," *Financial Analysts Journal*, July–Aug. 1960.
8. James O. McWilliams, "Price-Earnings and P-E Ratios," *Financial Analysts Journal*, May–June 1966.

Chapter 8
The Amazing Two-Tier Market

1. *Indicator Digest* (Palisades Park, N.J.: Indicator Digest, Inc.).
2. "First Session: The Impact on Institutional Investors in the Stock Market," *Proceedings*, hearings by the Bentsen Committee, Subcommittee on Financial Markets, U.S. Senate Committee on Finance, 93rd Congress, 2nd Session, on S2787 and S2842 (Washington, D.C.: U.S. Government Printing Office), Part 1, p. 182.
3. Carol J. Loomis, "How the Terrible Two-Tier Market Came to Wall Street," *Fortune*, July 1973.
4. Ibid.
5. Robert L. Hunt, *Proceedings*, hearings by the Bentsen Committee, op. cit., Appendix, p. 38.
6. Reginald Jones, "Are the Institutions Wrecking Wall Street?" *Business Week*, June 2, 1973.
7. *SEC Statistical Bulletin*, Aug. 1974.
8. Ibid., Jan. 1974.
9. Nicholas Colchester, "A Sense of Irrational Values," *Financial Times*, London, July 13, 1973.
10. Carol J. Loomis, op. cit.
11. Ibid.
12. Reginald Jones, op. cit.
13. Bank holdings figures from Bentsen Committee hearings and fund holdings figures from Vickers.
14. Samuel R. Callaway, *Proceedings*, op. cit., Part 1, p. 59.
15. Quintin U. Ford, *Proceedings*, op. cit., Part 2, footnote 2, p. 123.
16. George M. Lingua, *Proceedings*, op. cit., p. 118.

17. Walter R. Good, "Valuation of Quality—Growth Stocks," *Financial Analysts Journal,* Sept.–Oct. 1972.

18. Roger C. Kennedy, *Proceedings,* op. cit., Part 2, footnote 6, p. 144.

19. Edward Malca, *Proceedings,* op. cit., Part 2, footnote 16, p. 100.

20. Chalkley J. Hambleton, *Proceedings,* op. cit., Part 2, footnote 5, p. 184.

21. Carol J. Loomis, op. cit.,

22. Roy A. Schotland, Georgetown University, *Proceedings,* op. cit., table, footnote 16, p. 70.

23. Samuel Callaway, *Proceedings,* op. cit., footnote 16, p. 108.

24. "The Terrible Two-Tier Market Continued," *Fortune,* Oct. 1973.

25. Alan Abelson, "Up and Down Wall Street," *Barron's,* Sept. 3, 1973.

26. Benjamin Graham, David Dodd, Sidney Cottle, and Charles Tatham, *Security Analysis,* 4th ed. (New York: McGraw-Hill, 1962), p. 411.

27. Benjamin Graham, *The Intelligent Investor,* 3rd ed. (New York: Harper & Row, 1965), p. 18.

28. Benjamin Graham et al., op. cit., p. 179.

29. John Quirt, "Confessions of an Underperformer," *Institutional Investor,* July 1973.

30. "The Terrible Two-Tier Market Continued," op cit.

31. Op. cit.

32. *Wall Street Transcript,* March 11, 1974.

33. Irving L. Janis, *Victims of Groupthink* (Boston: Houghton Mifflin Co., 1972), p. 87.

34. Ibid., p. 63.

Chapter 9
Panic

1. *Proceedings,* hearings by the Bentsen Committee, Subcommittee on Financial Markets, U.S. Senate Committee on Finance, 93rd Congress, 2nd Session, on S2787 and S2842 (Washington, D.C.: U.S. Government Printing Office), p. 70.

2. John Maynard Keynes, *The General Theory of Employment, Interest and Money* (New York: Harcourt, Brace & World, 1969), p. 160.

3. *Proceedings,* op. cit., p. 106.

4. "The Buyers Weren't There," *Forbes,* Aug. 15, 1970.

5. Fred Bleakly, "Illiquidity—Is It Becoming a Problem Again?" *Institutional Investor,* Sept. 1972.

6. Charles J. Elia, "Heard on the Street," *The Wall Street Journal,* July 3, 1974.

7. George Katona, *Psychological Economics* (New York: American Elsevier, 1975), p. 56.

8. Ibid., p. 213.

9. Benjamin Graham, David Dodd, Sidney Cottle, and Charles Tatham, *Security Analysis,* 4th ed. (McGraw-Hill, 1962), p. 424.

10. Bernard J. Fine, "Conclusion Drawing, Communicator Credibility, and Anxiety as Factors in Opinion Change," *Journal of Abnormal Psychology,* Vol. 54 (1957), pp. 369–374.

11. Jonathan L. Freedman, J. Merril Carlsmith, and David C. Sears, *Social Psychology* (Englewood Cliffs, N.J.: Prentice-Hall, 1970), p. 327.

12. "Inside Wall Street," *Business Week,* Sept. 15. 1975.

13. Samuel Callaway, *Proceedings,* op. cit., Part 1, footnote 3, p. 80.

14. Duane P. Schultz, *Panic Behavior* (New York: Random House, 1964), p. 49.

15. Charles J. Elia, op. cit., Feb. 11, 1975.

16. Ibid., Jan. 8, 1975.

17. Donald T. Regan, *A View from the Street* (New York: New American Library, 1972), p. 41.

18. Alan Abelson, "Up and Down Wall Street," *Barron's,* May 3, 1971.

19. Ibid., June 21, 1971.

20. Martin E. Zweig, "Uncanny Floor Traders," *Barron's,* April 22, 1974.

21. Charles J. Elia, op. cit., Oct. 2, 1974.

22. "Bear Market Fueled Recession," *The Wall Street Journal,* Nov. 26, 1975.

23. "How Sagging Stocks Depress the Economy," *Business Week,* Jan. 27, 1975.
24. George Katona, *Psychological Economics,* op. cit., p. 332.
25. Charles J. Elia, op. cit., April 15, 1975.
26. "Investment Clubs Are Dwindling Sharply," *The Wall Street Journal,* Dec. 17, 1975.
27. Charles J. Elia, op. cit., April 22, 1975.
28. Robert M. Soldofsky, *Institutional Holdings of Common Stock, 1900–2000* (Ann Arbor, Mich.: Bureau of Business Research, University of Michigan Press, 1971).
29. *Wall Street Transcript,* April 27, 1974.

Chapter 10
Market Information: The Forest and the Trees

1. James H. Lorie and Mary T. Hamilton, *The Stock Market: Theories and Evidence* (Homewood, Ill.: Dow Jones-Irwin, Inc., 1973), p. 100.
2. Robert Hagin and Chris Mader, *The New Science of Investing* (Homewood, Ill.: Dow Jones-Irwin, Inc., 1973), pp. 154, 193.
3. Ibid., p. 229.
4. Paul A. Cootner, *Industrial Management Review,* Spring 1962, p. 25.
5. "It's Time to Call the Auditors to Account," *Fortune,* Aug. 1970.
6. Abraham Briloff, *Unaccountable Accounting* (New York: Harper & Row, 1972).
7. Ibid., pp. 13–15.
8. William C. Norby and Francis Stone, "Objectives of Financial Reporting," *Financial Analysts Journal,* July–Aug. 1972, p. 39.
9. Abraham Briloff, op. cit., p. 36.
10. Joshua Ronen and Simcha Sadan, "Income Smoothing via Classification," *Financial Analysts Journal,* Sept.–Oct. 1975.
11. Arnold L. Thomas, "The Allocation Fallacy and Financial Reporting," *Financial Analysts Journal,* Sept.–Oct. 1975.

Chapter 11
The Foundations of EMH—Bedrock or Quicksand?

1. Burton G. Malkiel, *A Random Walk Down Wall Street* (New York: W. W. Norton, 1973), p. 47.
2. George Katona, *Psychological Economics* (New York: American Elsevier, 1975), p. 303.
3. Harold Leavitt, *Managerial Psychology* (Chicago: University of Chicago Press, 1972), p. 185.
4. Alfred W. Stonier and Douglas C. Hague, *A Textbook of Economic Theory* (London: Longmans, Green, 1953), pp. 87–88.
5. Ibid., p. 2.
6. Sherman J. Maisel, "Economic and Financial Literature and Decision Making," *Journal of Finance,* May 1974.
7. Robert Plutchuk, *Foundation of Experimental Research* (New York: Harper & Row, 1968), p. 239.
8. C. E. K. Mess, "Scientific Thought and Social Reconstruction," *Electrical Engineering,* Vol. 53 (1934).
9. James H. Lorie and Mary T. Hamilton, *The Stock Market: Theories and Evidence* (Homewood, Ill.: Dow Jones-Irwin, Inc., 1973), p. 203. [Cited in Friedman, ref. 10.]
10. Milton Friedman, "The Methodology of Positive Economics," in *Essays on Positive Economics* (Chicago: University of Chicago Press, 1953), p. 15.
11. Ibid., p. 9.
12. Peter F. Drucker, *Management: Tasks, Responsibilities, Practices* (New York: Harper & Row, 1973), p. 510.

The following publications have also been consulted while preparing this chapter:

Ackoff, Russell L., *Scientific Method: Optimizing Applied Research Decisions.* New York: John Wiley & Sons, Inc., 1962.

Crosser, Paul K., *Economic Fictions.* Westport, Conn.: Greenwood Press, 1957.

Davies, J. T., *The Scientific Approach.* London: Academic Press, 1965.

Harré, R., *An Introduction to the Logic of the Sciences.* London: Macmillan & Co., Ltd., 1960.

————, *The Principles of Scientific Thinking*. Chicago: University of Chicago Press, 1970.

Hutchison, T. W., *The Significance & Basic Postulates of Economic Theory*. Clifton, N.J.: Augustus M. Kelley, Publisher, 1938.

Krupp, Sherman Roy, ed., *The Structure of Economic Science*. Englewood Cliffs, N.J.: Prentice-Hall, 1966.

Morgenstern, Oscar, *On the Accuracy of Economic Observations*. Princeton, N.J.: Princeton University Press, 1965.

Papandreou, Andreas, *Economics As a Science*. Philadelphia: J. B. Lippincott, 1958.

Popper, Karl R., *The Logic of Scientific Discovery*. New York: Basic Books, 1959.

Scheffler, Israel, *The Anatomy of Inquiry*. New York: Alfred A. Knopf, 1963.

Von Mises, Richard, *Positivism*. Cambridge, Mass.: Harvard University Press, 1969.

Walker, Marshall, *The Nature of Scientific Thought*. Englewood Cliffs, N.J.: Prentice-Hall, 1963.

Zeuthen, F., *Economic Theory & Method*. Cambridge, Mass.: Harvard University Press, 1953.

Chapter 12
A Contemporary Investment Strategy

1. J. Peter Williamson, *Investments' New Analytic Techniques*, 3rd ed. (New York: Praeger, 1974), pp. 152ff.

The following publications have also been consulted while preparing this chapter:

Cohen, Jerome B., Edward D. Zenbar, and Arthur Zeikel, *Investment Analysis and Portfolio Management*, rev. ed. Homewood, Ill: Richard D. Irwin, Inc. 1973.

Douglas, Herbert, *Investments*, 8th ed. Englewood Cliffs, N.J.: Prentice-Hall, 1968.

Ellis, Charles D., *Institutional Investing*. Homewood, Ill.: Dow Jones-Irwin, Inc., 1971.

Emory, Eric S., *When to Sell Stocks*. Homewood, Ill: Dow Jones-Irwin, Inc., 1973.

Graham, Benjamin, *The Intelligent Investor*, 3rd ed. New York: Harper & Row, 1965.

Graham, Benjamin, David Dodd, Sidney Cottle, and Charles Tatham, *Security Analysis*, 4th ed. New York: McGraw-Hill, 1962.

Levine, Sumner L. (ed.), *The Financial Analysts Handbook*. Homewood, Ill.: Dow Jones-Irwin, Inc., 1975.

Loeb, Gerald M., *The Battle for Investment Survival*. New York: Simon & Schuster, 1957.

Sauvain, Harry, *Investment Management*, 3rd ed. Englewood Cliffs, N.J.: Prentice-Hall, 1967.

Tuchman, Barbara, *The Guns of August*. New York: The Macmillan Co., 1962.

William, John Burr, *The Theory of Investment Value*. Cambridge, Mass.: Harvard University Press, 1938.

Average total return for each holding period.

P/E Decile	After One Quarter	After 1 yr.	2 yr.	3 yr.	4 yr.	5 yr.	6 yr.	7 yr.
Lowest 1	4.5%	10.2%	22.8%	26.7%	36.9%	45.6%	35.3%	24.5%
2	2.8	9.6	22.7	15.4	41.4	38.0	27.4	22.1
3	2.8	8.4	17.4	12.3	26.7	38.6	23.0	9.7
4	2.3	7.5	14.8	8.9	30.2	38.8	24.5	13.7
5	1.2	7.1	13.5	7.0	26.7	40.3	24.7	9.6
6	1.2	5.4	11.2	6.6	21.7	22.7	4.0	−7.2
7	0.7	2.7	3.7	−7.2	11.4	15.6	−6.3	−16.5
8	0.6	3.0	3.6	−1.5	13.8	27.6	4.2	−9.1
9	0.5	3.4	5.1	−2.0	8.5	19.3	4.6	−7.3
Highest 10	−0.4	1.1	0.0	3.1	7.8	6.8	−11.4	−26.1

Appendix_____

In order to update the high-low P/E studies to cover the last 9 years and to examine some criticisms of previous results, a computer study was undertaken in collaboration with Professor William Avera of the University of Texas and Cliff Atherton, a graduate student, for the mid-1967 to mid-1976 period. The sample, taken from the Compustat tapes, is broader than any reported previously. It consists of more than 1,000 stocks on the New York Stock Exchange with 5-year records. (For methodological reasons, we excluded stocks with fiscal years not ending in March, June, September, and December.) Total return (capital gain or loss plus dividends) was measured for each period. P/Es above 75 were omitted to screen out some companies with nominal earnings.

P/Es were established by taking the latest 12-month earnings to the end of a period from the Compustat tapes and the price 2 months thereafter to allow the last quarter's earnings to be fully digested by the market. The stocks in the study were divided into deciles, with the company's P/E determining which decile it was in for each time period measured. The top row in the table represents the lowest 10% of P/Es and the bottom row the highest 10%. The table on the facing page gives the rate of return of investing in each decile and switching the accumulated investment after each holding period to the commensurate decile throughout for holding periods of up to 4 years. (5- to 7-year results of the original portfolios were also calculated.) The percentage in each column is the total return for the period.

The quarterly results are the most impressive. The overall results tend both to provide evidence against the random walk hypothesis and to substantiate an investment strategy of diversifying among low P/E stocks. $10,000 invested in Aug. 1967 (based on the latest 12-month earnings, in this case to June) in the lowest P/E stocks and switched to the lowest P/Es quarterly would increase to $49,944 by Aug. 1976 before commissions. $10,000 invested in the same manner in the top 10% of stocks would be worth only $8,650; $10,000 invested in the S&P 425 would have grown to $16,170.

All the samples, with the exception of the quarterly returns, begin with 12-month earnings ending Dec. 1967 and reflect Feb. 1968 prices. The volatile markets following this point result in the rate of returns varying rather significantly for the different holding periods. For example, the 6- and 7-year results end with prices at Feb. 1974 and Feb. 1975, respectively. These portfolios were thus assembled near the top of the 1967-1968 bull market and sold in the 1973-1974 cataclysm. Nevertheless, the low P/E groups consistently outperformed the upper deciles. Turning the portfolios over each year, the bottom 10% would have performed almost nine times as well; even if the original portfolios were held for up to 5 years, the lowest P/E stocks would have performed nearly seven times better than the highest P/Es.

Our statistics further indicate if we started the portfolios near the bottom of the 1969–1970 market (June 1970) the low P/E groups would have continued to outperform the high P/Es for periods of 1 to 6 years.

The time span (1967-1976) is particularly important because the results seem to refute the contention of growth stock advocates that during this period, unlike those of the past, the high P/E stocks outperformed the low. The findings, if anything, appear to magnify the disparity in performance between the high and low P/E groups. (See Chapter 7.) It then appears that all the empirical findings over 40 years strongly and consistently favor the purchase of the low P/E groups.

We also measured the volatility (beta) of our sample, as some random walkers have justified the higher returns on the low P/E stocks on the basis of their higher volatility. However, our beta measurements indicated that the low P/E groups actually had moderately lower betas, thus making them less risky and slightly enhancing the overall results.*

*In the text I have not discussed beta other than to define it briefly. For those of a theoretical bent, we used the following measuring procedure. We studied 37 separate quarters (starting with June 1967 and continuing through June 1976). In each period 11 portfolios were formed (the 10 P/E deciles and the group of stocks above the P/E filter of 75). In all, 407 separate portfolios were established. Once the portfolios were formed for each quarter they were kept intact and the computer identified all returns for them over the 1967–1976 period. The returns for each of the 407 portfolios were compiled early in the sample period, most of the observations used for the regressions were drawn from subsequent periods; conversely, for portfolios identified near the end of the sample period most of the observations for regressions were taken from past data. The betas starting with the lowest P/E group are as follows: 0.997, 1.054, 1.077, 1.104, 1.102, 1.151, 1.125, 1.122, 1.077, 1.049, 1.153.

An interesting sideproduct of this study was the fact that the betas in the sample did not appear to be stable over time. Within the same P/E groups, beta measurements based primarily on past data differed from betas based primarily on future data. These preliminary findings pointing to the apparent instability of beta over time mesh well with the psychological hypotheses of investor overreactions advanced in the text.

Index _____

Abelson, Alan, 178
academic criticism, 18–43
　flawed, 96
　of fundamental analysis, 32,
　　34, 36–37, 218–19
　of institutional research, 116
　of mutual funds, 37–38
　of technical analysis, 28–32
　see also efficient market
　　hypothesis; random walk
　　hypothesis
accounting, 229–35
　concept stocks and creative, 93
　creative, 233–35
　investment strategy and, 268
　LIFO and FIFO methods of,
　　263*n*
　National Student Marketing
　　and procedures in, 93
　practices in, 229–33
Achieving Society, The (McClel-
　land), 134
Adler Electronics, 78
affiliation, stress and impetus to,
　138, 197
airline stocks, 5
Alexis, M., 143
Alger, Fred, 84, 104
"All American Research Team,"
　123
American Home Products
　Corp., 189, 199
American Stock Exchange
　(AMEX),
　average stock on (by March
　　1973), 168
　liquidity and (1972–74), 205

American Telephone & Tele-
　graph (AT&T), 212
AMF, 79
Amivest Corp., 205
Anderson, Arthur, 92
antibiotics, knowledge of,
　among doctors, table, 228
anxiety, opinion change and,
　198; *see also* opinions
Arthur Lipper Rankings, 86
Asch, Solomon, 130, 131
Asch experiment, 134–35, 139–
　40
attitudes, reference groups and
　creating and changing, 128;
　see also groups; opinions
authority
　complying with, as influence,
　　134–38
　effect of opinion change of
　　authorities, 198
　effectiveness trap and, 142
autokinetic light experiment,
　131–33, 137–40
　illustrated, 132
Automatic Data Processing, Inc.,
　259
Avon Products, Inc., 15, 128,
　170, 171, 173, 174
　decline in stocks of (by 1974),
　　194, 195, 197, 198
　opinion change on, 203
　share of (1973, 1974), 183

Babson, Roger W., 64
Bache & Co., Inc., 208
Bachelier, Louis, 18

Bacon, Sir Francis, 242–43
bank trust departments
  assets of, 3–4, 7, 11, 12, 176
  decline in companies followed
    by, 210
  described, 11–14
  effects of overconcentrated
    assets of, 194
  increasing holdings con-
    centration of, 210–11
  in 1972 trading, 189
  in 1974 panic, 203–4
  one-decision stocks in, 174–79
  pension and nonpension assets
    managed by (1966–72), 176,
    177
Bankers Trust Company, 12,
  174, 176, 184
banks, *see* bank trust departments
Baruch, Bernard, 72, 113
Bausch & Lomb, Inc., 151, 159,
  191–92
Baxter Labs., Inc., 170
Bear Stearns & Co., 208
Becker Securities Corp., 13
beliefs, change in central, 196;
  see also opinions
Bentsen, Lloyd, 170n, 172, 174,
  178, 196, 199, 200
Berkeley, Bishop George, 117
best stocks, *see specific categories
  of best stocks; for example:*
  concept stocks; favorite
  stocks
beta measurement, 267n, 292
  defined, 36n
Black Tuesday (Oct. 29, 1929),
  73–74
  price action on, table, 72
Block, Inc., H & R, 192
Blume, Marshall, 14, 37, 272
Blunt, Sir John, 58, 60
Bogue Electronics Manufacturing, Co., 78
book value per share, 263
Bosworth, Barry, 206, 207

bowling stocks, 78–80
  1961–62, table, 82
Breen, William, 163n
Briloff, Abraham, 230, 233
Bristol Dynamics, 78
brokerage firms, *see entries begin-
  ning with term: institutional*
Brookings Institution, 206
Brown, Robert, 19
Brunswick, 79
Bubble Act (1720; British), 58
Buffet, Warren, 112
Bundy, McGeorge, 9–10, 103
  141n
Burlington Industries, Inc., 107
Burroughs Corp., 151, 205, 259
buy-and-hold strategy, 19–20,
  29, 30

Caesar, Julius, 74
Callaway, Samuel, 174, 178,
  199–200
capital, preservation vs. appreciation of, 103
Capital Guardian, 107
capital markets
  institutional role and, for pub-
    lic companies, 212
  and two-tier market, 172–73
capital structure, defined, 262n
Carr, Fred, 9, 85, 189
causation, correlation distinguished from, 243–45
Celanese Corp., 223
central beliefs, change in, 196;
  see also opinions
charting
  illustrated, 23, 25
  methods used in, 22–27
  reason for unworkability of, 36
Chase Manhattan Bank, 12,
  107–8, 176
Chemical Bank, 13
Christie, Agatha, 183
Citicorp (formerly First National
  Citibank), 12, 13, 174n, 176,
  212

closed-end investment companies
  defined, 14*n*
  performance of, 14
  portfolio through purchase of, 272, 273 (table)
Coca-Cola Bottling Co., 171, 203
cognitive processes, perceptual, 142–45
cognitive shaping, 142–43
Combustion Engineering, Inc., 202
commingled funds, *see* pooled funds
commissions, negotiated rates and, 118–19
common stock
  combined shareholders in (1970–75), 209
  percentage of pension funds in (1966–72), 176
  valuation formula for, 187–88
comparative appraisal, defined, 138–39
competition
  effects of, 102
  in institutional research, 115
  reason for rising, 104
  see also conformity; convergence, policy of; performance
compliance (behavior), defined, 118*n*; *see also* groupthink
compound interest, 77*n*
Compustat tapes, 163, 291
Computer Direction Advisors, 211
computer stocks, table (1967–70), 90
computers, 27, 29–31
concept companies, 34–35
  creative accounting and, 233
concept stocks
  avoiding, 260–61
  creative accounting and, 93
  favorite, table (1972–74), 159
  groupthink in, 156–61

gunslingers and, 84; *see also* gunslingers
  see also favorite stocks; glamour stocks; one-decision stocks
concepts (images)
  creating their own reality, 55
  described, 53
  of earnings power, 261–66
  electronics as basis for new, 78, 80–81
  gunslingers and, 87
  research in new, 122
  speculation and new, 76
conformity
  in earnings estimates, 120*n*–21*n*
  evidence of group, 130–39; *see also* groups; groupthink
  in institutional research, 116
  intraorganizational, pressures for, 139–45
  job security and, 119; *see also* job security
  mindless, 100
  pattern of, described, 121
  point of view of expert and, 124
  reactions to pressures of, 125–26
  see also competition; convergence, policy of; performance
Conformity (Kiesler and Kiesler), 137
conglomerates
  speculative mania in, 87–94
  stocks table (1967–70), 90
consumption, 1973–74 decline in, 206–7
Control Data Corp., 78
convergence, policy of
  in institutional research, 118–20
  performance and, 111, 112
  see also competition; conformity; performance

Coolidge, Calvin, 66
Cornfeld, Bernard, 4, 5
correlation, causation distinguished from, 243–45
Covington and Burling, 92
creative accounting, *see* accounting
Crockett, Jean, 14, 37, 272
Crowd, The (LeBon), 48
crowds
  definition of psychological, 48
  group behavior compared with behavior of, 100, 102; *see also* groups; groupthink
  manner of thinking of, 52–53
  shifts in behavior of, 58, 59

Damon Corp., 202, 258
Darvas, Nicholas, 81
decision making, effects of groupthink on, 99–102; *see also* groupthink; performance
defensive game plans, 231
Dennison Manufacturing Co., 269
deviance (nonconformity; dissent), 140–42
discount retailers, 80
diversification, 268–71
Dodd, David L., 8n, 117, 179–80, 197
dollar, devaluation of, 103
domesticated dissenters, 141–42
Donaldson Lufkin & Jenrette, Inc., 92
Dow, Charles, 24
Dow Chemical Co., The, 223
Dow Jones Industrial Average (DJIA)
  buying lowest P/Es on, 264
  Dec. 1968-May 1970, 94
  Goodyear on (1974, 1975), 265
  hemline and, illustrated, 244
  liquidity drop of (1972–74), 205
  1927, 67

1928, 1929, 71
1929 (Oct.), 73, 74
1954–59, 76
1961, 81
1962 (May), 81, 82
  and random walk hypothesis, 28
  test on 30 stocks in (1937–62), 163, 165
Dow Theory, 23–25
  random walk hypothesis and, 29
Drexel & Company Inc., 162, 163, 165
Dreyfus, 104
Drucker, Peter, 248–49
du Pont, T. Coleman, 64
Du Pont de Nemours & Co., E. I., 223
Durant, William C., 70, 74

earnings
  concept of earnings power, 261–66
  conformity in estimates of, 120n-21n
  EMH and changes in, 39
  recent past record of, 33, 34
  see also accounting
Eastman Kodak Co., 177, 203
economic behavior
  psychological influences on, 196–97
  see also rationality
economists, 226, 227
Edward, Robert, 20n
effectiveness trap, 141, 142
efficient market hypothesis (EMH), 238–52
  applied to fundamental analysis, 36–37
  applied to mutual funds, 37–38
  appraised, 42–43, 245–51
  assumptions of, 219–20
  and capability to interpret

market information, 221–29
defined, 35–36
and economic rationality, 42–43, 240–45
and eliminating distorting variables, 148
evidence contradicting, 147–56
flawed, 96
groupthink compared with, 213; *see also* market information and information interpretation problem, 235–37
inside information and, 40–42
interpretational and psychological reactions and, 252–55
and market performance of popular and unpopular stocks, 161–67
and problem of investor behavior, 238–40
spreading influence of, 217–18
tests confirming, 38–42
electronics firms
speculative fever and, 77–78, 80–83
stocks, table (1961–62), 82
Eli Lilly & Co., 127
Elia, Charles, 195
Elias, Christopher, 115–16
Ellis, Charles, 110
EMH, *see* efficient market hypothesis
Employee Retirement Investment Security Act (1974), 13
England, Bank of, 59
Enterprise Fund, 9, 85, 189
entrapment, 202–3
equity funds, *see* pooled funds
experts
dependence on, 271
using advice of, 266–68
Extraordinary Popular Delusions and the Madness of Crowds (Mackay), 58–59

Fairchild Camera & Instrument Corp., 77
Fama, Eugene, 28, 38
favorite stocks
accounting dangers in, 234*n*
concentration on, 117–18
consistently inferior results in choosing, 255–60
effects of overconcentration on, 190–92, 193 (table), 194–200, 201 (table), 202
see also concept stocks; glamour stocks; growth stocks; one-decision stocks; two-tier market
Federal National Mortgage, 159
Federal Reserve, 71
Fidelity Capital, 104
Fidelity Growth Fund, 84
FIFO (first-in first-out; method of inventory accounting), 263*n*
Fifth Annual Institutional Investor Conference (1972), 5, 149
filter techniques, 26
random walk hypothesis applied to, 29
Finance Committee (Senate), 172, 174, 178, 196, 199, 200
First National Citibank, *see* Citicorp
Fischer, Bobby, 236
Fisher, Irving, 72
Fisher, James, 77*n*
Fisher brothers, 70
fixed income funds, *see* pooled funds
Fleecing the Lambs (Elias), 115
Florida land boom (1920s), 60–66, 95
FNMA, 151
Food and Drug Administration (FDA), 127
Forbes, 79, 94
Ford, Henry, 66
Ford, Quintin U., 174

Ford Foundation, 9–11, 103, 175
Ford Motor Co., 151, 198
  valuation formula of, 187–88
Four Seasons Nursing Homes, 93
franchisers, 93
Frank Russell and Company, 7
Friedman, Milton, 246
Friend, Irwin, 14, 37, 207, 272
fundamental analysis
  academic case against, 32, 34, 36–37, 218–19
  defined, 32–33
  economic situation (1971, 1972) and, 179
  institutional research and, 116, 117
  and interpretational and psychological reactions, 252–55
  and one-decision stocks, 183
  P/E rule of thumb and, 264
  performance and abandoning, 111
  and psychological influence on decision maker, 213
  random walk hypothesis applied to, 34, 35
  technical analysis and, 31–32
"funny money," power of, 92

GAAP (generally accepted accounting principles), 229, 230, 235
Galbraith, John Kenneth, 69, 95n, 267
General Electric Co., 212, 239
General Instruments Corp., 77
General Motors Corp., 53, 69, 70, 212, 269n
Genesco, Inc., 191
George I, 54, 58, 59
glamour stocks, 95n
  in 1960s speculative fever, 79, 81
  table of (1937–1970), 96

  see also favorite stocks
go-go markets, 84, 95, 157
Goldsmith, Frederick N., 27–28, 40n
Goodrich Co., B. F., The, 172
Goodyear Tire & Rubber Co., The, 183–84, 265, 267
Goyen, Jan van, 52
Grace, 223
Graham, Benjamin, 95, 110, 112, 117, 197, 261n
  on professional investors, 7–8
  and rate of growth, 179–81
Granger, Clive, 28
Great Southwest Corp., 233
greater fool theory, 64, 69, 81
groups
  effectiveness trap and, 142
  influence of opinion of, on individual, 130
  perception of reality by, 56; see also social reality
groupthink (groupthink-compliance hypothesis or syndrome), 97–213
  accounting dangers in favorites and, 234n
  ascendency of, 146–67
  in concept stocks, 156–61; see also concept stocks
  continuing influence of, 212–13
  correlation of data and, 243–45
  defined, 99–102, 146
  EMH compared with, 213; see also market information
  empirical evidence of errors due to, 147–56
  factors influencing, see competition; conformity; convergence, policy of; performance
  investment errors due to, 147
  market collapse and (1973–74), 195–202

and market performance of popular and unpopular stocks, 161, 162 (table), 163 (table), 164 (table), 165 (table), 166, 167
testing hypothesis of, 250–51
see also institutional research; panic; two-tier market; visibility
growth, problems of, 179–82
growth companies, visibility of, 175; *see also* visibility
growth stocks
defined, 77
1967–70 (table), 90
principle of, criticized, 180–81
see also favorite stocks
gunslingers, 83–95
characteristics of, 83–84

Hagin, Robert, 35–36, 218
Hague, Douglas C., 240–41
Haig, Sir Douglas, 125
Hamilton, Mary T., 35*n*, 218
Handleman Co., 191
Harvard Endowment Fund, 92
hedge funds, 86–87
Hercules, 223
Hewlett-Packard, 203
"Higgledly Piggledly Growth" (Little), 34, 181
"high flyers," 169
Holiday Inns, Inc., 191
Honeywell, Inc., 145, 265–67
How I Made Two Million Dollars on the Stock Market (Darvas), 81
"How the Terrible Two-Tier Market Came to Wall Street" (*Fortune*), 169, 178
Hugo, Victor, 76
Huxley, Thomas, 245

images, concept of, 53; *see also* concepts
INA, 269

individual investors
institutional investors compared with, 6
1965–72, 170–71
1970 and 1974 declines and, 208–9
role of, 208–12
share of market trading by (1971–74), 10
inflation
effects of, on market, 103
as reason both for buying and selling, 16, 200
information flow, as influence on decision making, 126–29; *see also* market information
inside information, EMH and, 40–42
institutional favorites, *see* favorite stocks
Institutional Holdings of Common Stock 1900–2000 (Soldofsky), 211
institutional investors
appraisal of performance of, 3–9
assets under control of (1960–75), 3–4, 7
holdings of (1965–72), 170–71
leading, (table), 176
see also bank trust departments
institutional research, 113–21
"best," 117, 119
commission rates and, 119
coverage open to, 121–24
exaggeration in current, 253
failure of, 115–21
increasing institutional role in market and, 210, 211
job insecurity and, 119
institutional role
economic implications of, 206, 207 (table), 208
effects on market of increasing, 208–12
in 1974 market decline, 204–6

share of market (1971–74), 10
institutionalization, effect of increasing market, 208–12
insurance companies, *see entries
beginning with term: institutional*
International Business Machines
Corp. (IBM), 34, 35, 149,
151, 156, 173, 259, 265
determining a value for, 257–
58
as growth industry, 77
holdings in, 177
opinion change on, 203
trading in (1961), 81
International Flavors and Fragrances, Inc., 34, 170, 173
intrinsic value theory, 255
investment clubs, decline in, 210
investment strategy, 252–74
and concept of earnings
power, 261–66
diversification in, 268–71
expert advice in, 266–68
portfolio, (table), 270
pressures against, 271–72
proposed, 260–61
psychological variables in,
252–58
visibility and, 258–60
investment trusts
mutual fund managers of
1960s compared with, 85
in 1920s stock market speculation, 70–71
SBICs compared with, 79
see also bank trust departments
investor behavior, problem of,
238–42
investor confidence, restored
(1950s), 76–77
Investors Overseas Services
(IOS), 4, 5
Ivest, 104

Janis, Irving, 99–102, 141, 185,
250

Jersey Scrap (example), earnings, 232 (table), 233
job, capital investment required
to create one new, 172
job security
"improper behavior" and,
133–34
jobs lost (1969–75), 219*n*
Johnson, Lyndon B., 141
Johnson and Johnson, 259
Jones, Reginald H., 170, 173
Juster, Thomas, 207

Katona, George, 196–97, 208,
239
Kaufman and Broad, 233
Keane, James R., 28, 40*n*
Kennedy, John F., 81, 101
Kennedy, Roger, 106, 175–76
Keynes, John Maynard, 111,
112, 119, 190
Kidder Peabody (top 50), 160,
170, 186, 200
decline in (1972–74), 194
percent change in (1973–75;
table), 161
Kiesler, C. A., 137
Kiesler, S. B., 137
Kimmel, Adm. Husband E., 101
Kirby, Robert, 107, 110
Korvette, E. J., 78
Kresge Co., S. S., 199

Landau, Peter, 157
Leasco Data Processing, 35, 55,
122, 233
Leavitt, Harold, 135–37, 239–40
LeBon, Gustave, 48, 52, 53, 57,
69, 76, 99, 100, 102
letter stock, 85–86, 92
Levitz Furniture, 15, 35, 159,
171–72, 181, 192, 258
LIFO (last-in-first-out; method
of inventory accounting),
263*n*
Liggett & Myers Corp., 191

Ling, James, 89, 91
Ling-Temco-Vought, 55, 87, 89
Lingua, George M., 174
Lipper, Arthur, 84
liquidation of stocks (1974), 204
liquidity
in 1974 decline, 204–6
problem of, 189–90
Little, I. M. D., 34, 181
Litton Industries, 87
Livermore, Jesse, 64, 70, 75
Lorie, James H., 35*n*, 77*n*, 218

McClelland, David, 134
McDonald's, 15, 128, 129, 170, 171, 173, 178, 197, 199
Mackay, Charles, 58–59
McLuhan, Marshall, 127
McWilliams, James, 163*n*
Mader, Chris, 35–36, 218
Magee, John, 20–21
maintenance research, 122–24
Maisel, Sherman, 242
Malkiel, Burton, 116, 239
Management (Drucker), 248
Managerial Psychology (Leavitt), 135, 239
Manhattan Fund, Inc., 9, 84, 92, 104
Manufacturers Hanover Trust Co., 12
margin, shares carried on (1920s), 71
margin requirements
1920s, 67
1960s speculative fever and, 82
Marine Midland Bank, 13, 166
market information, 217–37
and accounting, 229–35
and assumptions of EMH, 219–20
interpreting, 221–29, 235–37
market timing, 269–71
markets, characteristics of, 111–12
Mates, Fred, 85, 189

Mates Fund, 85, 86, 189
Max Factor & Co., 191
Meehan, Mike, 75
Memorex Corp., 122, 233, 234
Merrill Lynch, Pierce, Fenner & Smith, Inc., 205
Milgram, Stanley, 135, 136
Miller, Paul F., Jr., 161, 162
Mississippi Co., 58
models, 245–48
Modigliani, Francis, 206–7
Modonics earnings, 232 (table), 233
Mohasco Corp., 261–64
Mohawk Data Sciences Corp., 122
Molodovsky, Nicholas, 256
Moore, Arnold, 28
Morgan, J. P., 73
Morgan Guaranty Trust Co., 12, 92, 108, 128–29, 174, 176–78, 189
as leading institutional investor, 177
opinion change at, 199–200
Morgenstern, Oskar, 28
Motorola, Inc., 191
moving averages, 26–27
Murphy's Law, 265
mutual funds, 14–17, 77
assets of, and 1972–74 market losses, 206
cash position of (1970, 1971), 205–6
combined shareholders in (1970–75), 209
EMH and, 37–38
gunslingers in, 84–86
institutional research and, 113
investment climate and, 103–4
investments of, in 1966–72 period, 177
in 1972 trading, 189
in 1974 panic, 203, 204
no-load, 272*n*
one-decision stocks held by, 174

trading in Motorola (1966), 191

turnover of stock portfolios by, 10

National Association of Investment Clubs, 210

National Liberty Insurance, 234

National Student Marketing, 5, 35, 91–93, 148–50, 233

Nature and Conditions of Panic, The (Quarantelli), 202

need-for-achievement (n-Ach), 134–35

Needham, James J., 170*n*, 172–73, 190

Nelson, Samuel, 24

Neu, Harold C., 228

New York, Bank of, 13

New York Society of Security Analysts, 119

New York Stock Exchange (NYSE), 129

   average return on all stocks on (1928–60), 77*n*

   average stock on (by Mar. 1973), 168

   charts on stocks on, 27

   and increasing institutional holdings, 211

   inside information and, 41

   Morgan Guaranty trading on (1972), 178

   most active trader on (May 8, 1974), 202

   mutual fund return and appreciation of share on, 14, 37–38

   1971–72 trading of favorites on, 191

   stock splits on, investigated, 39

   survey of (1975), on decline in shareholders, 209

   top 50 stocks on, 160

Newton, Sir Isaac, 245

Nicholson, Francis, 162, 163

"nifty fifty," 169, 189

Nineteen Eighty-Four (Orwell), 14

"1974: The Year Stock Picks Didn't Matter So Much," 123

no-load mutuals, 272*n*

norms, group, defined, 137

nursing homes, 93

Nytronics, Inc., 78

odd-lotters, new, 206

offensive game plans, 231

Omega Equities, 85, 86

one-decision stocks, 173–79

   best stocks as, 185–86

   effects of overconcentration in, 190–92, 193 (table), 194–200, 201 (table), 202

   liquidity problem and, 189–90

   as manifestation of group-think, 179–88

   1973–74 decline and, 212

   see also favorite stocks

opinions

   affecting change in, 128–29

   effectiveness trap and, 142

   elements informing change in, 196–200

   group opinion and individual, 130–39

   intraprofessional influences on, 125–30

   uniformity of opinion after change in, 196, 197, 203–4

Organization Man, The (Whyte), 140

Organizational Decision Making (Alexis and Wilson), 143

organizational pressures for conformity, 139–45; *see also* conformity

Orwell, George, 14

Owens, Hugh F., 191

Pan American Airways, 149, 156

panic, 189–213

economic implications of institutional investing, 206, 207 (table), 208
as effect of overconcentration, 190–92, 193 (table), 194–200, 201 (table), 202
institutional role in, 204–6
losses, table, 207
nature of, 202–4
psychological experiments on, 202–3
payout ratio, 255, 258
P/E multiples (price/earnings; P/E ratios)
calculating, 160
capital market and, 172
choosing stocks with low, 260–61
and concept of earnings power, 261–66
high-low studies, 290–292
of National Student Marketing, 148
one-decision stocks and, 179
periodic restructuring of portfolio with stocks of low, 269, 271
on popular and unpopular stocks, 161, 162–65 (tables), 166, 167
selected stocks (1971–75), table, 201, 254
and two-tier market, 174, 175, 184, 185
visibility and, 258
Penn Central, 233
Penney Co., Inc., J. C., 64
pension funds, 11–14
assets of, 13
bank trust management of, 176; *see also* bank trust departments
changes in money managers in, 105
corporate executives and, 105–6
and drop in consumption, 207
effects of overconcentration of, 194
flows of funds of (1973–79), 211
growth in assets (1966–72), 176–77
investment climate and, 104
purchases of (1972), 171
turnover of stock portfolios by, 10
perception, selective, 142–45
perceptual-cognitive processes, 142–45
performance, 104
as conforming pressure, 105–13
as image of new reality (1967–70), 83
investment decisions and, 9
as standard, evaluated, 9–11, 13
time element in judging, 104–5, 109
Performance Systems, 233
Perkin-Elmer Corp., The, 203
Philip Morris, Inc., 189, 199
Phlogiston system, 246, 247
pinsetters, bowling stocks and automatic, 78–79
Plutchuk, Robert, 242
point, defined, 67n
Polaroid, 35, 173, 174, 178
decline in, 194, 195, 197, 198
as growth industry, 77
Morgan Guaranty holdings in, 177
trading in (1961), 81
pool operators, tape reading and 1920s, 22
pooled funds (commingled funds)
annual returns on, table, 12
bank-managed, 11–12
defined, 11
pooling, uses of, in stock market

speculation, 69–70
price diverging from value, 236;
    see also value
price-volume systems, 26, 30
professionals, *see specific aspects
    of work of, and pressures on
    behavior of; for example:*
    competition;   conformity;
    fundamental analysis
"prudent man" rule, 103
Psychological Economics (Katona),
    196
Ptolemaic system, 246–47
Putnam, Samuel, 103

Quarantelli, Enrico, 202, 203
Questrion Research, 213

Randell, Cortes W., 91–93
*Random Walk Down Wall Street,
    A* (Malkiel), 116, 239
random walk hypothesis, 18–20
    applied to fundamental analy-
        sis, 34, 35
    applied to technical analysis,
        28–32
    earnings change and, 181
    evidence against, 291
    principle of, 18, 19
    supported, 28–29
    see also efficient market
        hypothesis
Raskob, John Jacob, 70
rationality
    assumption of economic, 240–
        42
    attack on assumption of ratio-
        nal behavior, 238–40
    concept of rational man, 240
    EMH and assumption of, 42–
        43, 240–45
reality, perceived and real, 142–
    45; *see also* social reality
reference groups, 127–29; *see
    also* groups
reflected appraisal, defined, 138,
    139

Regan, Donald, 205
reification of economic data, 241
reinforcement,   positive   and
    negative, of opinions, 133
relative strength (system), 26, 27
    random walk hypothesis ap-
        plied to, 29
"religion stocks," 169
Research-Cottrell, Inc., 35, 202
resistance to change of central
    beliefs, 196
Ringling Brothers, 64
risk taking
    excessive, 100
    excessive conservatism follow-
        ing excessive, 200, 202
risky shift, defined, 200n
Roche, James, 173
rumors, 129
Ruth, Babe, 112

"sacred cows," 169
safe research, 122–24
Samuels, William, 132–33
Samuelson, Paul, 19n
Santayana, George, 75
Schlieffen, Alfred von, 274
Schotland, Roy A., 178
Sears, Roebuck and Co., 177, 205
secondary offerings, EMH and,
    39–40
Securities   Exchange   Commis-
    sion (SEC), 6, 40, 80, 170
    EMH influence on, 217
    letter stock and, 85
    study of, on new issues (late
        1950s, early 1960s), 83
    study of, on stock holdings
        (1969), 210–11
SEC v. Merrill Lynch, 40–41
SEC v. Texas Gulf Sulphur, 40,
    41
Securities Industry Association,
    173
Security Analysis (Graham and
    Dodd), 179

Security Pacific National Bank, 170

shaping, cognitive, 142–43

Sherif, Muzafer, 131

shock effect phenomenon, 196

Simon, H. A., 143

Small Business Investment Companies (SBICs), 79–83
  table (1961–62 stock), 82

Smith, Adam, 240

social comparison processes (or theory), 121*n*
  described, 55–56
  factors abetting, 138–39

social perception, 144

social reality
  defined, 56
  and lessons of history, 75
  1967–70, 83
  shifts in, 59*n*

Socrates, 110

Soldofsky, Robert, 211

South Sea Co., 53–60, 93, 94, 171

speculative fever (mania)
  common characteristics of, 94–96
  in conglomerates, 87–94
  defined, 47–48
  over Florida land boom (1920s), 60–66
  gunslingers and, 83–84
  1920s, 66–75
  over South Sea Co., 53–60, 93, 94, 171
  tables showing drop in prices, 68, 72
  technology as basis for new, 77–83
  over tulips, 48–52
  see also favorite stocks

Stahl, George Ernst, 247

S&P 425 (Standard & Poor's)
  1965–72, 170
  stocks outperforming, 166

S&P 500, 5–8
  airlines in (1972), 149
  bank trust departments

  surpassing performance of, 13
  buying lowest P/Es on, 264
  composition of, 166*n*
  concept stocks and (1972–73), 159
  decline (1972–74), 194, 206
  highly volatile stock and, 267
  and Kidder Peabody top 50, 160, 161
  1971–73, 170
  P/E ratio of (1949–61), 81
  runners up on (1972, 1973), 151, 152–53 (table), 156
  runners up on (1973), 151, 155 (table), 156
  top ten in (1972), 149, 150 (table), 151, 156
  top ten in (1973), 151, 154 (table), 156
  "12–24 rule" and, 105

Steen, Jan, 52

stock exchange, founding of first, 4

stock splits, 38–39

Stonier, Alfred W., 240–41

"stop loss" order, 26

STP, 191

stress, and impetus to affiliation, 138, 197

support and resistance levels, 25–26

Survey Research Center (University of Michigan), 196, 208

synergism, 88

Tandy, 200

tape reading, 22

technical analysis, 20–32
  academicians criticize, 28–32
  reason for unworkability of, 36
  survey of, 20–28

Technical Analysis of Stock Trends (Magee and Edward), 20

Technimetrics, Inc., 204

technology
  as basis for new speculative
    fever, 77–83
  table of stocks (1967–70), 90
  see also electronics firms
Teledyne, 87
Teleprompter, 159, 258
Telex, 122, 233
Texas Instruments, 77
Third Annual Institutional In-
    vestor Conference (1970), 3,
    148
Thomas, Arnold L., 235
Thomas & Betts Co., Inc., 203
Thomson, James, Jr., 141
Tobias, Andrew, 91, 148*n*
Tobin, James, 207
trendlines
  as charting tool, 24
  illustrated, 25
Truman, Harry S., 101
Tsai, Gerald, 9, 84, 92
tulips, 48–52, 94, 95, 238
two-tier market, 168–88
  capital market and, 172–73
  favored upper-tier in, 173–79
  institutional buying in, 170–72
  as manifestation of group-
    think, 179–88
  see also panic
Trans World Airlines (TWA),
    151
"12–24 rule," 105

Unaccountable Accounting (Bri-
    loff), 230
Union Carbide Corp., 212, 221–
    23, 226
U.S. Home, 233
U.S. Steel Corp., 15, 72, 73, 171
U.S. Trust of New York, 12
University Computing, 35

value
  determining, 253–58
  earning power analysis and,
    261–66

Value Line Composite Index, 6*n*,
    206
Value Line Index, 159
"vestal virgins," 169
Vickers Associates, Inc., 151
Victims of Groupthink (Janis), 99–
    100, 101, 141
visibility
  danger of overemphasizing,
    182–83
  investment strategy and, 258–
    60
  of one-decision stock, 173,
    179–86, 194, 195
  of top-tier, 192
volatility, 36*n*

Walt Disney Productions, Inc.,
    128, 129, 170, 174, 178, 189,
    197
  Morgan Guaranty holdings in,
    177
  opinion change on, 203
Walter Kidde, 87
Wang Laboratories, Inc., 191
wash sales, defined, 69
Westergaard, John, 212–13
Westinghouse Electric Corp.,
    200, 203, 212
White Sewing Machine, 74
Whitney, Richard, 73–75
Whyte, William, Jr., 140
Wiesenberger Services, 169
William Wrigley, 191
Williamson, J. Peter, 255–58
Wilson, Charles, 143

Xerox Corp., 34, 35, 128, 173,
    174, 178, 199*n*
  as growth industry, 77
  holdings in, 177
  1974 decline in, 205
  opinion change on, 203
  trading in (1961), 81

youth market, 91–92

Zulica, Tony, 208